TED BU MURDEKUUS MYSTERIES

THE MANY VICTIMS OF AMERICA'S MOST INFAMOUS SERIAL KILLER

KEVIN SULLIVAN

WILDBLUE
PRESS

WildBluePress.com

TED BUNDY'S MURDEROUS MYSTERIES published by:

WILDBLUE PRESS
P.O. Box 102440
Denver, Colorado 80250

WILDBLUE PRESS is registered at the U.S. Patent and Trademark Offices.

ISBN 978-1-948239-15-8   Trade Paperback
ISBN 978-1-948239-14-1   eBook
Interior Formatting/Book Cover Design by Elijah Toten
www.totencreative.com

THE MANY VICTIMS OF AMERICA'S
MOST INFAMOUS SERIAL KILLER

TABLE OF CONTENTS

AUTHOR'S NOTE

In 2006, I began the long process of writing a biography of Ted Bundy, perhaps the most infamous sexual serial killer this country has ever produced. Indeed, it's fair to say that when the subject of American serial killers comes up, Ted Bundy is the first, or certainly one of the first, murderers that comes to mind. Even a quick study of the facts of his life will show you why this is the case.

Nevertheless, as I began the two-and-a-half-year journey into the life of Ted Bundy and the known murders he committed, I had no idea where it would ultimately lead, and how one book would stretch into what has now become four volumes.

That journey first produced *The Bundy Murders: A Comprehensive History;* a book that broke new revelatory ground, including additional new information having to do with some of the murders. This work also turned out to be my break-out book into the world of true crime writing, and my literary and personal life changed forever.

At that point, the thought of writing another Bundy book was far from my mind. As the years rolled by, I wrote about other killers, and it was a refreshing change to be leaving Ted Bundy behind. But in 2015, I learned about an individual very close to the case who was very ill and his life was drastically changing. Being aware also that another of my Bundy contacts had recently passed away, I made the decision to write what I called a companion volume to my first book, and this became, *The Trail of Ted Bundy: Digging up the Untold Stories*, published in 2016. And like my first book, *Trail* also turned up new and never before published information that added new dimension to the case as people came forward to tell of their dealings with Ted Bundy. In 2017, I followed it up with: *The Bundy Secrets: Hidden Files on America's Worst Serial Killer*. And having written a trilogy of books on this most infamous case, totaling some 600 plus pages, I absolutely "knew" I'd said all I was going to say about Ted Bundy.

I have now learned that it's best to never say "never" …

Of course, I have a lot of "fans" of my Bundy books, and some of them are Facebook friends, and we communicate on a regular basis. Very often, however, they would direct their communication toward me and ask if I would consider writing another book about the Bundy case! Flattered, I would quickly thank them, but just as quickly I'd remind them that after three books I couldn't imagine writing anything more than the occasional article about Bundy. It all made perfect sense to me … at the time.

And then, during the summer of 2018, I appeared as a guest speaker in three separate Ted Bundy documentaries. It was no doubt this national exposure that sparked a small, but steady stream of people to contact me, wanting to tell their personal stories and their roles in the Bundy case. After a little investigation, a number of them were proven to be valid players, to one degree or another, in these high-profile murders committed by Bundy. Now, people like this occasionally reach out to me, and that's normal. But never in such numbers and in so short a time span. Not only this, but some of these contacts were giving me the names of other Bundy contacts, so it wasn't long before I began thinking the unthinkable: If I can locate even more people to interview, then perhaps I could delve back into the case and seek out additional information, especially about the lives of the victims, and ultimately, write another Ted Bundy book. It wasn't an easy or expected decision, but having had another of those epiphany moments, I could see how well this book could come together, and not just from these new testimonies, but from a deeper look at the official record that is teeming with exceedingly important and interesting information that, by and large, will never been seen by the public. Bringing this information to light, be it from new voices or from what the detectives obtained through lengthy interviews and the investigative material they gathered, is of utmost importance so that this information will be available to students of this case for decades to come. And so, because of all of this, once again the journey began.

A word about delving deeper into the lives of the victims (the real reason for this book): When I was penning *The Bundy Murders*, I brought out a great deal of information on the victims of Ted Bundy that had remained hidden; a fact that was recognized by many readers. With the two successive books, even more information came to light, but mostly from those who knew Ted Bundy or were otherwise closely involved in the case. But for this book, besides the interviews, it will be a book about the victims, where I will be going back into the case files, bringing far more to light about these murdered innocents, such as the letters between Kathy Parks and her boyfriend, during a time that was clearly stressful for Kathy, as well as other incidentals that you won't find in the usual books written about the case. And in fact, new information about the case has emerged once again from the depths of the record.

Once again the voluminous case files of the Ted Bundy murders will play a great part in our understanding of who these young women were, how they functioned in their daily lives, and not just what they were doing when they were murdered by Ted Bundy. Far too often, the victims of crime are defined in the public's mind solely by the murder. I know that I changed that focus with the publication of *The Bundy Murders*, but for this book, I'll be going even further so that you, the reader, will have an expanded view of the women and perhaps who they could have been had Ted Bundy not become a killer of women.

Kevin M. Sullivan

Louisville, KY

Fall 2018

CHAPTER ONE

LYNDA ANN HEALY

On January 31, 1974, Ted Bundy made the decision to enter a home at 5517 12th Street NE in Seattle for the purposes of abduction and murder. Without question, Bundy knew it was a home housing college coeds and, in fact, it is believed that he was at a nearby tavern (Dante's) earlier in the evening when Lynda Healy was there with a few of her friends, unwinding over a pitcher of beer. Having followed them home, he watched as they entered the residence. After a time, he checked the front door and found it unlocked. He had no intention of entering at that time, but would return and do so in the middle of the night.

When I was writing about the strange abduction of Lynda Healy for my book, *The Bundy Murders*, I had access to the entire police file which included the sworn testimonies of Lynda's housemates. By having this material, I was able to turn it all into a quick-paced narrative nonfiction story, quoting certain portions of the record as needed. This is the way books are written, be they fiction or nonfiction – the stories will have (or should have) a proper flow, and for nonfiction, you weave the facts from the case files into the narrative. One thing you don't do is just reproduce police case files, as they alone would give you plenty of facts, but no cohesive story. However, there is a place for the reproduction of case files—with commentary included— and which can serve as a companion volume to a previous book (the main book). In this case that would be *The Bundy Murders*. Indeed, this is the third companion volume I have written for that primary work on the killer.

Because this is a deeper look into the lives of the victims—from the record as well as (whenever possible) new testimonies—it is appropriate to allow you, the reader, a chance to see the full statements of the young women who knew Lynda very well, as they were her housemates. What follows are statements taken from the King County Police investigative file pertaining to the murder of Lynda Ann Healy, which include the testimonies of Joanne Testa, Monica Sutherland, Ginger Heath, and Karen Skaviem, all students at the University of Washington:

February 6, 1974

Statement of Joanne Carroll Testa

My account begins Thursday evening, January 31, 1974. Lynda, Ginger, Pete (Author's note: Pete Neal was a friend that came over that evening), *& I had dinner around 6:00 – 6:30. Then Pete, Lynda, and I decided to go drinking at Dante's Tavern. Before we did, though, Lynda used my car to go to the grocery store. This was about 7:00 – 7:30. She came back about 40 min. later and the three of us walked to Dante's. We sat upstairs at a table by ourselves, Lynda bought the first pitcher as we walked in. Pete bought the second and last one. During that time, Lynda was in very good spirits – she was lively & talkative but not nervous. She remarked that her recent stomach pains had gone & she felt good. Our conversation was light – from music to psychology to old friends – no subject being dwelled upon. Lynda and I talked to no one else as I can remember. Pete, however, approached a fairly large table of people next to us. They were playing a game with dice. He went to their table, inquired as* *to what game they were playing, and after just a few minutes, returned to our table. And we did not hear him speak but were watching him. We finished our beer, Pete wanted to catch the 9:41 p.m. bus home, so we left shortly before that – perhaps 9:20 – 9:30. He walked us home. He picked up some record albums he had left at our house, and left within 5 minutes or so. I do not recall anyone following us or approaching us on our way home.*

We all watched TV for a while (The Autobiography of Miss Jane Pittman). Lynda made a phone call to (redacted, but it was her boyfriend) *who had called her earlier and was staying in Seattle. She talked to him for some time – maybe an hour or so. When she went to the phone – it was then that I recall some of her clothing. She had on a pair of Levis (navy bell bottom style) somewhat worn ... and there was a black triangular patch - I believe on the lower inside – right side of her pants. I also assume she had on her waffle stomper shoes – they are missing & she most always wore them. They are lace boots - ankle high – brown vinyl – square toed. I am sure she had her two turquoise rings on as well. She always wore them. As for her top blouse – I do not remember that she had something white on stick in my mind, but I cannot recall.*

After watching TV, I went to my room. Lynda came in to talk with me – she was in a good mood – we talked about our upcoming party, about Dante's, and about a letter I had received from my boyfriend in Phoenix. It was again, light conversation – she said good night. She gave no indication of stress, physical or mental, and no indication of leaving. I do not know what she was wearing. She either had on the same clothes as before or she had on her long green robe – which indicates she had gone to her room. I'm not sure, my best guess would be the robe. I believe was (Author's note: I think she meant to write: "I believe **I** was the last ...") *the last of the known persons to see her.*

About ½ hour later – Karen, who also lives in the basement, came home. She also came into my room and talked to me for maybe 15 – 30 minutes, then she went to bed. My door was closed; I heard no sounds that night. I went to bed around 1:30 a.m. My first suspicions concerning her absence came the next - day about 4:00 p.m. Karen was worried that she didn't come home. I called Dick Shearer's house & (redacted)'s dorm – but with no success. Neither (redacted) nor (redacted) were home & I had talked to other people. Mrs. Healy called – I told her Lynda was not home yet. Her father and brother arrived at our house about 5:00 – 6:00. We all were home by this time and somewhat worried. She had planned to have her parents come to our house for dinner. She had been looking forward to it – it was most unlikely for her not to show. The fact that she had not shown up for work added to our concern. Shortly after, the police were called.

The circumstances were odd. Her coats were there and her bike which she rode every morning to work. She had worn a long, brown hooded coat to Dante's the night before. I remembered that she had only taken her wallet with her & when I checked – found it still there. Her red and grey backpack was gone.

Before the police went to Lynda's room I had gone in it. I found her curtains to be closed. I believe it was usual for her to open them during the day & close them at night. I noticed her room was neat and her bed was also neatly made. To my knowledge it was not customary to make her bed on those mornings that she had to work. It also seems to me that she did not always put her pillow under the bedspread – rather sometimes placed it on top. She had two pink satin pillowcases. I was there when the policeman pulled back the spread for the first time. I saw that the pillowcase was gone and that there were bloodstains on the pillow as well as one fairly large blood stain on the sheet – near the pillow. As far as I know, Lynda always kept a pillowcase on her pillow.

In regard to the side door – I can't say much. I never examined (it) right after her disappearance. I do know, though, that it was difficult to unlock from the outside even with a key & it was used primarily to take our bicycles in and out. I do not recall seeing it open as the newspaper said, but Karen did say it was unlocked in the morning when she checked it.

The matter of the keys – Lynda and I had both lost our keys. I lost mine after she did & I don't know how or where. They were not recovered. I had a key to the front door on my set but not the side door. I don't think Lynda did either, but she did have a front door key. She was quite sure she had lost her keys from her coat pocket. Hers were not found either. In fact, we had planned to go Friday afternoon to have spare keys made.

An incident happening before all of this, maybe 1 ½ months ago, I will tell as I remember Lynda telling me:

She was in the laundromat, alone (this was on the avenue near our home). She noticed a guy in an orange pickup who stopped in front of the laundromat and stared in. He came in – walked around - had no laundry there – but fooled around with a machine. He checked the back door – he left - then he pulled up again – again staring at Lynda – and came in again, I believe. She said he did drive away then, and by this time she was very frightened. She had had an earlier bad experience with a guy in a car who had offered her a ride which she accepted and since that time she was very afraid of situations like this. The guy never spoke to her or approached her, but she came home (I think on her bicycle with her clothes) very upset about the incident.

The only thing I can add is that Lynda and I were close friends. We confided in each other a great deal. She is not one given to moodiness or despondency. I have always known her to be reliable and responsible. She is a lively, healthy, person. I know others would confirm these traits.

February 5, 1974

Statement of Karen Mary Skaviem

Thursday evening, January 31, 1974, was the last time I saw Lynda Healy. It was at our house on 5517 12th Avenue N.E. At this time, she seemed to be in good spirits in comparison to how she had felt earlier that week. She told me her stomach cramps were gone and that she was looking forward to having her parents and boyfriend over the next evening for dinner. I asked her if she had been back to see a doctor about her stomach and she said "no." That night I went out and did not return until 12:00 p.m. (I had been to the library studying and then out for a drink with my boyfriend). (Author's note: an obvious mistake; she means 12:00 a.m.)

When I returned, a single living room light was on, and I could see the light from Joanne Testa's room on. I know she was still up so I went in to talk to her. We talked until 12:45 p.m. (Author's note: same mistake as before) *when at which time I went downstairs to my room in the basement. As I went down the stairs I didn't notice whether or not the side door was locked. The basement light was on but the light in Lynda's room wasn't. I assumed she was asleep and went to bed. I couldn't sleep right away but fell asleep about 1:30. The rest of the night I heard no sounds and didn't awaken until 5:30a.m., when I heard Lynda's radio alarm go on. I went back to sleep until 6:00 a.m., when my alarm went off. I got up and Lynda's alarm was still going. I went past the room & heard her radio but thought she was lying in bed listening to it & didn't have to work.*

At 6:30 a.m. the phone rang. Ginger and I both answered it. It was Northwest Ski Promotions asking why Lynda wasn't at work. I went to her room and called out to her. When she didn't answer, I turned the light on and went in. Her radio was still going and her bed was made, perfectly. I was convinced she hadn't slept in it as there were no wrinkles and the spread was neatly tucked under the pillow (which is unusual for Lynda to make her bed that way). As I walked back up the stairs to the phone, I noticed her bike was there and the side door was unlocked (which also was unusual.) I told the girl on the phone that Lynda wasn't there and we hung up.

A few minutes later the phone rang again and it was the same girl asking if Lynda's bike was there and I said "no" and we both got a little concerned. (Author's note: Karen made a mistake here, as Lynda's bike was there, and Northwest Ski Promotions was actually told by someone else that her bike was in fact still at the house). *I then hung up and asked Ginger and Monica if either of them knew where Lynda was and they didn't. I wasn't too worried because I thought she could be with her boyfriend and also* (redacted), *a friend from Olympia was in town. I thought Joanne would know where Lynda was for sure, but Joanne had left for work.*

At 12:30 I saw Joanne on campus and asked if she knew about Lynda and she didn't. Then I became worried because Lynda always told one of us where she was going. When all of us were home from school we knew something was wrong because her parents were due to be over any time and we know she had planned on being home all day to cook and clean. (I had come home at 2:30 and waited for the rest before deciding what to do.) We decided to wait until the father and brother arrived and tell them the story. When they came, Mr. Healy called his wife in Bellevue and told her not to come for dinner. She wanted to call the police but Mr. Healy said to wait. A few minutes later the phone rang and Mrs. Healy said a police officer would be over to the house in a few minutes. That officer was Officer Marshall, who took the first report.

The last time I saw Lynda she had on blue jeans and brown scuffed hiking boots. I think she may have had on a white smock-type blouse with blue trim on the sleeves and along the rounded collar. The blouse is an imported type from Mexico. She probably had on knee socks because this is what she always wears.

Lynda does her laundry about every two weeks (not more than this) at which time she washes everything. But if Lynda has an accident and gets something particularly dirty she washes this by hand.

February 6, 1974, 2:15 p.m.

Statement of Monica Louise Sutherland

The following statement is made of my own free will and is as accurate as I can be.

On the afternoon of Thursday, the 31st of January, I returned home from school around 1:00 p.m. Linda (Author's note: Monica will continue to misspell Lynda's name throughout her statement.) *was home at that time. Conversation,* (I cannot read the word here) *to daily jargon, and I inquired about her health. She said she felt much better, and would wait to see a doctor the following week. At 2:30 I drove her to the university – for her choir practice at 5:00 p.m. I picked up Ginger Heath at the university, and then picked up Linda – and returned home.*

About 6:00, I went upstairs to bed as I was not feeling well. Linda had stated prior to this when we were all sitting around she felt like going over to Dante's for a couple of beers, and then back home to bed. (redacted) *apparently came by, sometime around 6:30 or so, because he knocked on my door – and asked for me but I refused to answer him. He stated that Monica must be asleep. Around 8:30 – the phone rang, it was* (redacted) *asking for Linda. Upon getting up to answer the phone, I decided not to try and sleep anymore. Came downstairs, fooled around, and turned on the TV. Within about 15 minutes, Joanne, Linda, and* (redacted, but this is Pete Neal), *arrived home, shortly followed by Ginger. (*Redacted, Pete Neal) *said goodbye at the door, as he had to catch a bus. Ginger's brother and friend came by about 9:45 or so. We were all watching the Jane Pittman show and commenting. About 10:30 or so, I went up to go to bed and Linda was talking to* (redacted) *on the phone. She seemed in very good, relaxed, somewhat jovial mood.*

Friday morning at 6:30, the phone rang. Karen yelled up to see if we knew where Linda was, I yelled down that maybe she went to see (redacted, but it's Lynda's boyfriend) *after talking with him and everyone said no, she wouldn't bother to go see him. Went to school, did my laundry, shopping, picked up Ginger at 5:00 p.m. from the U of W. Upon walking in the door, Karen reported still no sign of Linda and her parents were due any time. The house was a mess. Not all the food had been purchased for dinner, and it was beyond us where she was. This was when I realized that something serious was wrong, besides just not showing up for work.*

We started to call her boyfriend (redacted), *and also called* (redacted) *to see if we could locate her. Around 6:00, her father & brother arrived for dinner – no Linda. Mr. Healy, after our talk about Linda, called Mrs. Healy, who I guess called the police and had a dispatch unit sent out. A young officer came (and) took a missing person report and left. The phone rang intermittingly from there on. 3 calls (...). – 7:00 – 9:00 -were dead by the time we said hello. Around 10:30, my sister Donna had called and said we should go around to all stores and bars – she proceeded to do this. When they asked in the Stop N Go on Ravenna and University Way the clerk told them, that a girl had come in around 2:00 Thursday night – and purchased Pepto Bismol. Thinking along the lines that Linda was sick -we took a photo down (for the clerk to look at). The man stated it could have been her* (Author's note: the following few words are illegible and undecipherable, which I have also indicated elsewhere by the use of question marks in those places where the original text cannot be deciphered) *he was quite rude and not interested. We then flagged down the patrol car to see if they would try questioning the clerk, they said no, but to call the patrol car in the university area.*

Sometime after midnight I think this was, another unit came out, got the story, and proceeded down to her room. *Within minutes, I followed down to see that they had ripped open her bed, and the blood was visible. I was not present when they pulled back the (????). A sergeant then came through and was downstairs for a time. We talked with the other police (officer) for a time and then they left. Joanne, Karen, Ginger, (redacted,) and I stayed the rest of the time in the living room until (Saturday) morning.*

Concerning Linda's room prior to the time police came through, I recall being surprised that things were so neat. Not a stitch of clothing anywhere and her bed made to perfection. Usually her bathrobe, shirt, or books (????) were within the room – not messy but a lived-in look. And her bedspread just thrown up over the pillow. I believe Linda's curtain is usually open during the day just to bring some light into the room. Also she attends to her plants almost every day, and so she was likely to have the curtain open to observe the (????) on the window.

Pertaining to the habits of our backside door. The door is used almost primarily for transferring our bikes outside, in fact that is the only reason, because it is too difficult to lock from the outside. Ginger and I had been driving to school that entire week so we did not ever use our bikes. Ginger and Karen are the two who are the most concerned about locking the doors, and they are the ones who often have (????) and locked it. I never check it. Neither Karen nor Ginger could recall if they had locked it Thursday night.

I don't think that any of us can stress how unlikely it would be for Linda to have left by herself that night. It just isn't her. I don't believe I have had many good friends as basic and good of a (????) as Linda was.

She is a reliable, considerate - (no temper) jovial person – it just doesn't add up that she would go out alone after dark.

I believe it was a month or so later (after Christmas though) that I was alone and had just come home and undressed for bed. Our neighbor's dog started barking considerably, much more so than usual. I grabbed a robe and ran downstairs not being fully dressed & looked through the door, and saw a young man standing on our lower step and holding this little dog around the neck shaking it fiercely.

I rushed out – and found many neighbors already outside & yelled at him - he replied something like this dog was attacking me and then fled on foot – I believe he was dressed in dark blue sweatshirt and pants – white male- 21 -25.

In reference to Linda's clothing, I can only be positive about her navy jeans, (????) and brown hiking boots of a plastic leather look. Two rings, one on the ring finger of each hand. Her hair was down straight shoulder length that night. In reference to the white smock type blouse I can recall vaguely seeing it but am not sure if Linda had it on. A triangular patch was across the right side of the jeans on the lower tip of the pocket. I can't describe the top though as I feel I remember it but I think it is just what everyone else has said I think.

I would be more than happy to take a polygraph test concerning my knowledge of Linda Healy, and her whereabouts. As stated before, the previous knowledge is absolutely true as I recall.

February 6, 1974, 2:15 p.m.

Statement of Ginger Renee Heath

The above and following information is all correct and given freely.

On Friday morning, February 1, 1974, I was awakened by a phone call from Lynda's work, saying she hadn't shown up, two minutes later they called again wondering if her bike was gone. Karen then checked for her bike, which was still there, she also checked Lynda's room, the room was very neat and the bed was made, something Lynda rarely does before going to work.

I left for school at 8:00 a.m. and came home at 5:00 p.m. Lynda had still not come home. She had plans for a special dinner for her family and boyfriend at our house, at 6:00 p.m. or so. She was planning on being home all afternoon to clean house and to cook the meal. Since it is so unlike Lynda to miss making dinner for her parents and to not call and tell us, we waited for her dad & brother to come to the house about 6:00, the police were then notified. In the meantime, we made calls to all her friends that may have seen her that day. No one had seen or heard from her.

Around 8:00 p.m., after Lynda's dad and brother had gone home and after the first report was made, we got a phone call which Monica answered, there was no one on the other end. We got two others similar to that within the hour. Later that evening, Monica's sister and friend went to the Stop N Go market, a block or so away from our house, asking if possibly someone had stopped in Thursday night or Friday morning. The man at the store said someone had come in around 2:00 a.m. Friday morning and bought some Pepto Bismol. Monica, her sister, and I then took a picture down to see if he would recognize it, he didn't seem to recognize the face.

We got in the car afterwards about midnight Friday and saw a patrol car so we stopped them and showed them Lynda's picture, thinking maybe they saw her walking somewhere late Thursday or early Friday morning. One officer said he thought he recognized the picture but he couldn't remember where, they then referred us to the district officers.

We then went back home and called the district police. They came by our house and got the picture of Lynda and took it back down to the Stop N Go market, they got the same response from the man at the store. The district officers then asked if they could see Lynda's room. On showing them her room, they went through the waste paper basket and pulled back the bedspread and blankets on Lynda's bed finding blood. The first thing I immediately noticed was the missing pillow case. Also the bed was made differently from the way Lynda usually makes it. The bedspread was tucked under the pillow whereas usually she just throws it over the pillow without a crease under the pillow. Also the bedspread was so perfect, in that there were no wrinkles on the bed. I thought too, that when the officers pulled back the blankets, the sheets were folded in such a fashion that the blood wasn't as visible.

The blood was in the upper right-hand corner, if you were looking from the foot of the bed. Also, there was a spot of blood on the pillow on the right side, and there was blood on the opposite side, somewhat in the center. I later went down to her room to see about clothing missing, this is still on Friday night & early Saturday morning. I then found her nightie draped across the bottom pole in her closet, finding a smear of blood on it on the shoulder. I think the curtains were slightly opened, but I don't know if possibly one of the officers had opened them.

I remember Karen saying Friday morning that the side door was unlocked. We usually try to make a habit of locking it, but I don't remember checking it Thursday night to see that it was locked. The door is primarily used for taking our bikes in and out of the house. I didn't ride my bike that Thursday, so the side door was not used by me at all. Usually if someone does ride their bike they take it out the side door and then go back in the house through the side door.

On this night (on Thursday night) we were all watching TV and Lynda was wearing waffle stomper boots, navy blue jeans, a white smock peasant-like top with multi-color fringe on the sleeves and around the neck (blue was a predominant color). She also had on two rings on each ring finger.

All of Lynda's coats were still at our house, also, her wallet and all of her purses were still there. Her red backpack was missing, but most of her books were still at the house.

We had thought that possibly the person that bought the Pepto Bismol could have seen Lynda because she had been complaining of stomach pains, also she was saying she was having trouble focusing on various objects.

On Thursday evening I came home from my night class just as Lynda, Joanne, and (redacted – Pete Neal) *were coming back from Dante's. We watched TV, then my brother and his friend came and visited at about 9:45. I went to bed about 10:30. Between about 9:30 and 10:00, Lynda was talking to* (redacted – her boyfriend). *Joanne last talked to her.*

The above statements were given to the detectives on my own and in my own handwriting.

The following information from this same report is a bit interesting, as it brings up a "possible" connection between Ted Bundy, Lynda Ann Healy, and Bundy's cousin, Edna Cowell. Also, you will notice that the detectives often place material within the report that offer dates of events, and they do not appear in chronological order. Why this occurred is unknown, it is probably due to the compilation of a great deal of material that was formed into the reports over time, and not all of it was done "neatly" as it were. This was an unimportant aspect to the investigators, as they were absorbing the material before them and their understanding of the case was not diminished in any way by having the report appear this way. Because it is the official report, I have left it all as is.

During the months of June through August 1972, Lynda Healy lived with Karen Covach and Kathy Henderson at a house on Ravenna Blvd. That June, Edna Cowell, a good friend of Karen Covach, came to visit. Edna Cowell is also Ted Bundy's cousin. Edna Cowell related she had met Lynda Healy while visiting Covach at Ravenna. Neither Karen, Kathy, nor Edna recall Ted meeting Lynda Healy. Edna recalls discussing Lynda's disappearance with Ted in 1974, but she thought the content of the conversation was that it was a "terrible thing."

In the fall of 1972, Kathy and Karen moved to 816 N. 47th Street, in Seattle, while Lynda remained on campus.

Karen Covach recalled seeing Ted in the Greenwood area in the summer of 1972, and also at 816 N. 47th during the summer after Lynda's disappearance.

Karen Covach and Kathy Henderson last saw Lynda Healy on January 29, 1974, at 816 N 47th. Lynda had come over to invite them to her party the next weekend.

In the summer of 1974, Enda moved in with Karen and Kathy. Edna's previous address for two years was 905 NE 43rd Street. This address is about two blocks south of Northwest Ski Productions where Lynda Healy worked. Edna knew that Lynda worked at Northwest Ski but did not know if Ted knew. Ted was a skier and had taken Edna skiing. Ted's address was about four blocks from Northwest Ski.

Ted Bundy frequented the Safeway store at 49th and Brooklyn where he often cashed checks. Also, Lynda Healy shopped at the same Safeway store. In fact, she wrote a check to Safeway on January 31, 1974, the day she disappeared.

During the month of January 1974, Ted Bundy had been going to night school at University of Puget Sound Law School. Normal class times were on Monday (1700-2245), Wednesday (1700-2130), and Friday (1700-2130). Healy was missing after 11:00 p.m. on January 31, 1974, which was a Thursday, a night when Bundy was not in class.

Since about XXXX, Bundy had been living at 4143-12 NE, Seattle. At the time of her abduction, Lynda Healy lived approximately fourteen blocks away from Bundy at 5517-12 NE. Bundy's girlfriend (Author's note: redacted here, but this is Liz, and this is her address, usually redacted in previous reports), *lived at 5208-18 NE, six blocks from Healy.*

The chance that Bundy either met or saw Healy prior to her abduction is significant.

In 1972, both Healy and Bundy were enrolled at the University of Washington (redacted), *where both were majoring in psychology. When comparing their transcripts for the winter quarter of 1972, investigation revealed that both were enrolled in similar classes, Psych 498 (Readings in Psych) and Psych 499 (Undergraduate research). These classes were not the type that met in a typical classroom setting. For these courses, the student would arrange with an advisor or instructor regarding specific readings to be completed or approval for a topic to be researched. No investigation has yet affirmatively concluded that Healy and Bundy met each other regarding these Psychology classes, or even in the building.*

CHAPTER TWO

GEORGANN HAWKINS

What follows are reports and information pertaining to the abduction and murder of Gerogann Hawkins. During the writing of my main Bundy book, *The Bundy Murders: A Comprehensive History*, I spoke with individuals who had been friends of the victims, and very often, they did not want to talk or be a part of the project. Occasionally, they would tell of their experiences, but did so off the record, which meant that I was not to reproduce what they'd told me for the printed page, and I always adhered to their wishes. And there have been occasions where friends of the victims did speak openly with me for the record, and I remain grateful for such assistance. Occasionally, folks would not learn of me until after the publication of *The Bundy Murders*, and when they did contact me, they were, of course, willing to talk. Yet even here (as in the case of Lorraine Fargo) they found it difficult to discuss what had happened, even after all these years, and wondered if dredging up these terrible memories was the correct thing to do. Therefore, I have always appreciated any efforts they have made to share their stories with me.

One individual who did return my call concerning the Georgann Hawkins abduction was Duane Covey. Incidentally, Duane was the last person to speak with Georgann Hawkins, literally only minutes before Bundy encountered her. And as with most of the others, Duane did not want to be interviewed about those events, so when we finally spoke, I kept my questions very brief, and basically asked him to confirm a couple of things that he'd told a reporter for *The Seattle Times*, and he confirmed that those statements were correct. As such, I'm going to begin this additional look at Georgann's abduction and murder from the record. And I will complete it with some quotes from an article published in Arizona that contains the thoughts and feelings of Georgann Hawkins' mother. First, however, a preface of sorts from me:

The evening of June 11, 1974, was a nice one, with pleasant temperatures, and a clear night sky. Georgann Hawkins, a first-year student at the University of Washington, was looking forward to closing out what had turned out to be a good freshman year for her. She was excited about getting back home to her family in Tacoma. She was just starting to enjoy her life as a young adult, a time for her to experience life and make wise choices, as she began her trek into full adulthood. She had plans for her future.

Georgann was also aware that a number of young women had disappeared from the area, and she was doing everything she knew to do to keep herself safe. So, when she took a break, from studying for a Spanish test scheduled for the next day, to go to a party, she left her sorority house on Greek Row with a friend, planning to return for more study time in just a couple of hours. Later, on her way back, she stopped at her boyfriend's fraternity house, and visited with him for about thirty minutes. I covered the below sequence of events in my book, *The Bundy Murders*.

For the next thirty minutes she visited with Marvin, the conversation apparently consisting of small talk and the upcoming test. After a brief kiss, George, as she was called by friends, walked out the back door and stepped into the alley. It was around 1:00 a.m. on

June 11. Duane Covey, whose second-floor room faced the alleyway, heard the slamming of the back door and jumped up just in time to see Georgann leaving. Covey called out to her, and the two spent the next five minutes chatting, mostly about her Spanish test, now only hours away. As they talked, Covey said they could hear someone laughing somewhere down the ally, and Georgann would occasionally glance in that direction. The two friends bid farewell to each other in Spanish, and Georgann Hawkins left to continue the short walk to her residence. Covey watched her, he said, for about forty feet, as she continued south toward the sorority house, before losing sight of her in the darkness. Naturally, he then turned away from his window. As Bundy strolled very slowly up the alley, he saw a door open and a woman emerge. He heard the faint sound of the door shutting and he watched as she began walking in his direction, only to stop. As she turned back around, he knew from the angle of her head that she was talking to someone in the window. With anticipation, he watched and listened, his mind already beginning to seize the opportunity in the making, to sense that he would soon have her, as that subtle rush of sexual arousal, began coursing through his being. As she said goodnight and then resumed what would have been a very brief walk to her place, she noticed the lone individual hobbling his way in her direction.

Had Covey continued standing at the window for another minute or so, he would have seen Georgann re-emerge from the darkness holding a briefcase and walking beside a seemingly disabled man hobbling on crutches, sporting a leg cast. They would, in fact, pass just below Covey's window as they ambled their way up the alley to 47th, where they crossed the street, turned right on the sidewalk, took a quick left at the corner, continuing north on 17th for about half a block. Just as they were about to pass a makeshift parking lot, unpaved and without proper lighting, the injured man motioned that his car was in the lot. His vehicle, a light brown VW Beetle, was the only one in sight. Unlike Greek Row, this area was completely devoid of human activity.

This lie of disability he presented worked perfectly on Georgann, who must have found the pitiful form approaching her completely non-threatening. So when he asked for help with his briefcase she didn't think twice about it. It just seemed the right thing to do. She could help him, she believed, and in a few minutes be on her way. There was still plenty of time to conquer the Spanish language.

Approaching the car, he guided her from behind to the passenger side door. It is unknown if the car was unlocked (probably not), or whether she unlocked it at his request. He may even have turned the key himself and then stepped back, giving Georgann room to open the door; still, the exact sequence of events here is a mystery. But what happened next is not. As Georgann stayed focused on the task at hand, he reached underneath the rear of his car for the crowbar he'd placed there earlier, and with one lightning-quick movement, he struck her in the skull, knocking her out cold.

What follows is from the official report and it contains the statement from Marvin Gellatly, Georgann's boyfriend, who was the second-to-last person to speak with her prior to her disappearance:

June 12, 1974, 2000 hrs.

Received a call from a Marv Gellatly LA2-7211. Gellatly states that he is a friend of the Hawkins girl and has been out with her on several occasions. He states that she was of high morals and never did anything with him other than drink beer. Gellatly also stated that the Hawkins girl carried some ID that belonged to another woman. He did not know where she had gotten it, but stated the Hawkins girl carried it with her all the time. She used it for getting into taverns and such. Gellatly he had looked thru the Hawkins girl's billfold several times and this was usually the only ID he ever saw in her wallet.

Gellatly states that he does not remember the name on the ID, but will attempt to find out what it is and call it in. To the best of his recollection he thinks the first name was Marsha, with a birth date making her twenty-three years of age.

Gellatly also stated that another girl by the name of Debbie West, who had been living in a sorority house in the district, has seen this suspect with the white/black two-door Cadillac hanging around in the district watching various houses. West told Gellatly that she would recognize the suspect in a second, as they have observed him on several occasions and had turned out the lights in the house and watched him. She claims he wears a silver colored watch on his left wrist, wears colored glasses, black hair, with sideburns, smokes cigars, and is probably in his late 40s.

West's parents have made her move home and she can probably be contacted at the phone number given.

The writer of the following report makes numerous mistakes by referring to a sorority house as either a fraternity or frat house. After several pages, someone came behind him and made the corrections from frat to sorority in black pen ink on this typed-up report. Therefore, the location will be inconsistently referred to as both a fraternity and a sorority, but both are referring to the victim's sorority house.

SEATTLE POLICE DEPARTMENT

MISSING PERSON: Hawkins, Georgann

Reporting Person: Bates, Mary House Mother

Last Seen By: Covey, Duane

Last seen by Covey, Duane (witness) in the alley behind Greek Row at approximately 0110 hours 6-11-74. Witness was talking to victim at this time and victim told witness that she was going back to the house to study.

6-12-74 0800 hours; Assigned case for further investigation from Sgt. Beeson, to work in conjunction with Det. Jelberg, Missing Persons bureau.

On becoming familiar with the missing person report, the report states that victim did live in residence at 5521 17th Avenue NE. and when last seen by witness Covey, Duane, was in the alley approx. 1 block from residence. Looking at census map, this is location due west and north from victim residence.

Also check with census map reveals that victim's residence is approx. 4 blocks south from where Healy was living and approx. 4 blocks east of the Healy home. This would place the radius of approx. a 5 block radius.

Det. Jelberg has contacted the parents who live 10422 Delwood Drive SW, Tacoma, Wash given phone number as JU8 XXXX and business phone as GR 2 XXXX Tacoma, Wash. The father, Mr. Hawkins states that his wife will be at home all day this date, and further contact can be made with her or him at his place of business. In interviewing the father, Mr. Hawkins this date, he stated the victim talked to her mother on Monday 6-10-74 and appeared to be in very good spirits and was talking about taking the final exams at the U of W. Mr. Hawkins stated he will obtain dental charts of victim and will either bring them to the office or mail them.

Called the frat. house and they stated they have not seen victim since time of reporting. Det. Jelberg to Communications requesting all information be given to units on the missing victim.

6-12-74 0810 hours. Miss Laura Heffron of 4521 17th Avenue NE, roommate of victim, called stating she had information which detectives might be interested in pertaining to a suspicious vehicle seen in the area prior to victim's attempt to return home. Advised her that we would be out as soon as possible this date to talk to her.

6-12-74 0845 hours: Detectives along with Sgt. Beeson to 4521 17th Avenue NE. Checked the alley behind above address, and found that the sorority house where victim lived is approx. ¾ of a block south of NE 47th (BETA Frat house 1617 NE 47th). Upon our arrival, uniformed officers arrived and sealed off alley waiting for Mr. Ishii and his lab crew to arrive for a methodical search of the alley.

Sometime after the securing of the alley was accomplished, and after an additional swarm of police descended upon the area, Ted Bundy rode his bicycle through the area to retrieve from the parking lot the earrings that flew off Georgann's ears after he'd struck her with the crowbar, as well as the one shoe that had come off her foot at the same time. Peddling through the area, Bundy had an up-close and too personal look at the detectives and patrolmen who were working the alley and the surrounding area. Apparently, they hadn't yet ventured one block away to the parking lot where Georgann was assaulted and rendered unconscious. Had the police spotted a single woman's shoe lying in the lot, they'd have cordoned off the area as a potential crime scene. Once again, however, luck had gone Bundy's way and, soon after picking up the clog shoe and earrings, he again left the area.

The report continues:

0900 hours: Detectives to room #8 victim's room and found a Miss Laura Heffron who stated that she was the roommate of the victim. At this time numerous ladies (residents) of the frat (Author's note: there he goes again, obviously not understanding the difference between a sorority house and a fraternity house) *house (Kappa Alpha Thema) appeared at the room. At this time detectives requested from House Mother Mary Bates if there was an area where we could converse with the girls. We were taken to a visiting room on main floor lobby. On talking to girls whose names will appear in order of conversation, the following was obtained:*

Laura Heffron: She states that she and victim were freshman at the U of W, and when she saw victim on evening prior to incident, the victim was wearing the following: navy blue good quality slacks which buttoned on the left side. These slacks were supposed to have four blue buttons but Laura stated that victim had only one button left and with this she went back to her room and obtained one of the buttons that was missing. White T-shirt halter top with collar. This was tied in the back and the back was bareless (sic).

Red, white, and blue long sleeved shirt. This was not tucked into victim's slacks but was tied by the tails in the front. Skin-toned or light tan Jack purse (leather) with red stains on it. The purse supposedly contains the following items, in a large purple wallet:

U of W ID card with photo

WSOL (info from Major Report) HA WK IG 453NO

Checkbook from Sea 1st Bank, Lakewood Branch, Tacoma, Washington

Other contents in JACK purse:

One bottle Heaven Scent perfume approx. 5" tall and ½" in diameter

One small brush with black bristles

One small jar of Vaseline

Laura further stated that victim's habits were of a normal pattern. That whenever she went out she would always let some Frat girl know where she was going and would always leave a telephone number. When asked if the victim was an indulgent of alcohol, she stated that she drank beer of any type, and that when she drank hard liquor it normally was Vodka mixed with a Tom Collins mix. She never seemed to get tipsy but always maintained her demeanor. Laura also stated that the victim was supposed to be going home to her parents in Tacoma on 6-13-74 (this would be upon completion of exams). Laura was then asked pertaining to any jewelry victim was wearing. She relayed that victim was wearing a rectangular shaped ring on her middle left finger. The stone was a black onyx type, with a very small diamond inserted in center of ring. The band was of gold metal. On the victim's right ring finger was a gold band ring with a small pearl inserted at the top. Victim was not wearing any wristwatch, and according to Laura, the victim's eyesight was not the best and she normally wore glasses or contact lenses. These the victim did not have with her when she disappeared. They were still in room #8 this date. Victim's teeth were good but not solid white. She had very good body stature, and the last thing recalled was that victim did have freckles about her nose. Her hair length is shorter than the photo attached to this case.

0930 hours. Talked to another lady who resides at the sorority (corrected again) *house with the victim, and given name is Jennifer Roberts, also a freshman at the U of W. Jennifer Roberts states habits and description are identical to what Laura describes. Jennifer stated that on June 10, 1974, she and victim and some other girls went to a frat party located around 50th NE. She states that Georgann had three beers while at the party and when they left the party approx. 0030 hours on 6-11-74 she and victim walked to the corner of NE 47th and 17 NE, where victim stated she was going to stop in at the Beta Fraternity House and see her boyfriend Marvin Bruce Gellatly WM 22, 1617 NE 47th. Jennifer states the victim told her to walk on down to their Frat* (sorority) *house, and, when she arrived, for her to yell back that everything was okay. Jennifer states that she did this, and stated upon arriving at the front of her house, she yelled back to the victim, and the victim in turn yelled back at her that all was okay. This was the last she seen* (sic) *of the victim. Jennifer then showed detectives the back* door and stated that this door is always locked in the afternoon, the majority of traffic within the house is from the front door. She also mentions that victim had seeing (eye) trouble and could not see at distances.

1000 Hours: Detectives talked to Marvin Bruce Gellatly WM 22 given address as 1617 NE 47th, LA 2 7211, home address away from U of W: 1220 1st Street, Wenatchee, Wash. Gellatly states he and victim have been going steady for the past quarter approx. three mos. That she did arrive at his roommate's Jeff Eckman's room at approx. 0030 hours 6-11-74 and that she sat and talked to him for approx. ½ hour. The conversation was of normal tone, school work, etc. After she finished talking, she stated that she had to be going home (four houses south of the Beta House). Gellatly stated he does not know whether she went out the front door or the back, but figured she went out the front.

1000 hours: This was the last time he seen (sic) victim, as she stated she had to do some serious studying for Spanish exam this date. Gellatly is very concerned and became very cooperative with investigators. His description of clothing is almost identical to others.

1000 Hours: Det. Cuthill talked to Duane Covey 1617 NE. 47th BETA HOUSE, and resides on second floor facing the alley of the above house.

At approx. 0115 hours, June 11, 1974, Covey states he was sitting in his room and heard the back door slam, and when he approached the window to see who it was, he saw the victim heading south down the alley, and he asked her where she was going, and she stated she was going home to study her Spanish. Covey states they talked for approx. five minutes. They said their goodbyes in Spanish and the last he seen *(sic) of victim, was she was walking down the alley southbound. He heard no cries nor screams, and has not seen victim since.*

Note: In talking to girls and men about the Frat houses, they all appear to have the same description of the victim as far as demeanor goes. She was outgoing in conversation, very friendly with all concerned, and would not go out with any person unless she knew the person personally. Girls state that she went out on a blind date last Friday with a WM by name of Greg Knowles, and that he has since left school as his exams are finished, giving telephone number as 858 – XXXX Gig Harbor Washington. Greg is supposed to have been living at the Pheta house on 21st and 47th.

The following is a letter sent to Det. Jelberg by Georgann's parents. It also contained a draft of a missing person's bulletin for Georgann which they had prepared.

June 20, 1974

Det. G. Jelberg

610 Third Avenue Room 529

Seattle, Washington 98104

Dear Det. Jelberg,

As you requested, we are forwarding a written statement posting a reward for information leading to the return of our daughter, Georgann. Also enclosed are the pictures and description of the jewelry she was wearing at the time of her disappearance. I talked with her roommates Laura Heffron and Phyllis Armstrong last evening, and they indicated that a description, as well as a drawing, of the rings were given to Det. Ted Fonis of your Department.

In addition to requesting your help in securing the printing of posters and distribution concerning the reward, we would also appreciate having an account of the disappearance and Georgann's description printed in the Crime Digest, which it is my understanding, is distributed throughout the country.

Mr. Hawkins and I are most appreciative of all of the hard work that you and your associates have put into trying to determine what has happened to our child. We know that you will continue to do everything possible to bring about a resolution of this problem.

God bless you in your work.

Sincerely,

Edith E, Hawkins

(Mrs. W. B. Hawkins)

P.S. It is also our understanding that the flyer or poster will contain a picture of Georgann and that you have the same available. If this is not correct, will you please contact us immediately? We feel that neither of the likenesses are good ones of her.

$5000 REWARD

GEORGANN HAWKINS, 18 years old, disappeared from the alley behind the 4500 Block of NE 17th Street, Greek Row, of the University of Washington, Seattle, Washington, on June 11, 1974. A reward of $5000 for information leading to her safe return has been posted.

The police have indicated that the circumstances of her disappearance were very serious. If you have any information concerning Georgann, call Seattle, area code (206) emergency number "911," (206) 583-2343, or your local police.

Description: White female, height 5'2," weight 118 to 120 lbs., shoulder-length, medium brown hair, brown eyes, olive complexion, heavily tanned at time of disappearance. Last seen wearing (please complete from your records).

What follows is a portion of a Seattle Post-Intelligencer article, which was published on Wednesday, June 19, 1974.

Seattle police stated yesterday they have turned up "absolutely nothing" in the way of clues in the search for Georgann Hawkins, 18. When told that the parents of the girl, Mr. and Mrs. Warren Hawkins, of Lakewood near Tacoma, appear to be losing hope that their daughter will be found alive and well, a homicide detective said, "So are we."

"Every day I'm a little bit lower," the girl's father said. "You'd like to hope. But I'm too realistic. She was a very friendly, very involved youngster. I keep saying 'was.' I shouldn't say that. It's a job raising kids," Hawkins said, holding his head in his hands. "You steer them along and we figured we had both these kids over the hump."

Warren and Edith Hawkins, devastated at the loss of Georgann, went through the years by withdrawing from the public conversation about Ted Bundy and the death of their daughter. They never gave press interviews (she once gave a single sentence to a reporter after Bundy's execution, but that's it) and writers of books and articles were always turned away as well. It was the only way to survive, Edith Hawkins would explain later. It would be almost four decades to the day before Georgann's mother would allow the world just a peek into their lives. And it must have been a somewhat painful decision to do so.

Nevertheless, on June 11, 2014, the fortieth anniversary of Georgann's disappearance, an article was published where Edith Hawkins, ninety-three years old, sat down with a reporter from the *Green Valley News & Sun*, an Arizona paper. As Edith explained, she and Warren had moved to Green Valley, Arizona, after they retired and built a house, which the article's author describes as "a large home, bright and well-appointed." It was just the two of them living there until 2003, when Warren Hawkins passed away.

Of course, it's an interesting, well-written article, and it gives us a look into what their lives were like. But we must remember that the loved ones of the murdered never really come back from it. They manage and they adjust, but their lives will never be normal again. And above all, this is the unspoken thread that runs through this article. When the reporter spotted a scrapbook and other mementos of Georgann, Edith Hawkins explained, "That's it," she says. "That's all I have left of my daughter." Despite all the recounting of the many good things about Georgann's life and all her accomplishments, the painful reminder of her death seeps through every word.

When her high school and college classmates held a memorial service to honor Georgann just days after Bundy was executed, they chose not to attend. "My feeling at the time was, what was it for, you know? It wasn't going to help me any." And Edith Hawkins was right, of course.

CHAPTER THREE

KATHY PARKS

When I first wrote about Roberta Kathleen Parks (better known as Kathy to her family and friends, and now to the world) for my book, *The Bundy Murders*, I was able to touch upon her personality as well as the tragic circumstances of her death at the hands of Ted Bundy. A native of California, she enrolled at Oregon State University at Corvallis, and had the misfortune of encountering Bundy a little after 11:00 p.m. on May 6, 1974, as she was sitting in the Memorial Union Commons cafeteria. Bundy, speaking in the third-person to a writer, said he approached Kathy as she was sitting alone at a table. And chances are, there weren't many in the cafeteria at that time as it was only minutes away from closing, so there'd be little to no witnesses. By some ruse, he was able to convince Kathy to leave with him in his car. After he cleared the environs of the university and no prying eyes were upon them, he took control of Kathy, and now it was just a matter of time.

During the writing of the Kathy Parks murder I had a great deal of material from the case file and was able to reconstruct the events of that evening of May 6, 1974. I did not, as in the case of almost all the other Bundy murders, speak with any of the investigators about Kathy as everything I needed was already in the record. That said, once *The Bundy Murders* was published, a number of people, all close to Kathy in one way or another, contacted me to tell me their stories.

One of these individuals was Lorraine Pickard, known in my book as Lorraine Fargo, a friend of Kathy Parks and the last person to speak with her before Bundy led her away to her death. I believe of all the people who've contacted me over the years, Lorraine Fargo made the greatest impression on me. Indeed, if it wasn't for one of her sons searching out his mother's name on the internet per her connection with the Bundy case, she would never have known that she was mentioned in my book! The bottom line was we became good friends (for the relatively short time she had left; Lorraine contacted me in 2010 and she passed away on March 12, 2011), and we exchanged a number of phone calls and numerous emails.

Because Lorraine had carried a lot of emotional damage from Kathy's murder, she was a bit angered when she discovered that I had written about her role and her activities in the case but had never spoken with her. But once she got to know me, and I shared with her the information from the case files that allowed me to write about her role so accurately, she softened and we became "fast friends", so to speak, and I like to think that over the time we "worked" together, her facing her fears and bad memories surrounding the event acted as a catharsis of sorts; something she confessed to me as things unfolded.

Not only did Lorraine open up about her role during those days, but she also confirmed two things I believed about the night that Kathy was abducted, but couldn't prove. As such, when, I started writing *The Trail of Ted Bundy: Digging Up the Untold Stories* in 2015, I added some of the material I had collected from Lorraine that explains this. I also included where she goes into some detail about the emotional pain she's experienced through the years, and how the specter of Ted Bundy became a type of haunted essence that would pop up occasionally to spook her once again.

The information I'll be including here will be new testimony from my time with Lorraine, and it all relates to her relationship with Kathy Parks. And, as is my custom, I will not be repeating the information she provided that I included in *The Trail of Ted Bundy*, but for quick access you can read this info on pages 35–38 in that book. While this particular info from Lorraine came from a blog I chaired, much of it—but not all of it—had been copied and pasted by Lorraine from previous emails she'd sent me (why write it out twice, she mentioned), as we messaged each other about her role in the case. For this book, rather than copy and paste from her saved emails—I have them all—I found it easier to copy the blog and present it here.

Kathy and I met shortly after my roommates and I had moved to Sackett Hall at the beginning of winter term, in the 1973-1974 school year. We immediately identified that we were both from the San Francisco Bay Area. Kathy was from Lafayette, and I was from Novato, just a hop skip and a jump across the Bay. We were California girls, and most of the girls in our dorm were native Oregonians. Somehow silently deeming ourselves "more worldly" (young women can be so funny!) we both knew that we related to a similar "reality" that the other girls didn't share. As silly as I know this sounds now, it was actually the basis for our friendship, and we really did see ourselves alike, and different from the rest.

Kathy was a sophomore, and I was a freshman. More significantly, she was 20 (when we met) and I was 18, so I both looked up to and admired her. She was a quiet girl, but had a sharp, quick wit that could be utterly ruthless, though she was careful to never share it in a way that would be hurtful to anyone. I liked Kathy a lot.

At the time of her abduction, Kathy was dealing with a number of things in her life that were troubling. She was in love with her boyfriend Christy, but he wanted her to settle down and commit seriously, as in marriage, and Kathy was sure she wasn't ready for that. He was due to visit in about a week's time, and she knew he wanted her to make a decision. She didn't want to lose him, but she knew she wasn't ready for marriage. She also wasn't thrilled with her overall experience as a student. She felt that she was paying out-of-state tuition and going through the motions of her classes without feeling a direction. She questioned her major many times, and once declared that she would change her major to "underwater basket weaving" and leave it at that.

Prior to the conversation that Kevin mentions in his book (this is the conversation Kathy and Lorraine had on the sidewalk just across from the Memorial Union Commons where Kathy would soon encounter Bundy, and can be found in The Trail of Ted Bundy), Kathy and I had spoken earlier in the evening. At that time, she expressed her ongoing confusion about "what to do" about Christy, and her father's heart attack earlier that day, which her sister had assured her was not life threatening. She was very concerned about a Spanish test scheduled for the following day, for which she felt totally unprepared. While she was a sophomore and I was a freshman, I was, in fact, in a more advanced Spanish class than she was. She asked if I would help "quiz" her later that night. "Yes, I would be happy to."

Kathy and I were the "night owls" of our section of the dorm, so when I told her I had a literature report due the following day, which would require several hours in the library to complete, she said, "That's fine, just come and get me when you get home."

I went to the library (more on that later), finished my report, and left when it closed at 11:00 p.m. It's about a seven-minute walk back to the dorm. I had made my *way past the Memorial Union Commons, crossed the street, and saw Kathy heading my way. I said, "Oh, I was just going to come and get you to quiz you on your Spanish."*

She said, basically, "Forget the Spanish, I am still not prepared, and right now I don't even care." She went on to say that she was really having a rough time, trying to decide what to do about "everything" and that she had just smoked hashish. When I initially spoke to the campus police, after she disappeared, I wasn't forthcoming with that information, because I didn't want to get Kathy into any trouble. She said she was going to the Commons for a hot fudge sundae, and she would be back to the dorm in a while. I mentioned that I still had some things to do to complete my report, and that she could find me in the dorm "lounge" if she changed her mind about the Spanish help. I would be up late, and didn't want to disturb my roommate while I continued to work.

Lorraine did, in fact, go to the lounge, continued working, and after a while, finished her report. But by 2:00 a.m., she was headed to bed. Kathy's failure to return to the dorm bothered her, and Lorraine felt it was very odd she hadn't returned home. Not only did Kathy fail to return by 2:00 a.m., which was the standard curfew at OSU, but Lorraine knew Kathy hadn't made prior arrangements which would have allowed her to stay out and sleep somewhere else without ramifications. Indeed, everything about this was very troubling to Lorraine.

The next morning, Lorraine ran into Miriam "Bunny" Schmidt, Kathy's roommate, before class, and Schmidt said Kathy never returned home and they just looked at each other. Lorraine said she could tell Miriam was as concerned as she was. It was, although they didn't know it at the time, the beginning of their own personal nightmares. The following information is from the Office of Campus Security, Oregon State University.

Since Kathy's disappearance all points teletype bulletins have been sent to all police agencies in Oregon, California, and Washington, notifying them of her disappearance, her description, and several possible destinations. She has indicated to friends in the past that she would like to get away from Oregon State University and possibly go to The World's Fair, or return to her sister's residence in Black Point, California. On another occasion she mentioned that she would just like to leave campus and go to Portland and walk the streets. It is extremely doubtful at this time that she intended to return home because of her father's heart attack, as she has not arrived, after being missing for over a week. We have made inquiries of the main hospitals in the Portland, Corvallis, Albany areas with negative results. Each of these hospitals have been requested to contact the Campus Security Office immediately if they receive information as to her location.

The Corvallis Police Department, Benton County Sheriff's Office, Oregon State Police, and the FBI have been alerted as to her disappearance, and are coordinating their efforts with the Campus Security Department to locate her.

Her boyfriend, Christy McPhee, and her brother-in-law, Paul Kaehler, believe that Kathy may have gone to the Newport Beach area to seek solitude. We have placed telephone calls to various police agencies in the Newport, Florence, and Lincoln City areas, notifying them of her disappearance, and have also sent photographs to each of these departments and have requested that they be on the lookout for her. We have also received cooperation from the local and main channels of the news media which have broadcasted Kathy's description, listing her as a missing person, and asking anyone that may have seen her to notify the Campus Security Department. This information has been channeled through the OSU Department of Information.

The local Greyhound Bus depot has been checked for possible leads to the location of Kathy. It was learned, however, that the ticket office closes at 9:00 p.m. on weekdays and that individual drivers would have to be located in order to possibly identify her. At this time attempts are being made to locate drivers of Greyhound buses who were in Corvallis the night of May 6th or early morning hours of May 7, 1974.

One positive lead which has been developed is Kathy's checking account at Citizen's Bank, downtown branch, Corvallis. On May 6, she received a $50 check from her mother, of which she deposited $35 into her checking account. An interview of several friends of Kathy's at Sackett Hall revealed that she repaid approximately $10 in debts on this date prior to her disappearance. This would indicate that she had less than $10 on her person at the time she disappeared. A check with the employees of Citizen's Bank revealed that Kathy's bank balance is presently $40.50. They have agreed to immediately notify the Campus Security Department in the event that they receive any checks written on her account at that bank.

The OSU Department of Information has supplied the Campus Security with copies of photographs of Kathy which have been sent out to police departments in areas which it is believed that Kathy may have gone.

Christy McPhee and Paul Kaehler have also contacted the Corvallis Gazette Times and had missing persons bulletins printed (800) which they are distributing in the area in an attempt to locate her. Information from Paul Kaehler is that Kathy's grandfather has offered $500 reward for information leading to her location.

Kathy's oldest sister, Sharon Kaehler, has stated that Kathy may have gone to the World's Fair in Spokane, Washington. Kathy did tell her about wanting to go to the fair, however, Sharon does not think she would go until she was out of school this term. Information was recently received from Mr. Paul Kaehler, (Kathy's brother-in-law) that her father is now aware of her disappearance.

Christy McPhee indicated that over Christmas vacation last year, he and Kathy had hitchhiked to his aunt's residence in Canada, and that she had become very fond of this area. His aunt, Mary McPhee, area code (removed by author), *was contacted, and she advised that she had not seen Kathy, but will call the Campus Security Office if Kathy arrives at her residence.*

A telephone call was also placed to the Spokane Police Department and a photograph of Kathy sent to them. They will furnish to the Security Department at the World's Fair in Spokane, and notify us of any information they receive.

A telephone call was also placed to Berwick, Louisiana where Christy McPhee resides. They were alerted to the information of the disappearance of Kathy and a photograph and a description was sent to them. They will notify us immediately if she arrives in their city looking for her boyfriend, Christy McPhee.

Kathy indicated to Christy that she would like to get a job dancing in a night club or "Go" club if she decided to live with him in Louisiana.

What follows are statements given to officers from the campus security office from those who were Kathy's dorm mates at Sackett Hall, and others who knew and interacted with her:

Nancy Nicholas

5:10 p.m.

May 20, 1974

She knew Kathy Parks pretty well and she knows she is missing. Nancy last saw Kathy on Sunday, April 21, 1974. She said Kathy talked about how unhappy she was with school and about the second thoughts she was having about going south to either live with or marry her boyfriend. Kathy told her she would probably go.

The whole time Nancy has known Kathy, Kathy did not strike her as the type who would just disappear; she was always very sensible and level headed. She was shocked at Kathy's disappearance and emphasized that Kathy "wasn't abnormal."

In the below reports, the detectives often refer to Kathy as Roberta, in that her full name was actually Roberta Kathleen Parks. However, she preferred to be called Kathy by her family and friends, but in official reports only, it's Roberta.

May 9, 1974

Roberta Parks' mother telephoned the Campus Security Office at 9:50 a.m. and requested that the area hospitals be checked to see if her daughter had been admitted. She seems to think it's possible something may have happened to Roberta. Mrs. Parks also had

Roberta's room checked to see if her makeup box was still there, as Roberta never goes any place without it. The makeup box was still in her room.

At approximately 8:22 p.m., 10 May 1974, an interview was held in the Head Resident's quarters at Sackett Hall and was attended by the following named persons: Mr. Ray Hoyt, Head Resident, Sackett Hall; Renee Ferguson, student, West Hall room 323 (has food class with Roberta Parks); Edward Warren Sumida, student, Sackett Hall room 223 (friend of Kathy Parks); Miriam Joan Schmidt, student, Sackett Hall (friend and roommate of Roberta Parks).

Missing from the interview but are very close friends of Roberta Parks: Joanne (Joey) Stevens, student, West Hall room 329; Sarah Dugan, student, West Hall room 313

The following information was received from Miss Schmidt, Miss Ferguson, and Mr. Sumida. All agree Miss Parks had only a few friends with which she talked or went out with and then only around campus. For instance, trips to the library building were very few as most of Miss Parks' studying was done in her room. All agreed she was a little moody at times and in many instances would stay be herself.

Miss Parks does take classes in Scuba Diving, conducted by the men's gym by Mr. Cramer. It was learned she has some of the equipment in her room but rents tanks and wetsuits from the Divers Den, 2744 SW 3rd Street, City (telephone number). This class (a hobby) she is most interested in and has taken at least three (3) trips to the coast with the class.

At times Miss Parks would ride her bike on campus and also the bike paths at Avery Park. A check was made on her bike and it was found to be in the regular place with the chain and lock (lock is broken). Check of her room by roommate Miss Schmidt indicated that the leg light which she used was still in her room, indicating this was not used on the night in question.

When asked if Miss Parks would hitch a ride to go anyplace away from campus, all indicated she would never hitchhike, but would ask Edward Sumida to take her. For instance, if she wanted to pick up a wetsuit or tanks for her diving class, he would take her. On one occasion Mr. Sumida did take Miss Parks to Portland to go shopping and they returned early in the evening.

Miss Schmidt stated that on the night in question both she and Miss Parks intended to go to another room (334) in Sackett Hall to visit, this was around 10:55 p.m. to 11:00 p.m. When departing their room, Parks said "Go ahead and I'll be over in a while." Miss Schmidt went to room 334 in Sackett and about fifteen (15) minutes later she went back to see why Miss Parks was not coming over. This was when Miss Schmidt found her roommate missing.

Each of those interviewed stated they could not understand why or what has happened and also why none has been called by Miss Parks as each considered they all are best of friends.

The interview closed at approximately 10:15 p.m., 10 May 1974.

L. Glass, Investigating Officer

This supplementary report by L. Glass goes deeper into the background of Kathy Parks in an attempt to discover what happened to her. It includes statements from Miriam Schmidt and Edward Sumida.

10 May 1974

An interview with Miss Schmidt (roommate) indicated Roberta Parks did in fact have a problem as she (Parks) had been going to the Mental Health Clinic (OSU Student Heath Center) for quite some time. One of her problems was that she and her father did not get along and then she was recently notified her father had just been hospitalized with a slight heart attack. She did state she believed he (her father) would be in good hands.

Miss Schmidt stated lately Miss Parks had been reading the World Bible but she did not think she had gone overboard with religion. When asked about habits (good or bad) Miss Schmidt replied no drinking, only that she smoked. When asked about drugs, Miss Schmidt was reluctant to answer and finally said Miss Parks was a frequent smoker of pot but used pot only while in Sackett Hall.

One other problem was a boyfriend living in Louisiana, who she had planned on living with this summer, but had changed her mind and had called him about her change of plans. Instead Miss Parks mentioned a trip to visit her sister (who lives out of state) sometime during the summer months.

Whether the information about her father, religion, pot, boyfriend, and the fact her Mental Health sessions were not helping may have brought a new low to Miss Parks could not be determined. But it should be considered a factor in her disappearance.

Miss Schmidt stated to this officer she could not understand why the two (2) friends of Miss Parks had gone to Portland when her roommate was missing. She was referring to Joey Stevens (west Hall) and Sarah Dugan (west Hall). Both are Oregon State University students. She believed both of these persons were holding information back as neither wanted to talk to the police about this incident until Sarah Dugan talked to her father who is an FBI agent in Portland. Both parties are in Portland this weekend and will be back Monday, 13 May 1974.

An interview with Edward Sumida showed he was at a complete loss as to the disappearance of Miss Parks and could give no reason for her leaving.

When questioned regarding pot and how often Miss Parks used it he was afraid to answer until this officer indicated this was for information of Miss Parks only. At this time Sumida stated he would give her a joint or two whenever she asked. When questioned if it was possible she (Parks) went off campus to obtain pot Sumida stated he did not think so. When asked about other drugs, a negative reply was given.

Mr. Sumida stated he had taken Miss Parks to rent wetsuits and tanks as he is the only one who has transportation (vehicle) that Miss Parks is friendly with.

L. Glass, Investigating Officer

Campus investigators interviewed numerous people connected to Kathy Parks. Some are close associations while others are not. While some of these are very revealing, they did not lead investigators to any real answers into Kathy's disappearance. What follows is a detailed report of the interview of Paul Kaehler.

PAUL KAEHLER – 51 Oak Street, Black Point, California

Mr. Kaehler arrived in Corvallis on May 11, and offered his assistance locating his sister-in-law. He advised that on May 6, Kathy's father had suffered a heart attack, and was taken to the hospital in California.

His wife, Sharon Kaehler, telephoned Kathy to advise her of her father's condition. At 8:20 p.m. on that date, he also telephoned Kathy to inform her of her father's present condition, which was fair. He further advised that Kathy did not become excited because of her father's condition and he assured her that he was in good hands and that it was not necessary for her to return home. She gave no indication at that time that she was intending to return home for any reason.

Paul Kaehler further advised that Kathy was under a great deal of pressure from her boyfriend, Christy McPhee, who she was at that time attempting to break up with. Christy McPhee was at that time employed as a scuba diver in Louisiana. He has corresponded with Kathy regularly in an attempt to convince her that their relationship continues. When Kathy enrolled at Oregon State University in the fall term in 1973, Christy McPhee came out to Oregon and they lived together in an apartment above the Oregon Museum Tavern in Corvallis. She continued to maintain her room in Sackett Hall during the time that the two of them lived together in October '73 until around Christmas.

Just prior to Christmas vacation, Kathy began experiencing pain in her abdomen, and was taken to Good Samaritan Hospital by ambulance. After several days she was released from the hospital and she and Christy hitchhiked to Canada over Christmas vacation. They stayed in Canada several days and then hitchhiked back to Corvallis where they lived together at the aforementioned residence until early March 1974, when Christy hitchhiked back to Louisiana. Mr. Kaehler believes that Kathy was a very independent and sensitive girl and would not have run off on her own. He also believes that she would not have been easily picked up by a passing motorist.

A search of Kathy's room revealed that nearly all her clothing, luggage, cosmetics, toilet articles, etc., were still in her room. Numerous letters, found in her desk drawer from her boyfriend, Christy McPhee, indicated that Kathy was attempting to break off their relationship, that she wanted to be on her own and maintain her independence rather than being burdened with a marriage and a permanent responsibility. Information from Kathy's closest friends indicate that she was in a very depressed condition due to the fact that she could not make a decision as to if she should break off her relationship with Christy or return to Louisiana after spring term and attempt to explain her feelings to him.

The following statements were given by girls who were close friends of Kathy's:

JOANNE STEVENS – 329 West Hall

Home address: Lafayette, California

Joanne attended junior high school and high school with Kathy. She knows that Kathy was very close to Christy, who lived with her during fall and winter term. She also knows that Kathy has been seeing a psychiatrist while she has been a student at Oregon State University as well as a high school student in Lafayette, California. Kathy took frequent walks in the evening from her room in Sackett Hall to the Memorial Union Commons to get refreshments. This was usually between 9:30 p.m. and 11:00 p.m. Kathy had recently told her she had received a $50 check from her mother which she had deposited in her checking account at Citizen's Bank in Corvallis. When Kathy failed to return to her room on the evening of May 6, she did not report her missing for the first two days because she *did not want to alarm anyone and thought that Kathy probably just wanted to be alone and get away for a day or two as she was quite upset over her relationship with Christy.*

SARAH ANN DUGAN – 313 West Hall

Home address: Portland, Oregon

She met Kathy through Joanne Stevens. They last saw Kathy when the three of them were playing basketball outside of Sackett Hall around 8:00 p.m., Monday, May 6. Kathy had already been notified of her father's heart attack by her sister Sharon, earlier that afternoon. Kathy was in a good mood, indicating that she probably should have been there when her father was in the hospital but that her sister had told her that her father was all right and that she was not to worry about it. Kathy told her that she takes walks in the evenings and has invited her to go with her, however, she never has.

MIRIAM JOAN SCHMIDT

She has been Kathy's roommate since fall term of last year. Kathy receives letters from Christy on a regular basis, and to her knowledge, she has dated only one person during the time she has known her. She knows this person only by Larry, and believes him to be weird and Kathy complained that he was bothersome to her.

GEORGINE THOMPSON, OSU Mental Health Center, psychiatric social worker

Mrs. Thompson advised that she has counseled Kathy on several occasions during the past year. She believes Kathy is very unpredictable and capable of running off by herself and possibly having suicidal tendencies. She *also stated that Kathy has been treated by Dr. Peter Winters, 310 N.W. 5th Street, Corvallis. Dr. Winters was contacted and advised that Kathy had been receiving extensive psychiatric tests. She has been hesitant to accept therapy and that he talked to her on three or four occasions. He believes her to be rebellious and very emotional. She had a poor family-social life, was highly rebellious and a very nervous person to the extent that she bit her fingernails until they were bleeding. She was a very angry and depressed person. He attempted hypnosis to quell her problems, however, this was unsuccessful. She was very reluctant to accept therapy, a very touchy person, very restless, destructive type personality, very unpredictable, and did have possible suicidal tendencies. *She was not close to her father, and was seeking someone whom she could confide in. Dr. Winters last saw Kathy on March 8, and he never did prescribe any medication for her, nor did she request it. She talked at length of her problems with her boyfriend Christy whom she was living with at the time he was treating her.*

Dr. ROBERT WILSON, M.D., Corvallis Clinic, 530 N.W. 27th, Corvallis

Dr. Wilson first saw Kathy in December when she entered the hospital with severe abdominal pains. He found no physical abnormality of Kathy, however, he was successful in getting her to confide with him and found that she did have a definite conflict with her parents. He communicated with Kathy's mother by telephone until Mrs. Parks came up from California and took Kathy home. During his visits with Kathy she stated she did not want to confide in her family in regard to her sex life and her relationship with Christy. Christy was not accepted by her family, and this bothered her a great deal. He believed her to be a very erratic girl and he could perceive her running off or possibly committing suicide. She is very confused and depressed, however, very close to her sister, Sharon Kaehler. She was not happy at OSU, and he last saw her in January of 1974. He discussed her condition with Kathy's mother, who came to Corvallis to visit her before taking her home.

KENNETH NAFFZIGER, OSU Mental Health Center

MR. Naffziger stated Kathy talked with him about "getting away," taking a boat to see the world. She was not interested in her studies, her career, future, or OSU. She disliked her mother, was very lonesome, and just was trying to find herself. Dr. Naffzinger's diagnosis was basically the same as Dr. Winters.

WENONA CHRISTENSON, Counseling Center, Lafayette, California

Kathy first came to her about three years ago for emotional instability. She was experiencing family problems, unable to communicate with her parents, particularly with her father, had a great deal of insecurity as to her future, and what she wanted to do with herself. Mrs. Christenson stated that she had not seen Kathy in approximately two years and believes that unless she has improved a great deal from when she last saw her, Kathy would be capable of "excluding herself from society, her friends, family, and anyone else that she ... (Author's note: unfortunately, page 5 of this report is missing and contains the remainder of this statement).

Christy arrived in Corvallis from Louisiana on May 13, after learning that Kathy was missing from OSU. He gave the following statement:

CHRISTY J. MCPHEE, Berwick, Louisiana

From the best of my knowledge I last talked to Kathy on Thursday, May 2. I believe she called me collect in Louisiana. She just wanted to talk. There was nothing striking about her conversation. She just seemed relieved that I wasn't giving her a bad time about wanting to be on her own for a while. She seemed to think that would be best and nothing but good could come of it. The last letter that I received from her was on Friday, May 10. It was dated May 6 and postmarked May 7. In the letter she sounded depressed over her father's heart attack and other things not specified. She seemed to have had a bad day that day and just said that she wanted to go out and walk around. That was the last I have heard from her. From what I have heard of her actions immediately prior to her disappearance, just doesn't sound like her (tearing the picture off the wall I drew for her, throwing away one of my letters.) Everything is so unusual it's just not like her to take off like that. I just don't know where she could be.

Following is a copy of a letter Kathy wrote to Christy dated May 6, 1974, postmarked May 7, 1974. First, a quick explanation about dates of letters and how they appear in this section. These letters are being presented in the order they're contained in the official report. However, some letters appear with earlier dates than the date of the letter preceding it, and it does so without explanation as to why they're not in chronological order. This juxtaposing of information occasionally occurs in police files, and it's almost always human error that's responsible for it. Because it's important to remain true to the order of the information presented by the official record, I have left these in the order in which they originally appear.

Dear Christy,

I got your letter today. I often wonder what you think of me, being so far away. I had a usual day today, somewhat. Ma reports my Aunt Mary opened her eyes a few days ago, and actually looked human again for the first time since she got sick. That's a relief. Sharon called from my folk's house this morning (Ma is still in Alabama). Dad had a heart attack last night around midnight. Evidently, he was conscious enough to call the doctor; get Sue out of bed to take him to the hospital. He's in the intensive care section for cardiac patients now. Sharon says he's O.K. now. I'm shook up about it, and I know dad must be, also. I hope he changes his lifestyle after this. I'm feeling down right now, due to a combination of things, I suppose. To tell you the truth, I don't even feel like finishing this letter. I think I'll go walk around outside a while. I'm sorry this is such a bum letter. I really am. But, after all, everyone has their ups and downs. This day has especially had its share of bad news. Well – I'm looking forward to seeing you – very much. When you come, please put your arms around me and make me feel like everything is O.K. I really miss you. I'm needing the comfort of your presence now.

I love you,

Kathy

Following is a transcription of an undated letter from Kathy to Christy McPhee, which is postmarked May 6, 1974.

Christy, it was wonderful speaking with you – you lifted my cloud of loneliness for you. Bless Ma Bell! Even though she's damned. I've just completed my ½ hour of overall exercises. Yes, this is my "May month of physical fitness program", 2nd night of ½ hour exercises. I always feel so relaxed and limber afterwards. Going to keep at it for at least a month, this time around. I'm also playing a lot of basketball and riding my bike lately, so it's not as if I don't get enough exercise as it is. Right now, I think I must feel the same way a kitten does asleep before a fire. I'm content after talking with you, relaxed from doing those exercises, sleepy because I'm stoned, and drifting on a wave of classical music. Today I heard "Nutcracker Suite" for the first time in years, it seems. It sounded beautiful to me. I love certain classical pieces very much, and too often I miss hearing them. What they have got on the radio right now is okay, but I especially like old familiar favorites I grew up with.

I love you – I feel I always will. You've lightened my heart tonight. I'm happy you were there – it was nice to hear your voice. Well, I'm very sleepy now, so, I think I'll go to bed. Remember – I care for you.

Friday night

I saw B.B. King tonight. God, he is really something else! I'll never forget him as long as I live. He radiates warmth and good feelings like no other performer I've seen or heard. He puts his heart into his music. A wonderful, wonderful man and musician! I wanted to shake his hand, just touch him to let him know how he touched me. He moved me very deeply. Sort of the feeling I have for Ray Charles. B.B. King truly is the "King of Blues" dedicated to the core. Tony Joe White also played (Poke Salad Annie). He was okay, in my opinion, in an a.m. radio style. B.B. King had the whole show, though I wish you could have heard him with me.

I sat out in the sun for two hours with Joanne today. Love to feel the sun's warmth on my body.

Kathy Tornow is getting married tomorrow, today now -April 4th (Author's note: Believe she meant May 4th). *I've been thinking about her a lot off and on today. I smoked some hash with Ed a while ago. I'll finish this tomorrow – I'm very, very sleepy – so sleepy I can barely think. Goodnight – I love you.*

Saturday Evening

Christy – it was beautiful today! The weather is great. I sat out with Joanne again in the sun a long while. This is "Moms" weekend. Mothers abounding everywhere. Everyone seems to be enjoying themselves. With this sun, how could they not? I just got back from riding my bike in the country. The setting sun threw a goldish hue over everything. I also did my exercises for ½ hour, and there was a fair up in the M.U. Quad this morning. All the usual arts and crafts. The one where I got you your ring had better craftsmanship, I thought. Still, it was fun. I bought a long, full, dark green skirt, very light material, and the blouse that went with it. It cost eleven dollars. I got a good deal.

I'm stoned again, so I think I must be letting myself ramble on pretty much in my writing. That's been my day, quite a bit of it, anyway, I want you to know I've been thinking of you. Oh, Christy, please don't worry about ever losing me, don't ever give it a thought. You are in my heart, and I think of you often, no matter whom I'm with, or what I'm doing. Nothing you could ever do could make me love you less. I accept you completely. If I loved you any less because of the way you are and live, I would not really love you. But I do, so I can say I love you, and I will, all my life. I know I'll never find another you. You are a vital person, and have a hell of a lot to offer this world. I care for you, I want you to be happy, give yourself a good time and feel absolutely free in doing so, knowing that I'll love you, simply because you are you. I miss you, Christy, and I love you very much. Guess I'd better get this off to you.

I love you,

Kathy

The following is a transcribed copy of a letter which was written by Kathy and found in the wastebasket in her room. The letter bears no date or salutation and appears to be a recording of her thoughts at the time. It's unknown when Kathy wrote this letter which was never mailed.

I have been thinking seriously about this coming summer and my future. I want to live and work in California for a while. I do not want to live or work in Louisiana. The only reason I'd want to be there is because you are there. I've asked myself if I honestly feel ready to settle down and live with a man. Living together and being married have no difference, in my mind. In both situations, emotional bondage and dependency are present, as are other binding factors. To be completely honest with myself, which is not an easy thing to be sometimes, I have decided that I am not ready to settle down. It is only fair to be honest to you, in turn, and tell you of my thoughts. I think it a better thing to be honest now, rather than sorry later.

There is something I feel I must do in becoming completely happy and at ease with myself inside, before I settle down. I must have the certain knowledge inside of me of realizing I can go it alone in this world. At this point, I know I am insecure and more than a little unsure of my own ability to cope with the world by myself. I want to have that feeling inside of me, and I want to build up my self-confidence and faith in myself. After this is done, then I can think of settling down, knowing I am a better person for it.

This decision is nothing against you. You are a good man, and a loving one. I love you as much as ever. My feelings toward you have not changed in the least. My plans for my own future have, though.

It hasn't been easy for me to ask myself what I truly want for myself but I did, and I know, I just know I need more time to become my own person. I need time to grow, and feel worthy of myself. If I come to live with you now, I will never know complete personal independence. I feel I must know this before I can give completely without any reservations ever blocking my love.

I also think any ties of commitment should not be binding if they are decidedly going to interfere with one's personal happiness and well-being. If I promise to jump off a cliff, I think it's only fair to me to be able to change my mind, if I think it would be unwise for me to go through with the commitment. I'm not equating living with you as being throwing myself off a cliff, but, in a way, it is. I think after a year or so I would become discontent, simply because I have never had the chance of being on my own. I want to give myself that chance. I think it's best for me.

I feel as though I've just changed the course of my life before the future has even arrived. "Set me adrift in a sea of hope — I'll set my sail to a new horizon". Keep the faith in me, Christy. I love you, more than ever.

Trust in me, I've got to have more time. I've got to know when I'm ready to settle down. You've got to accept that I have to know that if you love me like you tell me you do, you've got to give and take. We both do. Don't turn your love away from me, just give me time. I need time to grow and let my love grow. Please try to understand my feelings.

That letter is unsigned.

The following is a similar transcribed copy which is undated and unaddressed, written by Kathy and found in her room.

This is something I wrote a while back, there ain't anything like the "real thing," Christy, if what we feel for each other is the real thing, I think very strongly it can only grow stronger and stronger, and higher and higher.

There is someone you never forget, no matter who you may be with. There is always someone in the back of your mind. I think you are the one I'll never forget.

My mother waited for her man five years, not "waited," actually, more always had him in the back of her head, and he always had her in the back of his mind. They had an understanding between them. They were to go their separate ways, each was to go out with anyone they wanted. My father insisted that my mother go out and not sit at home. Both of them did just that. When my mom felt ready to settle down, she had her self-respect, confidence, and an honest liking for herself. She was sure my dad was the right one for her, just as dad thought she was the right girl for him. Now, neither one of them asked the other to wait, it wouldn't be fair to either of them. More than likely they would end up hating each other if they had promised to wait for each other, fingers crossed. My ma came to dad when she knew in her heart she was ready to settle down. Their love for each other was true, and they were ready for each other.

Following is a transcribed copy of a letter written to Kathy from Christy dated April 23, 1974.

Dear Kathy,

I'm laying here in my bunk on the barge. I'm afraid Kathy, I'm afraid that we may be drifting apart. I don't want that to happen, Kathy, I love you. I love you more than I could love anyone else, and I'm pretty sure that you love me. I don't know why you made such a turnabout in plans I thought we had made. You said something about wanting to be independent and not have to be dependent on me. But then you say you're going to be living at your sister's. It seems to me you're just transferring it from me to them. I want you to be dependent on me to a certain extent. You really mean something to me, Kathy you're the most important thing in my life. You make it seem like there's some meaning to my life when I have you, but without you there just doesn't seem to be very much. You give me something to work for, certain goals to achieve. Without you those goals are unachievable. Sure, I could find something else to work for, but the life with you is the happy one. I don't want to be away from you for so long. I'm afraid you'll drift away from me and I might never see you again. When I think of not having you I get this really empty feeling or something in my gut. It happens all the time now because, since you dropped the bombshell last night, I think about it all the time. Tonight, while eating dinner I thought about it and I couldn't eat. When I looked out the window at the ocean and thought of what it would be like without you I felt really sick, and all I wanted to do was go lie in my bunk. Writing this now makes me feel the same way. I'm confused, Kathy. I love you. I never want to be without you. Please stay with me. I'm very weary Kathy, I must sleep.

April 24, 1974

Kathy, I got the word this morning I'm going home, the job is over. I'll be talking to you tonight but I'm sending this anyway. I really wonder why it is you changed your mind. I love you Kathy, I don't want to lose you.

The following is a transcribed copy of a letter to Kathy from Chris dated May 1, 1974.

To my dearest Kathy:

I hope you've been alright lately. I've only gotten the one letter from you so far. I hope you've written more than that. You know when I said that James and I were going to Baton Rouge to look at cars? Well, we never made it. Jeff still hasn't come back with the truck we're going to drive there in. But we'll probably go whenever Jeff comes back. I sure do miss you sweetheart. I wonder what you think of me when I'm so far away. I wish I was with you Kathy. I want so bad to be able to hold you in my arms. I love you so much Kathy. I'd be happy just to wait for you. If I knew you'd be waiting for me also. I want you Kathy. I can't see myself with anyone else. You're the girl I want. I only hope I will be able to keep you as "my girl." Well hon, I've got to go now. I've got some things to do. I love you. I'll write or talk to you soon.

Write me often!

Love ya always,

Chris

What follows in a partial inventory of the items Kathy Parks left behind. Each item had to be catalogued by investigators before they could be turned over to the Parks' family. For this book, I'll be highlighting those items that most reveal what Kathy enjoyed such as reading material, and other objects she obviously had emotional attachments to. Hence the reasons why I have chosen to skip some items such as an umbrella and "a brown coffee cup."

INVENTORY OF PERSONAL BELONGINGS OF ROBERTA KATHLEEN PARKS

On the morning of June 13, 1974, William R. Harris, Investigator, and Amos Shaw, Director of Security, removed the following items from room 325 Sackett Hall "B" which was occupied by Kathy Parks. These items are presently stored at the OSU Campus Security Office in Gill Coliseum.

* *A total of sixty-two letters, most of which are from Chris McPhee to Kathy. Five of these letters arrived since her disappearance.*

* *Seven envelopes containing bank statements and canceled checks from Citizen's Bank, Corvallis, in the name of Kathy Parks.*

* *One savings account book, Lafayette Federal Savings, Lafayette, California, in the name of Kathy Parks, showing the most recently withdrawal of $16, on January 4, 1974, with a balance of $44.87.*

* *Three statements from OSU Department of Housing to Kathy Parks showing a balance due of $309.*

* *One cardboard box containing six books of personalized checks from Citizen's Bank of Corvallis in the name of Kathy Parks.*

- *One OSU general information booklet.*
- *One wedding invitation from Mr. and Mrs. Tornow and Mr. and Mrs. Roy T. Sutrow announcing the marriage of Kathryn Colman and Thomas Michael on May 4, 1974, in Walnut Creek, California.*

Here we begin the cataloguing of items that, for the most part, reflected the personality of Kathy Parks and those things she enjoyed.

Cardboard box containing the following items:

- Eighty-six paperback novels
- Four paperback books on university subjects
- Assorted hand-written pages on the origin and history of Belly Dancing
- One paperback book titled *Astrology Made Simple*
- One university paperback book titled *Cognitively Oriented Curriculum*
- One paperback book titled *One Family*
- One blue-colored spiral notebook containing notes on Hinduism and world religions
- One dark gray-colored three-ring spiral folder titled *Food and Man*
- *Old English Ballads*
- *Golden Treasury of Songs and Lyrics*
- *New Hudson Shakespeare*
- A novel titled *My Cousin Rachael*
- Very old book from the Sacramento Public Library titled *Cyril Hamilton: His Adventures by Land and Sea*
- *The Prophet*
- *Collected Poems by Robert Frost*

- *Rubaiyat of Omar Khayyam*
- *The Prose and Poetry of John Milton*
- *Chinese Fairy Tales*
- *Flower Thoughts*
- *The Indispensable Edgar Allan Poe*
- *Wuthering Heights*

Closing out the information on Kathy Parks, I'm including two letters that are worth noting. The first is from Kathy's father, Charles Parks Jr., and it's clear from this communication that he wants—and is grateful for—the press getting the word out about these terrible murders.

August 21, 1974

Mr. Kerry Webster

The News Tribune

1950 So. State Street,

Tacoma, Washington

Dear Mr. Webster:

I sincerely appreciate your letter of August 15, together with the copy of the special report on the missing girls, including my daughter.

I'm afraid that the similarities of these unplanned disappearance(s), together with the personal knowledge of my own daughter's character, are too coincidental to be anything other than foul play.

Thank you very kindly for your courtesy in sending this very fine, well-organized and highly descriptive article. I would hope that the Bay area would pick this whole story up.

Again, my deepest appreciation.

Very truly yours,

Charles E. Parks, Jr.

What follows is a letter from Captain Nick Mackie to the parents of Kathy Parks. Although the brief communication appears almost "standard," if I may use that word, nothing could be farther from the truth. The law enforcement community in Washington State, and especially those in the Seattle area, were not just doing everything they knew to do to catch this killer, but it was taking an emotional toll on them as well:

April 28, 1975

Mr. and Mrs. Charles Parks

1117 Rahara Avenue

Lafayette, California 94549

Re: Roberta Kathleen Parks

We wish to take this opportunity to express our sympathy for you and your family over the loss of your daughter. Be assured that our detectives are exhausting all possible leads in connection with the death of Kathy.

We have enclosed a certified copy of the death certificate as Mrs. Parks requested. If you have any questions about the investigation, please contact Detective Roger Dunn or Detective Robert Keppel.

Lawrence G. Walt, Sheriff-Director

Joseph N. Mackie, Captain

Criminal Investigation Division

CHAPTER FOUR

SUSAN RANCOURT

I first told the story of Bundy's travels to Central Washington State College (CWSC), and the murder of Susan Rancourt, in my first Bundy book, *The Bundy Murders*. I was not able to visit this college, or any other Washington State location for the writing of the book, but that wasn't a hindrance as I had all pertinent case file material for all of the Washington murders, as well as photos (both from the time of the murders and current), as well as numerous maps, which allowed me to sort it all out.

However, for my second Bundy book, *The Trail of Ted Bundy: Digging up the Untold Stories*, published in 2016, I traveled to Washington and visited all of the sites where Bundy had hunted and abducted his victims, including CWSC. In 1974, Bundy, ever the sly and attentive-to-details type of killer, had parked his VW in an isolated area of the campus, so that as he led his unsuspecting victim to his car, he'd have a much better chance of overpowering her and quickly getting away without being noticed by anyone.

When writing the first book, I had a general idea where Bundy parked his car, where the railroad trestle might have been located, and the approximated distance Bundy had walked with his intended victims, including his actual victim Susan Rancourt, but I had no knowledge of where the pond was located or the bridge which spanned it. Not until a Facebook friend who had, through much research, figured out conclusively where they were located. Knowing this allowed me to recreate for the printed page, step by step, where the path was located that Bundy and Rancourt took to his car.

What follows is from *The Trail of Ted Bundy*, and the information contained herein will give you a good picture of how this abduction unfolded. Never leaving things to chance, the scheming Bundy parked his VW in what may have been the most isolated spot on campus:

The area of Bundy's hunting centered on the Bouillon Library (now Bouillon Hall), which sits between Walnut Street, in front, and Chestnut Street, which runs along the rear of the library. If one stands in front of the library, Black Hall is on the left, facing the side of the library. Squeezed in between these two buildings was a round structure known as the Grupe Conference Center (still standing today). In 1974, there was a small man-made pond that ran between the conference center and Bouillon, and the bridge spoken of in the record ran over this pond and parallel to the library. So, walking this bridge means you're either walking toward the library or away from it, as students could only enter the building through the main front doors. Knowing this is critical to understanding Bundy's movements in conjunction with one of his potential victims, and I'll have more about this shortly.

At one time, the Milwaukee rail line angled its way through the campus, but the railroad trestle Bundy made use of is now long gone. I brought along for my visit a copy of a map of this area that investigators used and on which they had marked locations pertaining to the murder victim, potential victims, and location of Bundy's parked car. At the time Bundy pulled into this area, which is approximately 150-plus feet from the library (and only a slightly bit closer to Black Hall), it was very much a desolate area. The closest building, Black Hall (not the Black Hall of today, where additions have been added, making it appear from the air like an "H" shape rather than one elongated structure), was not giving off much light. And the two parking lots available to students for this area were both north and south of this location and too far away to provide sufficient illumination.

Today, buildings sit all around this location, and the two parking lots have now joined to become one massive parking area, essentially gobbling up this infamous spot. So, with the trestle removed and the uninhabited now habited, you must, while standing there, mentally visualize what it must have looked like as Susan Rancourt walked with Ted Bundy to his Volkswagen on that dark night of April 17, 1974.

My first Bundy book told the story of the abduction (using case file material), and the second book answered some important geographic questions pertaining to the murder, as well as an in-depth look at Kent Barnard's experiences with Bundy that day. Barnard was at the campus that day visiting his girlfriend, and encountered Bundy while he was seeking a victim, both in the afternoon and again in the evening. This current work will be taking a closer look at the actual verbatim investigative reports on the Rancourt abduction, which will allow the reader to comprehend firsthand what the investigators had to work with as they searched for the answers as to what happened to Susan Rancourt.

What follows is from my book, *The Bundy Murders*, and tells of the events leading up to the abduction of Susan Rancourt:

A little before 8:00 p.m., and only moments before Kathleen D'Olivo would be entering the Bouillion Library for two hours of uninterrupted study, Susan

Rancourt placed some clothes into one of her dorm's washing machines and walked to Munson Hall, located at the southern end of the campus, where she attended a meeting for those wanting to be dorm counselors. The meeting was due to end about ten. The last people to see Susan said she was wearing a yellow, short-sleeved sweater, grey corduroy pants, a yellow coat, and a pair of brown Hush Puppies. At 10:15, as Barbara Blair was crossing Walnut Street at Eighth Street (the location of Munson Hall and close to the library, which is also on Walnut), she saw a man "in a green ski parka, who acted as though he were in a daze," as well as a young white female "wearing a yellow low coat going north on the Walnut Mall." This was no doubt Susan on her way home, on a path which would take her past the library, where she would turn right, and keeping to the sidewalk between Black Hall and the Bouillon Library, take a left on Chestnut and continue north towards Barto Hall where she lived. She was, in fact, traveling almost the exact route Kathleen D'Olivo had taken a short time earlier. But Susan never made it to her residence. And like Lynda Ann Healy and Donna Gail Manson, Susan Elaine Rancourt appears to have vanished into thin air.

What follows are the transcripts of Jane Curtis and Katherine D'Olivo, and they are presented in their entirety:

INTERVIEW WITH JANE CURTIS, 12/10/74 at 12:15 hrs

With DETECTIVE ROBERT R. KEPPEL

My name is JANE CURTIS; I am 21 years old, 5'8", about 140 lbs., hazel eyes, washed-out blond hair, a little bit over my shoulders. My birth date is March 10, 1953.

What day did your incident occur on?

JANE: Okay, it occurred on a Sunday evening after I worked a Curriculum Lab at Central Washington State College. It happened – I was leaving the college library between 8:30 and 9:00 p.m.

DETECTIVE: Were you in the Curriculum Lab with anyone else?

JANE: Yes ... it's kind of busy as it's used mostly by education students in the evenings, and I work shelving books for about two hours in the evenings. It's usually the same persons who come up during the evening.

DETECTIVE: Is this in the library, itself?

JANE: Yes ... upstairs on the second floor.

DETECTIVE: What did you do after you left the library?

JANE: After I finished work, I walked out the main entrance of the library, and was just minding my own business, I walked straight out, and I was approached ... well, there was this guy coming along and he had this huge stack of books, like about 8 or 9 books, and he had a cast on his left arm as I recalled later ... but he was carrying these books and all of a sudden he kind of drops them, right in the direction that I was walking in, so I just more or less ... offered assistance. I said, "Gee, well it looks like you have quite a load, would you like some help? So I helped him pick up the books ... no big deal, 'cause he didn't act like, uh, he acted like a very nice person. So I said, "Do you need any help?" He said that he could, so I ... he just happened to be walking in the same direction I was, so I thought it was no big deal if I helped him carry his books out to the car, 'cause the parking lot ... they usually park right behind the library which is just like across, or not even a block away, so I just more or less just helped him carry his books. We went past Black Hall and I was on his right-hand side, and he was on the left, and I remember he was shorter than I was, because I was wearing kinda high shoes, it gave me a couple inches, it made me about 5'9". I remember he was shorter than I.

DETECTIVE: What were you wearing that day?

JANE. I remember wearing my jeans, a sweater, and probably my ski parka.

DETECTIVE: Were they faded blue tight jeans ... baggy blue jeans?

JANE: No ... they were high waisted ... the one girls usually wear, those Navy blue jeans ... the ones that you buy down at the Navy store.

DETECTIVE: What kind of coat?

JANE: Uh ... my pink ski parka.

DETECTIVE: Is it a full-length coat, or ...

JANE: Just the waist length.

DETECTIVE: Did you have anything on your head?

JANE: No.

DETECTIVE: Was it dark outside?

JANE: Yes, it was dark.

DETECTIVE: Describe the person that you met.

JANE. Okay, the person I met was definitely shorter than I. I remember he had a stocking wool hat on his head.

DETECTIVE: What color was it?

JANE: You see, it was dark, so if it was a bright color it didn't stand out, so considering the lighting was kind of ... the lighting is the high lighting across the sidewalks and his clothes were a dark color, and he had on what would now be called hippie clothes, he had on kind of a long coat, kind of grubby, a wool hat with a brim that went up. I remember he kind of ... I can't recall the length of his hair...

DETECTIVE: What color was his hair?

JANE: It was dark.

DETECTIVE: Dark colored?

JANE: ... dark ... I remember that everything about him was lacking color ... no outstanding colors like red or yellow.

DETECTIVE: Did he have a mustache?

JANE: No.

DETECTIVE: Beard?

JANE: No beard.

DETECTIVE: How about glasses?

JANE: ... that's the thing that's been bothering me ... I've been thinking about that. He kind of looked at me sideways ... kind of turned his head and looked at me kind of funny like. He looked at me strangely. His eyes seemed weird. That's one thing I remembered, but I can't remember whether he had glasses on or not. And I remember his cast ... when we were walking it was on this ... side, so it would have been his left hand because his fingers were in my direction because I noticed that there was on one of his fingers some metal, kind of a metal type cast on his fingers, silver, splint-like. I asked him how that happened and he said it was a skiing accident. I asked where it happened and he said it happened at Crystal Mountain, and that he ran into a tree up there. I kind of stereo-type skiers, he didn't look like a skier-type to me. He didn't look like the athlete out there skiing.

DETECTIVE: Did the whole situation seem like a "line" to you?

JANE: In a way ... it didn't click because I asked how it happened, and he said he ran into a tree. Well, it could happen up at Crystal, but it's not very logical ... I don't know how that would be able to happen.

DETECTIVE: Do most skiers from Central go to Crystal, or Snoqualmie Pass?

JANE: It depends ... a lot of them go to Mission Ridge in Wenatchee. A lot of them don't go clear over to Crystal unless it's for the holidays or something.

DETECTIVE: Okay, with respect with the sling on his arm, was it in a sling?

JANE: No. It looked like ... when I was at Western I was in a cast for several months, and it looked like it wasn't hard ... not the plaster. It looked like the wrapping of gauze-type.

DETECTIVE: What color?

JANE: It was white. It was white wrapping. It was completely around his fingers, across here, around his thumb and up his arm, but he had his coat on. The coat was over it, but only part way so you could see it. Then he had that metal thing on his finger ... it looks like maybe it was something you could do yourself.

DETECTIVE: Does that seem unusual to you for him to have a broken arm and not have a cast on it?

JANE: Uh ... no, because I had the gauze on before the swelling went down, then they put a hard cast on. It looked like something anybody could do if they wanted to. I just sorta glanced at it, but it didn't look like a professional job. That little metal thing over his finger looked like it was just taped on.

DETECTIVE: Did you get the impression he was skinny?

JANE: No. His coat was big, kinda bulky looking – slouched over.

DETECTIVE: On the way to wherever you were going, did he wince, or say anything about his arm hurting?

JANE: No. That was the surprising thing ... the only thing ... only the times when he needed help, like when I was leaving, when I approached the car, then he wanted me to get in, then all of a sudden he started, like, ohhh, my arm ... he went on about his arm hurting him, and he said don't forget I have a broken arm – you feel sorry for me ... get in ...

DETECTIVE: Were those the words he used?

JANE: No. But more or less, that was the way he wanted you to think. Okay, when I approached his car, I remember it was parked on the side where you go under the railroad trestle there's a right road that goes out to another road by Big John's, kind of a drive-in, and it says no parking. His car was parked there on the side, and it's kind of like tall grass, and we went around to the passenger's side of the car.

DETECTIVE: Did he go with you?

JANE: Yes, he was right at my side ... my right-hand side, I was near the car door so he would have been behind the door if it had been open.

DETECTIVE: Okay, what happened then?

JANE: When we approached the door, he said for me to open it up.

DETECTIVE: Was he carrying any books?

JANE: Yes. He was carrying a couple of books, but I was carrying the majority of books. He said, "Open it up." I said, "What?" Then he handed me the keys.

DETECTIVE: He handed you the keys?

JANE: Yes. He got his keys for me.

DETECTIVE: Was the car locked?

JANE: Yes, the car was locked. So I said, no. He then unlocked it. I looked inside of the car, and the first thing that struck me was that the passenger's seat was gone.

DETECTIVE: What did he unlock the car with? A key? With his right or left hand?

JANE: The Key. That's a good question ... I can't remember that ...

DETECTIVE: What did he do with the books?

JANE: I can't remember if he gave them to me ... I was holding a bunch of them ... I can't remember if he ... I remember he unlocked the door, that it wasn't me that unlocked it.

DETECTIVE: What was he saying at the time?

JANE: He wasn't saying anything. He unlocked it, then he told me after he opened it up, "Get in." I said, "What?" Then he said, "Ohhh, could you get in and start the car for me?" I said, "I can't".

DETECTIVE: So he was wincing at the time about his arm?

JANE: On his arm more or less to make me feel sorry for him ... then when I looked, what really got me was that the passenger's seat was gone. That's what really bothered me was that it was gone.

DETECTIVE: It was completely gone?

JANE: It was completely gone ... it was just out.

DETECTIVE: What was there in its place?

JANE: Nothing ... it was just the flat surface of the regular car. It had a backseat, and it had those high back seats.

DETECTIVE: What color was it?

JANE: Yellow.

DETECTIVE: Yellow Volkswagen?

JANE: A yellow VW with the high back, black seats.

DETECTIVE: The Bug?

JANE: Yes, the Bug-type. We have one, and I know what a VW is. It was yellow because I remember looking right at the car, standing there, it was yellow.

The VW appeared yellow, instead of the light tan color it actually was, due to the poor lighting, the closest of which was at Black Hall.

DETECTIVE: Did the interior light come on?

JANE: No, it did not. I remember that it was dark, that when I looked in there it was really dark. The light never came on.

DETECTIVE: What else did you notice about the inside of the car? Anything? Any articles in the car at all?

JANE: No, it was just plain ... just the black seats; there was nothing ... wait a second ... I was thinking about that ... if there was a square box in the back, way in the back in a cubby hole behind the back seat. There was something back there, but there was nothing unusual that struck me except the whole passenger seat was gone.

The following Q & A's concern the exact date on which this occurred:

DETECTIVE: Okay, while you were in the Curriculum Lab, were there ... did you get the indications that anyone was watching you?

JANE: No ... never.

DETECTIVE: Had you ever seen this particular individual who confronted you before?

JANE: No. That's it ... I remember ... I spent a lot of hours in the "Sub" with friends, and a lot of kids come in there during the hours because Central is a small school and you look at faces. You recall them. I remember I looked around the next couple of days at school after this incident to see if I could see this person, as it would be easy to see if a person had a cast on his arm or not. It would be something you would remember as not too many people have casts on, or broken arms, and if you looked at them you would kind of recall. I never saw that person again. I remember before when I looked at him I had never seen that person before at Central. I mean he was definitely older.

DETECTIVE: What age?

JANE: He was definitely over 25 years. He was an older guy, because just being around kids my age you just can sorta tell. He just looked older from his appearance when I looked at him.

DETECTIVE: Did you notice what he had on his feet? What type of shoes?

DETECTIVE: How was his speech?

JANE: There was no accent or anything to it.

DETECTIVE: Did he swear?

JANE: No.

DETECTIVE: No profanity?

JANE: No, no profanity.

DETECTIVE: Did he seem to have an answer or explanation for anything you wanted to know?

JANE: Well, I asked him a question and he gave me an answer, like the accident.

DETECTIVE: Was it quick, or did he have to think about it?

JANE: Uh, think about it. Because I'm the one who more or less edged him on, like how did it happen ... he said he'd had a skiing accident, and I said, oh, I do a lot of skiing, where did it happen? He said Crystal Mountain, so he was aware it was a skiing area. When I said, how did it happen? He said he ran into a tree. I said, you ran into a tree ... I didn't question him anymore. It kind of struck me though, Crystal Mountain, and he ran into a tree??? It didn't seem to fit in because I've seen Crystal and there aren't that many trees around, especially in the main track. In the main track there aren't any trees.

DETECTIVE: Was there any particular odor about him?

JANE: No.

DETECTIVE: Like any after shave lotion?

JANE: No.

DETECTIVE: You couldn't tell when you opened the car door any odor at all in the car?

JANE: No. There was nothing.

DETECTIVE: Like he'd been smoking, or anything like that?

JANE: No. There was nothing.

DETECTIVE: How was the lighting around the car?

JANE: There wasn't much. In that particular corner there is no lighting ... it's kinda dark in there. There are lights further up, and behind the railroad thing. (Author's note: she means trestle here) There are no lights around there.

DETECTIVE: If you had a car, and were going to the library at CWSC, where would you park?

JANE: I couldn't park where he parked as there's no parking area there. It would be right across the street from where he parked, along the whole railroad side you can park there.

DETECTIVE: But he parked in a no parking zone?

JANE: Yes, he parked in the no parking area. I'm pretty sure that's a no parking area.

DETECTIVE: Why is that a no parking area?

JANE: Because it goes around a curve, and right in there there's a road and it has the block – wooden blocks, and there's a parking area for the tickets for the lower dorm, then right around the corner there's kind of a high grass and ditch.

DETECTIVE: Is it marked no parking?

JANE: I went back there and I'm pretty sure it said no parking, I'm positive. I rode my bike by and I remember it said no parking, there are two signs further down.

DETECTIVE: Is there a parking lot by the library?

JANE: Yes, you have to have a permit to park in there. And right across the road there on the library side, they're usually filled up and you don't have to have a permit.

DETECTIVE: *How far did you have to walk from where you exited the library to where you met him, where he dropped the books?*

JANE: *Oh, right smack in front of the library. The front door, right in front.*

DETECTIVE: *Was there anyone else standing around at the time?*

JANE: *I don't think so. At that time of night, it's kind of quiet. A lot of people don't use that ... well, a lot of people use that library but it was early in the quarter and there wasn't anybody else out there. There might have been someone who had just walked down, but never paid any attention. I don't remember.*

DETECTIVE: *In what condition were the keys he gave you? Were they on a chain, on a ring?*

JANE: *I didn't look at the keys.*

DETECTIVE: *Did they jingle as you held them?*

JANE: *Oh, he held them.*

DETECTIVE: *He held them ... he never did give them to you?*

JANE: *He never gave them to me because I wouldn't unlock the door.*

DETECTIVE: *Oh, I see, you never did receive the keys.*

JANE: *He took the keys out, and kind of put his hand towards me with them in his hand, and he said to unlock it. I wouldn't take it. I said, No.*

DETECTIVE: *Was it his right hand or left hand?*

JANE: *I never really paid that much attention. If he handed them to me ... I can't even remember. I wasn't paying that much attention, I mean he wanted me to unlock the door, and I didn't and said no, and I remember he took the keys out and I didn't pay any attention. I knew he wanted me to unlock the door and I said no.*

DETECTIVE: What type of books did he have? Were they paperbacks?

JANE: Hard bounds.

DETECTIVE: All of them were hard bounds?

JANE: All of them were hard bounds.

DETECTIVE: All big books?

JANE: No ... they were pretty good size ... not really thick. He had several ... they were all hard bounds. I can't say if they were from Central's library, or not.

DETECTIVE: Did they have any book covers on them?

JANE: No.

DETECTIVE: No book covers. If you had to characterize him, just from the experience you had with him, what would you describe him as, a college student, a guy who works at a gas station, what type of person would he be?

JANE: Oh, gee, I look at a person like him as being a kind of hippie-freaky type guy. He didn't look ... he looked like the bum-type. Not the kind who works at a gas station, or the student-type. Just kind of a do-your-own-thing person.

DETECTIVE: If you had helped him put his books in the car, and he'd have asked you to go to the local drive-in for a coke, or something, would you have gone with him?

JANE: No.

DETECTIVE: You wouldn't?

JANE: Hmm-mmm (Negative).

JANE: Well, I had an experience, not quite like this, and I just had my guard up against anyone strange who comes along. So I just more or less protect myself. I was telling a guy, if I looked at him I would never say he was a good-looking guy.

DETECTIVE: You wouldn't?

JANE: No. Not at all.

DETECTIVE: What is good-looking to you?

JANE: Tall, good build – athletic-type guy, just all around good-looking, but he was the more freaky, hippie-type. From just looking at him I could just tell. I remembered that when I looked at him.

DETECTIVE: Okay, when I think of a freaky guy, I think of a guy who says, hey man, what are you doin' tonight? And all that type of terminology. He never used any type of terminology like that?

JANE: No.

DETECTIVE: Not the street talk, right?

JANE: Not street talk, not at all.

DETECTIVE: Do you think he was a student at all?

JANE: Was a student, where at?

DETECTIVE: Do you think he was a student?

JANE: He could have been at one time, but I couldn't ... now his type, I see a lot of his type. I went to Western and there are a lot of his type up there, but they're all very intelligent individuals. He's a person like that. He's just kind of different. The way he looked at me bothered me.

DETECTIVE: How did he look at you?

JANE: I ... he put his head kind of sideways and stared at me.

DETECTIVE: *Like he was looking through you?*

JANE: *Yeah. Just kind of ... his eyes looked weird. He just stared funny.*

DETECTIVE: *Did his eyes have bags under them?*

JANE: *I can't remember.*

DETECTIVE: *Could you see them?*

JANE: *No. Just kind of big eyes that stared at me.*

DETECTIVE: *Did you get the impression at all that there would be any foul play?*

JANE: *No, never.*

DETECTIVE: *As you observed the car, did you observe anything like a ski rack on it?*

JANE: *No.*

DETECTIVE: *How about a bicycle rack?*

JANE: *No. There were none of those at all. All I remember was that it was a late model, yellow VW with high black back seats.*

DETECTIVE: *Was the top all yellow too?*

JANE: *Yes.*

DETECTIVE: *There was no convertible-type top?*

JANE: *No.*

DETECTIVE: *Did you get a look at the front?*

JANE: *No. I just glanced over it, it just looked to me like a VW Bug.*

DETECTIVE: *What type of tail pipes did it have? Did you notice that?*

JANE: *No.*

DETECTIVE: *Some of them have one, some have two that come up ...*

JANE: No. I didn't notice.

DETECTIVE: How about the wheels? Were they regular wheels, or mag wheels?

JANE: No, I didn't notice at all. There was nothing that really stood out that was different.

DETECTIVE: He physically opened the door for you, right?

JANE: Yes.

DETECTIVE: What did you do with the books?

JANE: When he opened the door, I dropped them.

DETECTIVE: You dropped them on the ground?

JANE: I dropped them right on the ground.

DETECTIVE: What did he say at that time?

JANE: When I dropped them ... we stood there ... I had the books in my hands and he said, Get in. I said, what??? He said, get in and start the car for me. I said, oh, I can't. And he wanted me to get in on the passenger's side.

DETECTIVE: He wanted to have you get in on the passenger's side?

JANE: That was to start the car up.

DETECTIVE: Do you think that's what he meant, to start the car up, or just to "get in."

JANE: That's just it, "get in."

DETECTIVE: Did he actually say start the car for me?

JANE: ... start the car for me ... I remember that. First of all, he told me to get in, I said what, then he went through his little pain bit, and said get in and start the car for me because I can't. He said because of his arm he couldn't start it. He wanted me to start it for him.

DETECTIVE: Where was the ignition on the Bug, right or left-hand side of the steering wheel?

JANE: Left hand side.

(End of tape)

This is the testimony of Kathleen Clara D'Olivo, who encountered Ted Bundy at CWSC, and almost became one of his victims. Here is her opening statement to Detective Robert Keppel, followed by their Q&A:

KATHLEEN: On Wednesday, April 17, 1974, about 8:00, I dropped off my roommates close to downtown Ellensburg and drove up to the library. I parked in the sub-parking lot next to the Hertz Music Hall.

DETECTIVE: Where is the parking lot in respect to the library?

KATHLEEN: Kind of caddy-corner to the library, I guess about a block span.

DETECTIVE: Which direction does the library face?

KATHLEEN: It faces west.

DETECTIVE: Okay, what did you do when you left your car in the parking lot?

KATHLEEN: I locked the door and went right over to the library, went in the main entrance to the library; I think I went upstairs, in the upper part of the library (that is called the Curriculum Laboratory). I'm not sure that's where I was that evening, but I'm almost sure. I stayed there until 10:00.

DETECTIVE: What were you wearing that particular day?

KATHLEEN: Most likely I was wearing blue jeans, and I'm not sure what I had on with it that time of year, I think I was wearing a blazer jacket.

DETECTIVE: What was the weather condition outside?

KATHLEEN: It was a clear night, I don't remember it being extremely cold or extremely warm.

DETECTIVE: How tall are you?

KATHLEEN: 5' 9½"

DETECTIVE: How much do you weigh?

KATHLEEN: 125 pounds.

DETECTIVE: During that time of the year, how long was your hair?

KATHLEEN: Long, way below my shoulders, long and straight.

DETECTIVE: What color is your hair?

KATHLEEN: Black.

DETECTIVE: Did you have anything in your hair?

KATHLEEN: Not that I remember.

DETECTIVE: Were you wearing any jewelry of any sort?

KATHLEEN: I had on two rings and a watch; I could have had on a bracelet, but I don't think so. Usually I just wear two rings and a watch.

DETECTIVE: Was one of the rings an engagement ring?

KATHLEEN: Yes.

DETECTIVE: How long did you stay in the Curriculum portion of the library?

KATHLEEN: As near as I remember, I was in one spot the whole time I was in the library, which was about two hours. I remember looking up and seeing that it was 10:00, and I normally called my fiancé on

Wednesday nights and (SIC) 10:00, so I gathered up my books and left.

DETECTIVE: What books did you gather up?

KATHLEEN: I think I had, most likely I had a couple of notebooks, possibly one or maybe two textbooks with me, no more than that.

DETECTIVE: Did you have a purse?

KATHLEEN: Yes.

DETECTIVE: What kind of purse?

KATHLEEN: A shoulder strap purse made out of navy blue fabric.

DETECTIVE: What route did you take to get out of the Curriculum Lab?

KATHLEEN: Most likely I went straight out of the lab, down the main stairs of the library, and out the front door, the main entrance. Now I'm not sure on that, I could have done something else in the library before I left, but I don't think so. I think I went from that area on out.

DETECTIVE: When you leave the library, do you have some sort of book procedure that you have to check through on the way out?

KATHLEEN: They don't actually check your books, but it's electronically done now, and you do walk through a certain path to get out.

DETECTIVE: What would happen if the electronic system went off?

KATHLEEN: That would mean you were carrying a book that wasn't properly checked out, or had some other property of the library. I went through it with no problems and left.

DETECTIVE: You left through the front door, then?

KATHLEEN: Correct.

DETECTIVE: Where did you go from there?

KATHLEEN: I walked out, I took a right, which was leading across the front part of the library, cement porch-like, whatever, and was cutting across a lawn that went between the library and Black Hall. I was aiming toward the parking lot where the car was parked. I hadn't quite gotten off the lawn, or sidewalk. Wherever I was, I hadn't reached the main mall stretch when I heard something behind me. It sounded like something following me, it didn't startle me or anything, it wasn't a loud noise and I turned around and there was a man dropping books, he was squatting, he was trying to pick up the books and packages was what he was doing, and so I noticed that he had a sling on one arm, and a hand brace on the other. I didn't really notice it at the time, I just noticed that he was unable to pick up that many things and I assumed that he was going to the library. I went over and said, "Do you need some help?" He said, "Yeah, could you?" or something to that affect. So I picked up what was to me felt like a bicycle backpack, it was light nylon material, kind of.

DETECTIVE: Do you recall the color?

KATHLEEN: No ... orange stands out in my mind, but there are so many orange ones around, that might be why. I'm not sure on that at all.

DETECTIVE: The backpack had what felt like books in it?

KATHLEEN: Yes, it felt like books.

DETECTIVE: Was he carrying anything else?

KATHLEEN: Yes. Some packages, three boxes that were small, not large. I think they were wrapped in *parcel post, or brown paper bag-type thing and I think some of them had string ties on them, you know, like ... I'm almost sure on that, but at any rate, I picked up the bag that I thought had books in it, the knapsack type bag, and he picked up the packages.*

DETECTIVE: Could you describe him to us, as far as how tall he was?

KATHLEEN: He was no taller than I am, possibly, he could have been a few inches taller, maybe 6'. He ... I don't remember thinking he was a lot shorter than I, nor a lot taller. I would say he was probably around my height. He had brown, light brown, kind of shaggy hair, no real style, no real cut, cut kind of long and shaggy. He was thin and his face is a blur to me, I don't remember his features at all. I don't really recall if he had a moustache or not. I picture him in my mind both ways, one with and one without one. The same thing about glasses – in one thought in my mind I picture him with wire rims, and another I don't. I don't really know. He was dressed kind of sloppily, not real grubby, but nothing outstanding.

DETECTIVE: Describe the condition of his arms.

KATHLEEN: His left arm was in a sling, no cast, no plaster of Paris cast, I know that, but it was in a sling. His right arm had like a hand brace, or finger brace.

DETECTIVE: Was it metal?

KATHLEEN: Yes. As far ... yeah, I think it was metal. He had bandages wrapped around it. It was supporting his fingers. I'm not sure if his arm that was in a sling was wrapped, but I think it was, I think his hand was wrapped. He told me he had hurt it skiing. He'd run into a tree or something and bent his fingers back, and dislocated his shoulder (or did something to his shoulder).

DETECTIVE: Where did you think he was going to take the books to?

KATHLEEN: I thought he was going in the library. He was headed that way, so I thought that's where he was going. But that same sidewalk actually leads up over a little bridge that runs right alongside the library, it's just a short bridge that goes over a pond (man-made pond) and that's actually the direction he was going in, but it's right next to the library and the same sidewalk will angle off to go into the library so that's where I thought he was going. We started walking and when we came to the bridge, it was obvious that he wasn't turning off to go to the library, and I said, wait a minute, you know, where are we going? He said, "Oh, my car is just parked right over here." I said okay, or didn't make any motion, but at the time I knew what I was carrying which I thought was books, or felt like books, was very heavy, and the way in was carrying them, I knew I could protect myself with it if the need arose.

DETECTIVE: Did he, at any time between his car and the library, stop and wince, or anything, or say that his arm hurt.

KATHLEEN: He never actually stopped at all. He may have mentioned that he was in pain, maybe once, but he didn't make a real big deal out of it; it was just so obvious that he was helpless that he'd have to be in pain, that's the way it appeared to me, anyway. He told me he'd been in an accident (ski) and this is what had happened, and the way he was bandaged up it all made sense, the sling on his arm and shoulder.

DETECTIVE: How far do you figure you walked from the library to where his car was?

KATHLEEN: Well, I couldn't give it to you in feet, possibly a block and a half, but it wasn't arranged in blocks...by any means. We walked across the bridge then to the edge of...I don't recall the name of the street, but it runs up the campus, kind of an alley street. It's not a real well traveled street. Then under the railroad trestle and then his car was parked in the first right under the trestle there, it was a dark road. There were no street lights on that road. But his car wasn't parked so far down that it was completely black.

DETECTIVE: Is this a no parking area?

KATHLEEN: I believe it is, I'm pretty sure it is.

DETECTIVE: What kind of car was there?

KATHLEEN: It was a Volkswagen. I think it was brown, it was a newer VW; there were no dents in it. It was shiny and fairly nice.

DETECTIVE: What happened when you got to the car?

KATHLEEN: I set the pack down, well first of all, he went to unlock the door on the passenger side, which is the inside...I mean, the car was parked right next to a log and there was room between it for a person, and he went to unlock the car on the passenger's side, and I set down the package (the pack) that I had been carrying and leaned it against the log and I think I said goodbye...anyways, my thought was well, I had done my deed and I was going to leave, and then he was supposedly unlocking the car and he dropped the key; then he felt for the key with his right hand and he couldn't find it apparently and he said, "Do you think you could find it for me because I can't feel with this thing on my hand. (meaning the brace on his right hand.) I was cautious at this time, I mean, even while we were walking, I thought well, I'm not going to let him get behind me, I'm gonna keep an eye on him, I've got these heavy books and I can use them. But I didn't want to bend over in front of him so I said, let's step back and see if we can see the reflection in the light, so we stepped back behind the car, kind of behind the car to the side, and I squatted down and luckily I did see the reflection of the key in the light so I picked up the key and dropped them in his hand and I said goodbye and good luck, or something with your arm, or something to that affect, and that was the end of the conversation.

DETECTIVE: Did he say anything to you at that time?

KATHLEEN: He may have said, "Thank you", or something like that. He didn't offer me a ride home, or ask me to come with him, or anything like that...that's about it.

DETECTIVE: At the time you put down the books, you said goodbye at that time, and then he dropped the keys?

KATHLEEN: I think that's how it went...I'm not real sure, but I remember then that my thought was to leave then, so I think I did say goodbye.

DETECTIVE: During your first confrontation with him, when he dropped his books, did you feel that it was a sincere gesture on his part, that he was dropping his books and needed help?

KATHLEEN: Yes. I did. Yeah ... and I thought he was just going into the library, it was just a short distance and he really did need help and I thought I could help him, you know.

DETECTIVE: AT what point in time did you fear there may be something else on his mind?

KATHLEEN: I became a little leery about what I was doing when I realized that he wasn't going into the library, when I asked him where are we going, and he said, "My car's just parked over there." At that time, I knew I had the books in my hand, I knew they were heavy and I knew I could handle him, you know. So that's about it.

Despite Kathleen D'Olivo's confidence that she could overcome Bundy, if anything happened, by use of the weighty bookbag, her escape would have been highly unlikely had Bundy initiated an attack. Although we don't know the exact mechanics of his plan of attack that night, if he placed the pry bar behind the right rear tire, as he had for the Georgann Hawkins' abduction, her ability to stop his attack would no doubt have been met with failure.

DETECTIVE: Did you notice anything unusual about his car, for instance, some sort of ski rack or bicycle rack, or anything like that?

KATHLEEN: No, I didn't. It looked, just very normal, like any VW on the street.

DETECTIVE: Were the tires wider than normal?

KATHLEEN: Not that I noticed. All I really noticed was that it was a nice VW, it was in good shape. It was shiny.

DETECTIVE: Did he appear to you to be the skier, or athletic-type of person?

KATHLEEN: No, not at all. No, he just ... he didn't fit the stereotype in my mind of an athlete, or even a skier.

DETECTIVE: At any time did he swear, or cuss?

KATHLEEN: No, not that I recall.

DETECTIVE: Did he use any street-type language at all?

KATHLEEN: No ... there was nothing unique about his voice, or the way he talked, or the language he used, at all. It was just a very ordinary conversation, really.

DETECTIVE: Did you get the impression that he knew just exactly what he was doing?

KATHLEEN: Not at the time, no. I thought it was on the up and up, really.

DETECTIVE: At any period of time, did you or he introduce each other?

KATHLEEN: No. No names were exchanged or where we lived, or anything like that.

DETECTIVE: Was there anything mentioned about classes, or school, or anything like that?

KATHLEEN: No, hmm-mmm. I didn't discuss what I had been doing at the library, or anything like that, no.

DETECTIVE: Did he indicate to you that he had come out of the library at all?

KATHLEEN: No. Not at all. He didn't say where he had been, or what he had been doing.

DETECTIVE: When you got to where the VW was, did ... was the door ever opened to the VW?

KATHLEEN: No. He went to open it, he dropped his keys and then we found the keys and handed it to him and I left before he opened the car.

DETECTIVE: Did you notice if there was a seat missing or not inside the VW.

KATHLEEN: No, I didn't notice it and I was right alongside of the car on the passenger's side. I think I would have if there had been a seat missing, but I can't be certain on that, but it seemed all intact to me and in good shape.

DETECTIVE: Did he have a particular odor of any type?

KATHLEEN: No. Nothing unique about him at all.

DETECTIVE: Where did you live on campus?

KATHLEEN: Knissen Village Apartments, apartment # 21, it was on 14th and "B" Street.

DETECTIVE: How far is this from the library?

KATHLEEN: Oh, nine, eight blocks ... maybe ten; it's up a ways. Well, the campus runs the stretch between 8th and 14th, and then ... but I was clear down on lower campus. So ...

DETECTIVE: You had to pass under a railroad bridge to get to where his car was parked, right?

KATHLEEN: Right.

DETECTIVE: In walking to the car, was there anything speeded up in his walk, did he seem to get faster as he got closer?

KATHLEEN: No, I didn't notice that at all because I was, I think I would have if he'd done that because I was being very cautious to stay right alongside of him and not let him ... get behind him at all, so I didn't notice his pace being unusual.

DETECTIVE: Did he ... which side of him were you walking on?

KATHLEEN: Uh, his ... left side I believe. I think his left side.

DETECTIVE: Did he ever get tough with you at any point?

KATHLEEN: No. He never changed his manner at all; he was just helpless and seemed grateful that I was helping him and that's about it. He never you know ... he was never rough or tough.

DETECTIVE: Did he demonstrate that he was disappointed when you left, or were going to leave?

KATHLEEN: No, not at all. That's why I wasn't suspicious, because it was just a small thank you for helping me, was the attitude that I picked up anyway, and uh ... he didn't seem nervous that I was leaving. He didn't say, "Hey, do you need a ride home, or how 'bout a ride, or get in the car" or anything like that. So I still felt it was on the up and up, and I was kind of mad at myself for being suspicious.

DETECTIVE: Did he give you the impression that he went to school there?

KATHLEEN: Yes, that's what I thought. Namely just because he was on campus and because I thought he had books and just assumed he went to school there.

DETECTIVE: Did you get the impression that you had ever seen him before?

KATHLEEN: No, but there was nothing unique about him really that would, I may have seen him in a crowd somewhere, I ... his face ... nothing about him was familiar to me. I don't recall ever seeing him before. But then, again, it's a possibility, you know.

DETECTIVE: Did he strike you as the type of person that would appeal to you?

KATHLEEN: No. He was shaggily, or sloppily, or however you want to say it, dressed and kind of scrawny looking. He didn't appeal to me at all.

DETECTIVE: Did you volunteer to take his books, or did he ask you to take them?

KATHLEEN: No, I think I said, "Can I help you?" He didn't say, "Will you give me a hand, or will you help me?" I think I was the one who volunteered it.

DETECTIVE: Do you normally walk from one place to another on campus?

KATHLEEN: Yes, I walk to all my classes. I'm all over the campus.

DETECTIVE: Was there any time that you feel this person would have been watching you earlier?

KATHLEEN: No. I never felt that anyone was watching me, however, that day I had been to most of my classes, and I imagine I had been in, or at least through the SUB where most of the people had congregated, and you know, I don't know if he could have been anywhere in the crowd, in the rush between classes, up and down the mall, you know anywhere like that. I can't exactly remember what I did that afternoon. Most of my classes were in the morning, but I think I was at home most of the afternoon, and then in the evening up until 8:00, or so.

DETECTIVE: What time does the library close?

KATHLEEN: 11:30 p.m.

DETECTIVE: What time does the SUB close?

KATHLEEN: Uh ... I don't know. I don't know what time they actually lock the doors.

DETECTIVE: Did you hear anything when you were walking, for instance, shoes squeaking? Possibly he was wearing some sort of tennis shoes, or anything like that.

KATHLEEN: No, but it seems to me, and it's the first time this thought has come into my head, that he did have tennis shoes on, like a boat shoe, not a regular Converse, or something like that ... but I'm not sure about that. I never thought about it, but I kind of picture that right now.

DETECTIVE: Do you recall what he was wearing, for instance, maybe a shirt or jacket of any sort?

KATHLEEN: It seems to me that he had a shirt on, like a sport shirt, it was very sloppy or wrinkly looking. It seems to me he had a shirt-tail hanging out. I mean, intentionally hanging out, wearing it on the outer side of his pants. I don't remember what type of pants he had on. Just all-around kind of grubby, like jeans or something like that.

DETECTIVE: The distance between the library and the car is about a block and one half, and was there any conversation other than what the ski accident was about?

KATHLEEN: No, I don't think so. I remember distinctly we gathered up the books, packages, and stuff and started walking and it was right before we came to the little bridge, next to Group Conference there, that I said, "Wait a minute, where are you going?" because it became evident that he wasn't going to the library.

DETECTIVE: How far was the bridge from where you started out?

KATHLEEN: Hardly any distance at all. Just a matter of feet, and uh ... so I said, "Well, wait a minute, where are you going?" He said, "Well, my car's just over there." I said, "Okay," so we started walking across the bridge and we were maybe a quarter of the way across the bridge and he began telling me about his ski injuries and that conversation took us up to by the other side of the bridge and a little way beyond that, and then I asked him again, "Well, where's your car?" I expected it to be parked on that street that's right behind the library. He said, "Oh, it's just right here." Then we walked under the trestle to the right there, and it was just barely down that dark stretch.

DETECTIVE: Did he volunteer the conversation about his ski accident?

KATHLEEN: I think so. I don't remember asking him what he did. I'm not sure about that though.

DETECTIVE: Do you think you ever saw him or the car after that incident?

KATHLEEN: No, I don't. If I had seen the car, it probably would have clicked back on me, and I would have thought back, but I didn't, as far as I know.

DETECTIVE: The particular type of jeans that you wear, were they tight for you, or baggy, or flared, or what?

KATHLEEN: They were tight ...uh ... they weren't exceptionally baggy, but they weren't new jeans, either, but I'm not sure. Anyway, they were flared and they had a cuff, and that's about it.

DETECTIVE: Were there any other people coming out of the library, or in the area where you were when you first confronted him?

KATHLEEN: I'm sure there were, that's a busy time of the night around the library, but there was no one walking the direction we were walking on the street or sidewalk that runs up and down behind the library, so once we left the side of the library I never saw anyone after that.

CHAPTER FIVE

THE LAKE SAMMAMISH REPORTS

Janice Ott

I am at Lake Sammamish, sunning myself.

-A note left by Janice Ott and taped to her front door.

The above heading and the quote "I am at Lake Sammamish, sunning myself," as well as the explanation as to where this note was found, was placed here by me as a type of introduction to the following reports, and does not appear at the top of the original report page.

Taken by ROBERT D. KEPPEL

Statement of SYLVIA MARIA VALINT

On July 14, 1974, at about 1230 hrs., I was at Lake Sammamish State Park, with Kathy Veres and Pam. We were sitting on the beach close to the water. A girl I have positively identified as Jan Ott came up near me and she was on a bicycle. She laid her towel down; she had a pair of cut-offs and a shirt that was tied in the front that showed her stomach. The cut-offs were jeans. She had a dark colored knapsack. She took off her cut-offs and shirt and lay down. She had on a black bikini. I think she had leathered colored thongs. She lay there for about ½ hour.

Then a guy came up to her. He is about 5'6" to 5'7", medium-build, blondish-brown hair down to his neck, parted on the side, had dark tan, left arm in sling. The cast started at wrist and bent around the elbow. He had on white tennis shoes, white socks, white shorts, and a white "T" shirt. He said, "Excuse me, but could you help me put my sailboat onto my car because I can't do it by myself because I broke my arm." She said, "Well, sit down and let's talk about it. Where's the boat?" He said, "It's up at my parent's house in Issaquah." She said, "Oh, really, I live up in Issaquah." She said, "Well, okay." She stood up and put on her clothes. She picked up her bike and said, "Under one condition, that I get a ride in the sailboat." He said, "My car is in the parking lot." She said words like, "Well, I get to meet your folks then." He had asked her who she knew in Issaquah. They left like they were going out to the parking lot. They were only on the beach for about ten minutes. He had a small English accent, kinda like a fag. He had tiny sideburns. He was smooth talking. He was definitely a white male and could not be mistaken for a Latin or Hawaiian. His clothes looked like he was rich and dressed to go sailing. He stated that his name was Ted, after she said my name's Jan. I was about two feet from Jan. We were about a hundred yards from the Rainier function. He walked up from the west.

I have read the above statement and it is true and correct to the best of my knowledge.

Sylvia Valint

July 17, 1974, 11:05 a.m.

The following report is from Katalin E. Veres, a friend of Silvia Valint, who was with Sylvia and Pam Okada at the park that day.

Taken by ROGER E. DUNN

Statement of KATALIN E. VERES

On Sunday, July 14, 1974, I went t to Lake Sammamish State Park with Pam Okada, 11111 Luther Street, S., PA 5-6887, and Sylvia Valint. We got there about 11:30, or a little later. We put our towels down on the beach right near the water's edge, right in front of the float. I'm really not sure of who was around us on the beach when we got there, but there weren't many people on the beach. I noticed a really foxy blonde girl sitting next to Sylvia on the beach, and she had a greenish-yellow girl's bike with her. The bike had thin tires, but I couldn't tell if it was a ten-speed, or not. She had a dark blue backpack with her. She was wearing a dark blue bikini. We didn't speak to her and I didn't pay too much attention to her. It didn't seem to me like she was waiting for somebody. Pam and I got thirsty so about forty-five minutes after we got there, we went to the concession stand to get snow cones. We were gone from the beach about fifteen minutes and when we got back to the beach, the blonde girl and her bike were gone. Sylvia stayed on the beach and told us about a guy coming by and picking up the girl. This happened before 1:30 p.m., because the loudspeaker announced that there were going to be slalom races by the boat launch some time after we got back to the beach. I didn't see the blonde girl talking with anyone or leave with anyone from the beach. I was at work last night when Pam called to tell me that this blonde girl might have been one of the girls who was missing. Today at about 10:20, Detective Dunn showed me a black and white photograph which I have identified as the blonde girl we saw at the park on Sunday. I have initialed the back and dated it. This two-page statement is true to the best of my knowledge.

July 17, 1974, 10:57 a.m.

Signed by Katalin E. Veres

July 17, 1974

Taken by DETECTIVE ROLF T. GRUNDEN

Statement of THERESA MARIE SHARPE

Sunday, July 14, 1974, I left my home with my five children about 11:00 a.m. We arrived at Lake Sammamish State Park about 11:45. I sat down and prepared my children for swimming. Approximately fifteen minutes had passed and a girl sat down next to me. She was approximately ten to fifteen feet from me.

She was dressed in blue jean Levi cut-offs, real short, similar to hot pants, and off-white midriff blouse with three or four buttons. She took these articles of clothing off and sat down in her swimsuit. The suit was a two-piece black bikini. She put coco-butter on — it comes in a small orange jar.

Prior to laying down, she laid her ten-speed bike down in the sand, in front of where she was going to sit. The bike was a bright yellow.

When she lay down, she lay on what appeared to be a white, ordinary towel.

She lay down until 12:30. I know this because I always look at my watch. At 12:30 p.m., a guy came walking up to her. He said something about a sailboat. It sounded like, will you help me with my boat. Or would you like to ride in my boat. The girl sort of hesitated, but then said, "Can I bring my bike with me?" He said, "Sure, okay." She though the boat was at the lake, and he said, "No, it was at (his) parent's house." She looked like she wasn't going. I couldn't hear what was said then, but then I heard her say, "Under one stipulation, that I meet your parents." He said, "Sure." Then she said, "I don't know how to sail." He said, "That's okay, it will be easy for me to teach you." She asked him if there was room in the car for her bike. He said it will fit in the trunk. She got up, slipped her blue-jeans and her top on, and she then picked up her beach bag. I don't remember what the bag looked like. The two of them then left.

Monday, I heard on the radio that two girls were missing. I didn't pay too much attention until today, then I heard they were missing from Sunday at the park.

The guy I saw looked to be about 6', 180 – 185lbs., his hair was brown and about collar length, wavy. He had a tan. It really showed up because of his white outfit. His shirt was a white T-shirt with some kind of design, I don't remember what it was. He wore white shorts, similar to a swim suit, I don't remember if he had shoes on. His left arm was in a sling. The sling was beige in color. I didn't feel his arm was really hurt. I do remember he took his arm from the sling and moved it around. I didn't notice any tattoos or any scars on him. He had real hairy arms and legs. If I saw the man again I can identify him. He looked to be twenty-five to thirty years old. I never saw any vehicle they left in. I do recall she sort of talked with an accent.

I have signed the back of the photo, who I've identified as the girl.

Theresa M. Sharpe

July 17, 1974, 1:15 p.m.

July 17, 1974

JANICE ELLEN GRAHAM

I left the house at 11:15 a.m. and arrived at Lake Sammamish State Park after 11:30 a.m. I looked around for a picnic table. There were none so I went to the bandstand to watch the races. A guy came up and said hello and I said hello. Then I kind of moved away. He asked me if I could help him for a minute. I said, "Yeah, what do you want?" He said he was waiting for friends, but couldn't find them. He said he wanted to load his sailboat on his car. I told him sure.

I would describe him as being 5'8" – 5'10", sandy blond hair, curly, short on sides, longer in back, 150-160 pounds, about twenty-four to twenty-five years of age, dressed in a white T-shirt with red trim (neck line was crew–type) and it had short sleeves, blue Levis type jeans (long length, I think), I didn't notice his shoes. Then we walked up to the car that was parked in the parking lot between the bandstand and restrooms. He asked me what I was doing. I told him I was waiting for my husband and parents. He said, "This is out of sight, there are so many people." He stopped many times to hold his arm against his body as if it was hurting. That was when I first noticed he did not have a cast on (Bundy actually wore his arm in a sling). *He said he hurt it playing racket ball. Then he asked me if I had ever played it, then he said it was a lot of fun.*

He asked if I lived around here and I told him Bellevue and where I worked. By that time, we were close to the car. This is when I noticed there was no trailer on the car or sailboat anywhere around. The car was a newish looking Volkswagen, bug, metallic brown in color. I asked where it was. This is when he said, "It's at my folks house; it's just up the hill." I said I really couldn't go with him because I had to meet my folks. That's when I asked him what the time was. I did not notice if he looked at a watch, but he replied it was 12:30, and I said I was late already because I had to meet them at 12:15. He said, "Oh, that's okay, I should have told you it wasn't in the parking lot." "Thanks for bothering to come up to the car."

He walked me about halfway back up toward the park. He went to the right toward the bandstand and I went to the concession stand and bought a snow cone. I stayed at the concession stand while eating it. It was about ten minutes later when I saw him walking with a girl to the parking lot. The girl had a yellow bike and it looked like a ten speed because of the curved handlebars. I thought to myself that it didn't take him very long to get someone else to go to the parking lot with him. They were walking towards the parking lot (he was on the side closest to me) and the girl was in between him and the bike she was pushing. I could not see the girl very well. I wondered where he was going to put the bike. I met my folks about 12:45, and did not see him for the rest of the day.

March 14, 1975

Taken by ROGER E. DUNN

Statement of DONALD STEPHEN BIRDSALL

On Sunday, July 14, 1974, I went to Lake Sammamish State Park with Darrell Greenwood. I rode over in his boat. He dropped me off at the point where my parents were picnicking and then we split. I got to the park around 11:00 to 11:30 a.m. There was a Ragtime

Band playing at the Rainier Beer party stand but the events hadn't started yet. I saw Connie Gregory and her boyfriend Terry at the park. We threw the frisbee around for a while.

At about 2:30 p.m., I was standing around in the crowd watching the keg throwing contest. I looked over and happened to notice a blonde girl talking to a guy. The guy was about twenty-three to twenty-four years old. He was about 5'8" – 5'9" tall, and weighed 155 – 160 pounds. He had blond hair that covered his ears. I don't remember what he was wearing other than he had a T-shirt on. He had his right arm in a sling, and his arm was bandaged through his palm. The girl with him was about 5'4" tall, and slender. She had on cut-off jeans and was wearing either a bikini or halter top that was orange or yellow. Her hair was pulled back and hung down to the middle of her back. She had a white or yellow girl's ten-speed bike with her. I only looked at them for fifteen seconds or so, and didn't see either of them again.

I recognized the girl as one I had seen riding her bike around the area. I first saw her about three weeks before riding past my parent's house at 19501 S.E. 51, which is on the southwest corner of Lake Sammamish. I saw her again about a week later riding past, and then about a week before July 14, 1974, down by VIP's Restaurant. I've seen photographs of Janice Ott, and I'm almost sure she was the girl I have described. The color composite drawing of "Ted" shows his hair as coming down too far on his forehead, and it is too dark. The eyebrows are too dark. The eyes are real good as are the nose and mouth. I think his face is a little too fat.

This three-page* statement is true to the best of my knowledge. *Author's note: this is a two-page statement.

Statement ended on March 14, 1975, at 11:35 a.m.

The following statement contains a description of a man that may have been Bundy, but if so, the witness has made some mistakes concerning his attire, or she may have been watching someone else who also wore a sling on his arm. Nevertheless, it's a statement from an individual who was present that day, and as such, I'm including it here.

Taken by DETECTIVE RANDY HERGESHEIMER

Statement of JACKIE M. TERRELL

On Sunday, July 14, 1974, my youngest daughter, Becky, five yrs., and I went to Lake Sammamish State Park near Issaquah. We arrived at the park at approximately 12:30 p.m., and by the time we found a parking spot and got out of the car, it was approximately 1:00 p.m. I parked across from the Ranger Station entrance in the grass parking area, and we walked from there through the wooded area toward the beach, past the concession stand. We stopped by the second life guard stand, south of the peninsula, and I lay on the sandy beach on a blanket while my daughter played in the sand nearby. I stayed in this area the entire afternoon, sunning and picnicking. We were about ten feet from the life guard stand.

Later in the afternoon, I observed a young white male walking toward me from the area of the small peninsula, north of me. The reason I noticed him, among all the people, was because he had his left arm in a sling. He walked slowly, looking around, toward me and passed in front of me at a distance of about six feet. He walked right by the lifeguard stand, just on the east side of it, in the sand. I paid particular attention to him because I have suffered four broken arms and the sling the man had his arm in was very unusual.

The man was about twenty to twenty-six years old, 5'6" or 5'7" tall, average build, with an even, medium suntan, and brown hair that I would call short by today's standards. The hair appeared to be combed back from the forehead, neatly groomed, exposing his ears. The hair would not have reached his collar. He had no mustache or sideburns. He was wearing an ordinary white-sleeved T-shirt, made of thinner material as I could almost visualize his tan through the T-shirt. He wore a red pair of boxer swim trunks with short legs. They may have had some white piping on the side where the seam would be. He was barefoot. I did not notice any unusual amount of body hair. I noticed no watch or jewelry. I would describe his facial expression as sort of expressionless without smile or frown. He casually glanced from side to side as he passed.

The most unusual thing about him was the sling on his left arm. It didn't look like a typical muslin sling, but rather a thin off-white dish towel. The sling covered from the wrist to the elbow and appeared to be frayed or worn along the outside edge toward the left shoulder. The sling was looped around his neck. The sling looked like he could take his arm in or out of it without untying it. The arm was not in the usual sling position. It hung lower than his wrist. Something unusual I noticed was a mustard-yellow colored cloth ribbon about 1 ½ to 2" wide which was coming downward parallel to his sling across his chest from the neck. The ribbon looked separate from the sling and didn't seem to have any purpose. I couldn't visualize any useful purpose for the ribbon.

After he passed me he seemed to head for the concession stand and I didn't observe him any further. I know the time was 4:00 p.m. because a swimmer asked me what time it was, and it was 4:00 p.m. It was just a few minutes after 4:00 p.m. when I observed this man I've described. It seemed unusual that he was alone because even with all the people around, almost everyone was with someone else.

I have looked at the #2 composite sketch shown me by Detective Hergesheimer and it is a close resemblance to the man with the sling except that I would make his face thinner and his lips fuller. I don't think he had a cast on under his sling as his arm did not look bulky.

This statement is true and correct to the best of my knowledge.

Signed by Jackie Terrell

July 22, 1974, 6:45 or p.m.

October 8, 1975, beginning at 11:44 a.m.

Taped interview between Detective Roger E. Dunn and Jerry Edward John Snyder, thirty years of age who is an undercover DEA agent assigned to Group One in the Seattle office, B/P XXX-XXXX. (This would have been a redacted phone number). *Agent Snyder is known by the nickname of Kelly.*

DETECTIVE DUNN: Kelly, could you in a narrative phrase start out with your activity on July 14, 1974, from the time you arrived at Lake Sammamish State Park, the approximate time, and what you did then.

KELLY: It was on June 14, excuse me, July 14, 1974, myself and my family, which is my wife and my two sons and at the time a pet Doberman arrived at Lake Sammamish Park and parked in the main parking lot. We parked in the southernmost part of the main parking lot and went directly from the parking lot to the beach area. I believe the time was approximately 10:15 or 10:30 in the morning. We went directly to the beach, like I said, and we put down mats and the kids went into the water and due to the fact that dogs were not supposed to be on the beach, I had to get a few feet back of my wife, where she was sitting, and I was about several yards back.

In the place where I positioned myself on the beach I noticed there was a young lady to my left, approximately twelve to fifteen yards away from me, dressed in a black two-piece bikini with blond hair. I remembered that earlier when we were arriving at the park, the same young lady was riding her bicycle, parallel to my vehicle. I don't know the brand name, but it was greenish-yellow in color, looked like a racing bike of some sort. I remember it more distinctly as a yellow bike and she was riding that particular bike into the park and when I first noticed her, she just went by the car.

DETECTIVE DUNN: Was it a boy's frame? Or a girl's?

KELLY: I seem to recall a boy's frame, but I'm not really sure of that. I'm just going to have to say that I think it was a boy's frame.

DETECTIVE DUNN: Did you notice anything about packs, or anything?

KELLY: Well, while riding into the park she had what I would consider a book backpack, in other words it wasn't very large, it was a rather small backpack that she had on her back. I believe she was wearing a white blouse and cut-offs, blue jean cut-offs.

DETECTIVE DUNN: What color was the knapsack?

KELLY: That burlap type fabric, the real thick fabric. Anyway, once we got into the parking lot I didn't really pay that much attention to her until going back to what I said earlier when I arrived at the beach, the same girl that was riding next to my vehicle was the same one who was lying on the beach. The reason that I noticed that of course was the bike and the clothes that she had were lying next to her. As far as my position on the beach, as I explained earlier, my family was located in front of me and I was approximately ten yards in back of my wife. I was located almost directly in front of the refreshment stand located on the back part of the beach and almost directly to the far left side of the floating raft which is located in the water. Approximately fifteen to twenty yards, excuse me, twenty feet away from my right side was at that time, a life guard stand. Approximately five to ten feet in that basic vicinity, in back of me were three fairly young females sitting on blankets, sunbathing themselves.

The young lady that I previously described that was to the left of me in the black bikini bathing suit ... the basic articles that were accompanying the young lady were the knapsack that I described earlier, the clothing that I described earlier, and the bike. I noticed that there were various books laying on the blanket that she had and they looked like paperback books and I didn't pay any attention to, or couldn't see what type or what the names were of the books. Other paraphernalia that might have been laying around that I can't totally recall, but it seems that there was sun tan lotion also.

Approximately 10:45 or 11:00 a.m., it was several minutes after we had been on the beach, I noticed a white male walking, he was to my right. Walking down the beach toward me and the reason I noticed him, or looked at him anyway, I noticed that he was looking at all the girls as he walked down the beach. He would stop, almost come to a complete stop, after he had walked up to a girl laying on the beach and as if what it appeared to me that he was trying to pick up a girl or trying to find someone that met with his qualifications. The man continued to walk up to me and then eventually walked past and stopped at the place where the girl with the black double piece bathing suit was laying down and he stopped and said something to the effect of "Hello, Miss" or "Excuse me, Miss" or words to the effect like that. And I don't recall any further conversation other than that he sat down in a cross-legged position and spoke with the young lady for maybe five minutes.

As far as the description of the white male, he was approximately twenty-five to twenty-nine years old, 5'10" to 5'11" or maybe 6' would be pushing it. He was approximately 165 pounds, and he had a hair style that was collar length, wavy, sort of light-brown color. He was wearing white boxer-type shorts with a stripe on the side, the leg side, I believe the stripe was red and he was wearing not a turtle neck but a pullover shirt which was beige in color and had what I would consider had a rust stripe type dual color in it. On his left arm I noticed he was wearing a shoulder harness to support his left arm which appeared to me to be wrapped in adhesive tape, could have been a cast but it looked like an adhesive bandage wrapping all around the arm.

As I explained earlier, the man I described and the female I described sat there for approximately five minutes discussing various and sundry things and eventually the young lady stood up and put on her clothing, the white blouse and the cut-offs, rolled up her blanket. Prior to that, she put all the books and various things that were laying on the blanket into her knapsack and put the knapsack, I believe, over the bike, picked up her bike and the two of them walked off headed in the direction of the refreshment stand, more to the right of the refreshment stand as you are facing it and at that time I lost eye contact or didn't bother to look any more at the individuals going away.

Subsequent to the young lady that I described earlier who was subsequently identified as Janice Ott, I was shown a series of photographs or a photograph of Janice Ott and on that date I positively identified the photograph of Janice Ott as being the young lady that I saw on July, 14, 1974, on the beach. And on the same date, I was shown a photograph of a similar type of bike which was owned by Janice Ott and I identified that photograph of the bicycle as being similar to the one that I saw Janice Ott have on the beach on July 14.

Approximately two days after Janice Ott was believed missing, or was definitely missing, I came home from work that evening and spoke to my wife and said something to the effect that they had information on a girl who was missing from the Sammamish Park and at that period of time we talked about the fact that we were there and how weird it was to be somewhere where someone would be missing and possibly dead. My wife, at that time, based on information that she had heard from the news, made comments on what the girl was wearing and that the police were looking for that individual and also said that the police had made a statement to the press that the man had his arm in a sling and they had somewhat a basic description of that person. Recalling what I had seen the two days prior to that I telephoned the King County Police Department and spoke to an officer and explained there was a possibility that I might have information that could assist them in the investigation, and I believe it was the following day or possibly two days later that I eventually spoke to a King County Police Officer and related all of the previous facts that I have given in this interview.

It should be noted that during the present time of this Janice Ott missing and this incident at the beach, I at that time was working in an undercover capacity for the Drug Enforcement Administration and brought this to the attention of the King County Police Officer for obvious reasons that they would not circumvent any investigation that I was involved in at that time. In addition, that same week that I gave information to King County Police Officers regarding the identification of this subject, I was taken to the Seattle Police Department Laboratory where I gave a composite description of the white male that I previously described to an illustrator employed by Seattle Police Department. Since the original date that I spoke with the King County Police Officers, on several occasions since that time during the remaining year of 1974 and all the way into 1975 to date, I have been shown a series of photographs estimated somewhere in the vicinity of 1500 to 2500 photographs of various individuals which King County have been sent and are investigating.

I have also spoken to a psychiatrist which was an interview basically on what I felt the man's characteristics on the beach that day represented and was questioned or interviewed regarding his composure and the type of person I felt personally he would be. *In addition to that, sometime in the early part of 1975 I was taken to a doctor's office in Seattle and placed under hypnosis to try to bring back to my mind basic facts that took place on July 14, 1974. During this hypnosis I related to the doctor, and to Detective Dunn what my memory was pertaining to this instance on that date.*

On October 8, 1975, I was contacted by King County Police Department and requested to once again come to their office to try to identify photographs of various individuals and after carefully looking over the montage I extracted or pointed out a photograph I believe to be the individual who I saw on the beach on July 14, 1974. As far as the gentleman I picked out in the montage in relation of his photograph to the others, his photograph is located in the middle of the montage. The reason I picked him was the basic physical description I described earlier and from my memory as best as I can recall, the man fits the description as the one I saw on the beach July 14. The only characteristic in this photo, well, two characteristics is that the man's face looks a little bit fatter and his hair is not combed in the manner of what I saw on that date. The relative length is, I would say, the same. The only difference, of course, would be the curliness, whereas in this photograph it appears to be somewhat of a receding hairline; it seems like there's a light over or above the man as he was being photographed, almost representing his hair to be blond whereas as far as I can remember it was brown or light brown and the hair looks a lot straighter and it was definitely curly or wavy the day I saw him on the 14. The first time I was ... that I had seen a photograph of the individual that I *pointed out in the montage was today and he has been identified to me this date as Theodore Bundy.*

I have heard of the circumstances surrounding his arrest in Utah in the news, however, because of job-related activities, I have not seen a lot of the press but I've heard news cast and radio communication relating to this individual and the basic coincidences that arise from his arrest in Utah and the circumstances surrounding the incidents that happened in the Washington area. The evening, I believe the same date he was arrested in Utah, this Bundy, I waited up for the 10:00 o'clock, I believe it was the 10:00 o'clock, or the 11:00 o'clock, news to see what this individual looked like for my own personal reasons and the time that they were having the photographs shown on television I had a telephone call work-related concerning the airport in a case which was developing out there, and was unable to see a photograph of the individual at that time.

On today's date, subsequent to being shown the montage of photographs and after tentatively identifying the photograph of Bundy, I was shown an additional photograph of Bundy and it was a color photograph and this particular photograph I was shown, to me is a more exact representation of what the man on the beach on July 14 looked like. The facial structure is very exact, the hair is exactly the same, total ... the same, the color is the same. The one thing I recall earlier that I didn't mention on the beach was that as the man was walking down the beach I noticed that he was very slender and what appeared to be athletically built and this man in the color photograph brings to mind or makes my recollection seem to be that he is exactly the same as the one I saw on July 14, 1974.

I have subsequently initialed the photographs I have identified on October 8, 1975.

DETECTIVE DUNN: This is Detective Dunn again, and the taped interview with Special Agent Jerry Snyder is terminated. It is 1231 hrs. on October 8, 1975.

What follows are reports of interviews of those who knew Janice Ott – her family, her husband, and others.

ISSAQUAH POLICE DEPARTMENT

STATEMENT OF RAY JACKSON

DATE: July 17, 1974, 12:30 p.m.

I first met Janice Ott approximately one month ago at the tennis courts directly behind Issaquah High School. Lester Gray, a friend of mine from the Freemont area, had come out to visit and he had called Betty Stover and told her to meet us at the courts. Jan had come along with her. We all then had supper together.

During the next few weeks, Jan came over to my house several times for dinner and on July 7, 1974, we went to a drive-in movie together.

July 9, she and I had a telephone conversation in which she said she might drop over later in the week. I have not seen or heard from her since.

On July 15, 1974, at about 11:00 a.m. or noon, Betty Stover called and asked me if I had seen Jan. I told her I had not. I then went over to her house, where Chief Prosise was already there. Betty and I spent most of the rest of the day searching all the area around Lake Sammamish State Park on foot.

The following report from the Issaquah Police Department includes interviews with Janice Ott's parents,

Don E. Blackburn and Ferol L. Blackburn, and Janice Ott's husband, James Ott:

ISSAQUAH POLICE DEPARTMENT

STATEMENT of FEROL L. BLACKBURN (mother) and DON E. BLACKBURN (father)

DATE: July 18, 1974, 11:50 a.m.

Janice is a bright, honor student girl, orderly, precise, considerate, outgoing, and sunny. She had a great desire to help others – always has seen good in everyone.

We last saw Janice on Sunday July 7. She had been home for a one-week visit. She visited all our family – everyone had a wonderful time. Our relationship was and always has been just great – beautiful.

Our last letter from her was written July 13 – postmarked the same date.

There was no evidence of depression – only happiness and a zest for the future in our visit, or recent correspondence. She was looking forward to visiting us again in late August and moving to California to be with her husband in September.

SPOKANE DENTIST: Dr. Harold Thomas (Northtown Office Building)

SPOKANE M.D. Dr. Horlacker (County Homes Medical Center) and Dr. Copsey (Rockwood Clinic)

JANICE (B/D 2/14/51) – McMinnville, Oregon, attended elementary and secondary school in Spokane. H.S. graduate (Shadle Park High School). Graduate of E.W.S.C. (Cheney), B.A. (Soc. Work) in 1972. Married to JAMES OTT in December 1972 – moved to Seattle at that time. Present employer: KING COUNTY JUVENILE COURT (caseworker) – (Probation Officer).

DENTIST: (Seattle) – Dr. George Kennaugh, University Way (U District)

DOCTOR: Groupe Health Cooperative – Dr. Weaver, Northgate Office; sometimes went to the Central Office on Capitol Hill, walk in clinic.

BANK ACCT: Both checking and savings at Seattle First National, University Branch. I have since closed the account on 7/18/74, 10:00 A.M. The accounts were both joint accounts.

STATEMENT OF JAMES OTT:

I met Jan at Eastern Washington State College in the spring of '72. We were married the 28th of December, '72, after which time we moved to Seattle where I was a student at the U of W and Jan started working at a daycare center on Alaskan Way, Seattle. Jan, after about three to four months, started working at the Juvenile Court, Seattle, Detention Unit. She found it a little difficult working in a position that offered no chance of advancement, as she was always wanting to improve herself intellectually, so that she could help others. She got the opportunity of moving up to the Probation Unit and was very elated to have such a chance to stimulate her growth as a person. Other than minor problems with some of the secretaries there in the unit, she was very satisfied with her job and herself. The problems encountered with the secretaries were personality conflicts. They seemed to gossip about everyone there, including her. This bothered her quite a lot, because she thought it was unfair that anyone would talk about another person behind their backs. She always wanted to be open with people, whether what she had to say was of appraisal or negative in nature, and if it was negative, she wanted to talk about it so as to resolve it. She wanted everyone to be happy. If she could do it, she would make the whole world happy.

Jan was a compulsive individual. She needed order in her life or she didn't feel satisfied with herself. Everything was to be planned and in order. If she went into something without some semblance of order she wouldn't feel like it would go over too successfully. She always wrote down appointments for everything from social engagements to doctor's appointments, etc.

Jan was very neat and conscious of her appearance. It was important for her to look attractive to others, as well as to herself. Without actually thinking about it, due to her naivety of others, she could be very sexually attractive, most of which was due to the fact that she was a very pretty woman without actually trying to be. She had a very attractive figure which adds to her attractiveness and sexuality.

Legally, I was Jan's husband. However, we liked to keep our marriage out of its traditional role. That is, being devoted only to each other, such that either of us could not expand ourselves in our work and with other people. We both felt a need to have an independence of our own, so that we could expand and in turn, enhance our relationship.

An important part of our relationship, so Jan felt, I too for that matter, was a need to communicate. This was an important facet of Jan's philosophy besides. She liked talking to people, helping them in any way shew could, just by being an honest person with whomever she dealt.

I last saw Jan on the 16th of June. She drove down to Corvallis, Oregon, where my parents live, as I was moving to California. She spent that weekend there and returned to Seattle that Sunday.

The last time I talked to Jan was Saturday night at 10:00 p.m., on the 13th of July. She was to call me again the following Wednesday evening until this terrible thing happened.

KING COUNTY DEPARTMENT OF PUBLIC SAFETY

Taken by: CHIEF PROSISE

Statement of: DAVID ALLISON MCKIBBEN

July 17, 1974

Occupation & Employer: Owner – Laundromat

I arrived at the Suds Shop at 32 E. Sunset approximately 10 a.m. on Sunday, July 14, 1974, to clean up. As I entered, a young woman entered carrying a basket of laundry who later identified herself as Jan Ott. She was wearing cut-off blue jeans, a white open collar button-up blouse, tucked in, no bra, and tennis shoes. I don't recall any jewelry. Her hair was about two to three inches longer than shoulder length, worn loose.

As I cleaned around the laundromat, we talked about whatever came up. Nothing in particular. She was going to the beach on her bike – she was a probation officer in Seattle. Lived with a friend who worked there too, but different hours. She finished about the time I did and I asked her if she wanted a cup of coffee since I was going too, and she said, sure, as soon as she took her laundry across the street to her house. I walked to the corner of Sunset and Front with her and she took her laundry in and came out about five minutes later, looking the same as before.

We walked down to Fasona's Restaurant, and sat at a small booth and talked over coffee. She said she was separated from her husband, a "liberated woman". Used to live in Seattle but moved because she was ripped off and lost most of her things. All she had now was her Volkswagen, bike, and clothes. She said she was planning to go to the beach but preferred to have nothing more to do with it. I talked a little about myself, that I had two girls, lived in North Bend, what I did for a living and how I got involved with my business. She was a very friendly person, very outgoing and easy to talk to. Mentioned that she had had breakfast, a week or two earlier, at the Snoqualmie Falls Lodge. Mentioned that her parents lived in Spokane, Washington. I believe we left the restaurant about 11:15 a.m. and walked back down to the house. She went inside after saying good-bye and I left for North Bend. That was the last I saw of her until hearing about her being missing on Tuesday evening.

Taken by DETECTIVE ROLF T. GRUNDEN

Statement by SUSAN JANE KINSINGER

July 17, 1974, 11:25 a.m. I have known Jan Ott since 1969. We went to Eastern Washington State College. We have been in pretty close contact since she has been in Seattle. The last time I saw her was June 27, 1974, we had lunch together.

I spoke to her two or three times prior to her being reported missing. We had set up an appointment to have lunch today, July 17, 1974.

She is the type of individual who is always very punctual. Normally she does not carry large sums of cash. She would have about $3.00 or $4.00. It would bother her very much to be in dirty clothing. I know she would contact her parents, roommate, or Jim, her husband.

Her strongest bond is toward her mother and father. They have always had high expectations of her.

Jim, her husband, is a calm type of individual. He is in medical school in California. I am sure that he would not harm Jan in any way.

Her past boyfriends were Greg Kinsinger, my brother, who lives in Walla Walla; Mike Casey, he also lives in Walla Walla. Those are the only boys I know she dated other than Jim, her husband.

This statement is true and correct to the best of my knowledge.

I have always found personal communications that are provided to police by witnesses and friends of the victims to be of utmost importance. For the police, it's an opportunity to obtain what they hope to be valid information that could lead them to the one responsible for the abductions and murders. And at the time, that was the primary focus, as these reports were for in-house use by the investigators only. But as the years rolled on and Ted Bundy was captured and ultimately executed, the files were opened up for all to see. It is from this perspective that the poignant aspect of this material comes forth. And this is especially true of communication that comes directly from the families, where the ever-present pain is always just below the surface of their words.

CHAPTER SIX

THE LAKE SAMMAMISH REPORTS

Denise Naslund

As a true crime writer, it is impossible for me to read stories of victims and the circumstances of their deaths, and not wonder about the "what-ifs" of each situation which led to an abrupt and untimely end to their lives. Such is the case of young and pretty Denise Naslund. In my book, *The Bundy Murders*, I mention that Denise wasn't even supposed to be at Lake Sammamish State Park on that beautiful and sunny Sunday of July 14, 1974, and that's correct. Had she and her boyfriend, Kenneth Little, not received a phone call that morning from another couple with an offer to go with them to the park, you wouldn't even be reading this story now, and we wouldn't even be aware of her name. Had Ted Bundy not been the lethal entity he was, or if he'd skipped hunting that day, Denise Naslund would no doubt be alive today, and may have become a mother and grandmother by now. But her inability to see into the future was something Bundy counted upon and would use to his advantage. He was a planner of murder, and from the moment he encountered Denise on that Sunday late afternoon, he already knew what her future would be, if only he could convince her to go with him …

Taken by DETECTIVE ROLF T. GRUNDEN

Statement of PATRICIA ANN TURNER

July 19, 1974

July 14, 1974, I went to Lake Sammamish State Park with another couple, Donna Ray, Kim Prior and my boyfriend Nick Bennett. We got to the park around 3:00 p.m. We first sat down in front of the concession stand, we sat there for about fifteen minutes, then moved to where the Rainier picnic was. Nick and I stayed at the Rainier picnic. Donna and Kim sort of wandered off – we met them about quarter to four at the Rainier picnic site. The four of us returned to the area in front of the concession stand and sat down on the beach – this was about 4:15 p.m.

I didn't feel good so I got up and walked toward the concession stand. As I was walking up the sidewalk, a man came walking toward me. He had a sling on his left arm. The sling was bleached white, clean. He had on white shorts, a white T-shirt, and white tennis shoes. He was about 5'8", 160 – 165, he was well built. His hair was dishwater blond, it was about neck length, cut in a shag; as far as I know he didn't have sideburns; it was parted in the middle more or less – his hair was messy. He was a very good-looking man. He was about twenty-four or twenty-five.

As I walked to the concession stand, he followed me. We talked to each other on the sidewalk and he said, "I need to ask a really big favor of you." He then said, "You can see I'm not very useful of my hand, would you please help me launch my sailboat?" I looked at him as if I didn't understand. He said: "I normally wouldn't ask this favor but my brother is busy and is unable to help." He sort of pointed in the direction of the parking lot. I said: "Well, I am sort of in a hurry to go." He said: "That's okay." He just stood there for a few seconds; that's when I walked on to the concession stand. I glanced off into the crowd and saw him walk away.

I didn't notice any accent in his speech. After I got to the concession stand, my boyfriend came up. I told him what the man said. Nick said he didn't notice the man except from the back.

We left about 4:45 p.m.

Today, July 19, 1974, I saw him in a composite drawing in the Seattle Times.

Today, Detective Grunden showed me a composite of him which I will sign on the back of the photo.

Taken by DETECTIVE ROBERT D. KEPPEL

Statement of JACQUELINE MARIE PLISCHKE

July 17, 1974

On Sunday, July 14, 1974, at about 4 p.m., I arrived at Lake Sammamish State Park on my bicycle. I was there for about twenty minutes. I had gone to the point on the beach where they water ski from. I was approached by a white male, early twenties, 5'8", medium build, dark blond hair, hair length was about to the middle of his ear, average skin tone, left arm in a sling and sling was beige in color. The sling was not neat, something, either a cast or wrap was over his arm. He had a wide face, average features and his speech was smooth. He talked clearly, no slang words – everything was distinct. The first thing he said was, "Hello, I was wondering if you could help me put my sailboat on my car?" I said, "I'm not very strong." He said, "It's better that I asked someone who was alone." He answered my comments right away. I said, "I'm waiting for someone." He then seemed to not have any interest in me." He said, "Oh, I see." Then he turned away and walked toward the bath house. I was about two feet from him.

About fifteen minutes prior to talking with him, I had seen the same guy look at me when I came in. I just noticed his face and sling at that time. I was riding my bicycle. I was wearing blue jeans, sort of cut-offs, and a pink, very brief bikini top.

About ten minutes after he left from talking with me, I looked at my watch and it was 4:30 p.m. I did not see him again. He did not act nervous. He was not pushy. He didn't seem disappointed when I told him I was waiting for someone.

I have read the above statement and it is true and correct to the best of my knowledge.

Taken by ROBERT D. KEPPEL

Statement by TAMMIE MICHELLE STEWART

August 1, 1974, 1:45 a.m. or p.m.???

On Sunday, July 14, 1974, at about 3 or 4 p.m., I was at Lake Sammamish State Park with Pam Culbertson. We were standing by the concession stand on the grass. A guy walked by us and Pam told me he had walked around us about eight times. I would describe him as about twenty-four to twenty-five years, 5'6", medium build, 150 pounds, blondish-brown curly hair covering ears and down the back of his neck, dark tan. I think the right arm was in a white sling; white cast; he wore cut-offs, unknown what type, a white or yellow shirt was tied around his waist; white low-topped tennis shoes, no glasses. He was a white male. This guy walked around us for ten minutes and a girl came up and sat down about four feet from us. The girl had on a pair of cut-offs, white earrings and a light brown shag haircut. The guy came up and talked to her. I did not hear anything that was said. He talked to her for about fifteen minutes. I did not pay any attention to them. We left and I did not see him again. The girl he was talking to was not one of the missing girls.

BOTHELL POLICE DEPARTMENT

Statement of SINDI JANE SIEBENBAUM

July 17, 1974, 1935 hrs

On Sunday, July 14, 1974, I was at Lake Sammamish State Park. At approximately 4:00 p.m., I was heading back from the restrooms towards the point where my friends were. I was about a hundred yards from the restrooms when a man who was walking toward me said, "Excuse me, young lady, could you help me launch my sailboat?" I then asked him what he had done to his arm; he stated that he had sprained it and that he couldn't find anyone to help him. I told him I was sorry, but I couldn't help him because I had people waiting. He told me that the sailboat was up on the beach and that it would only take a few minutes. It appeared to me that he meant the boat was up towards the restrooms.

I again told him I couldn't help, however, he kept on asking. I talked to him for five or ten minutes. I finally just told him I was sorry and left. The last I saw of him, he was walking toward the restrooms.

The man I was talking with was about 6'0" to 6'2". I'm not sure how much he weighed, but I remember he was really skinny. I would say that he had a small frame and kind of boney. His hair was salt and pepper colored about two inches below his ears. It was parted in the middle and bangs over his forehead. It was curly, but looked like it had been styled. I think his eyes were either green or blue, and he looked bug-eyed and set back. His pupils were real small. I would guess this man to be in his thirties. He was clean shaven. It appeared to me that he was nervous. He spoke rapidly and gestured with his hands. His left arm was in a sling and it appeared to be the type a doctor would put on someone. He was wearing sort of a bleached-white boxer swimming suit and elastic for a waist band. His body had a full tan, not real dark, but he was tan. He had sort of a pointed nose and thin lips. I don't recall him having any noticeable body hair.

Taken by ROBERT D. KEPPEL

Statement by PATRICK MICHAEL CULBERTSON

On Sunday, July 14, 1974, at about 3 – 3:30 p.m., I was at Lake Sammamish State Park with Tammie Stewart. We were waiting for friends near the concession stand on the grass. I saw this guy walking around us. I was standing and Tammie was lying down. I would describe him as a white male, 5'7", 145 pounds, thirty years, medium build, thin frame, light brown hair, parted in the middle, wavy down to back of his neck, blue eyes, thin nicely shaped nose, cheeks were hollow, pointed chin, hair over ears, nice tan, pants, white shirt hanging out back pocket, left arm in beige sling. The sling was around his neck. The left arm appeared to be wrapped. He gave me the impression he was foreign looking, like British, and he was good looking. He walked slowly and lightly. He looked odd to me.

He kept walking around a circle, staring at Tammie and another girl. He approached the other girl. She was lying down. She was wearing a bikini top and blue jean cut-offs. The guy knelt down and talked to her. He talked to her for about three minutes. The next time I noticed him, about five minutes later, and the girl he was talking to were (sic) *gone. I did not see him again. The guy was clean shaven. The girl he talked to was about four to five feet from Tammie and me.*

It seemed like he bent over a little bit when he walked. He did not appear to be with anyone. He didn't seem like he had anywhere to go. He was not real hairy.

I have read the above statement and it is true and correct to the best of my knowledge.

Taken by DETECTIVE ROBERT D. KEPPEL

Statement of BETTY J. BARRY

July 17, 1974, 12:30 p.m.

On 7/14/74 at 11:45 a.m., I was at Lake Sammamish State Park. I was with the Rainier Family Picnic. Around 3:30 or 4 p.m., I went to the ladies' restroom. I saw a girl in the restroom, which I have positively identified as Denise Naslund. She was leaving as I went out. There was another girl that walked out the same time, who was wearing a maroon knit bikini top. Denise had talked to the other girl. The other girl was about the same size as Denise. Denise had on faded cut-off jeans, and a light-colored halter top. Her shoes were a brown Mexican-type sandal. They both appeared to be good looking.

I have read the above statement and it is true and correct to the best of my knowledge.

Taken by DETECTIVE ROLF T. GRUNDEN

Statement of JACQUELINE CRAVEN

July 18, 1974, 12:00 p.m.

On Sunday, July 14, 1974, I went to Lake Sammamish State Park with my family. We got there at 3:30 p.m., and we stayed there until 4:45 p.m.

Between 4:00 and 4:30, I went to the women's restroom with my twenty-two-year-old daughter. The restroom is located in the middle of the park by the concession stand. As I was waiting for my daughter, I noticed a man with a sling on his left arm. He was walking back and forth in from of the restroom. He is described as follows: 5'7" – 5'8", 170 pounds, good build, tan, but fair complected (sic). He wore boxer-style swim trunks with Hawaiian print, with possibly a white waist band. He had some hair on his chest, but was not "hairy". No shirt. The sling on his left arm was a regular triangular bandage, beige in color. The sling was soiled. It had a safety pin on the outside of the left elbow.

His hair was dark brown, clean cut, sideburns about to the middle of the ear lobe. I don't recall if he had glasses.

Me and my daughter left the restroom area about 4:30 p.m. I don't recall if he was still there when we left.

This statement is true and correct to the best of my knowledge.

What follows are the statements of those who knew Denise Naslund. We begin with Robin Woods, and continue with the remaining three individuals, Kenneth Little, Robert Sargent, and Nancy Battema, who were with Denise on July 14, and finish with Elenore Rose, Denise's mother.

Taken by DETECTIVE ROLF T. GRUNDEN

Statement of ROBIN ROSE WOODS

July 30, 1974, 1:00 p.m.

I have known Denise Naslund since the seventh grade. We have known each other seven years. Denise was my roommate for seven months from October 10 to April 1, 1974.

From November on, Kenny Little lived at our house.

Denise is a person who has a good personality. She tends to get along good with people. I never saw Kenny or Denise fight physically, but I have heard them argue.

We have used various types of dope but we tend to use marijuana.

Denise always wore a black onyx ring. The band is yellow gold. The stone is tear-drop in shape. She also wore a gold wedding band on her little finger on either hand. On her right hand on her third finger she wore a ring with a light blue stone and a silver band. She wore a zodiac necklace, Libra sign. It was silver with black antique. She also wore a gold watch on her left hand.

The last time I saw Denise was on July 3, 1974. She came to my house with her brother Brock and Kenny Little. Kenny came over to get his fishing pole. They were going to Fish Lake over in the eastern Washington area.

Denise was mad and more or less didn't want to go. She said her and Kenny had been arguing. Brock normally took Kenny's side. She wished me and my boyfriend, Joe Alcon, could go. We couldn't because we had company from out of town. They must have stayed five minutes and left. They left around 10:00 p.m.

I left town to go to Nevada on July 9, 1974. I returned home July 14, 1974, at 10:30 p.m. From July 3, 1974, on, I have never heard from Denise. I am sure if she were around, I would have been the first person she would have contacted.

I know she would never go anywhere with any motorcycle people because she feared them. She knows how they are from what I've told her.

At one time Denise worked for Sellect Enterprise. It was a dating and escort service. She was a receptionist and bookkeeper. She never went out on dates.

I would like to make it clear that Denise never worked at a body painting studio.

I would like to add that Denise is the kind of person who likes to talk about herself to people who are interested or people she is interested in. If she was high on July14, 1974, she would be loose. If the guy was a smooth talker and good looking, Denise would then help him.

This statement is true and correct to the best of my knowledge.

Taken by ROBERT D. KEPPEL

Statement of KENNETH LEROY LITTLE, JR.

July 16, 1974, 8:30 p.m.

On 7/14/74 in the afternoon, I was with Denise Naslund, Bob Sargent and Nancy. We met Bob and Nancy by Charlie's East at 1230 hrs. to go to Lake Sammamish. We left Bob's car there. We met Bob inside. We took Denise's car. We got at the park at 13:30 hrs. There were no arguments between anyone and everything was cool. We met a couple of Bob's friends. We sat at the park in front of the restroom. I had my dog with me. I kept having to get up and get my dog. I told Denise, she could get up once in a while and go look for him. She gave me a dirty look. Bob's friends left sometime after the keg throw. Denise had dozed off. Then I lay back and went to sleep. We had stayed up late over the weekend and we were both pretty beat. I don't know what time it was, but when I woke up Denise was gone. Nancy told me Denise had walked towards the restroom. Nancy had asked Denise what time it was and it was around 4 or 4:30. Denise had left her purse in the trunk of her car so no one would steal it. She usually goes nowhere without her purse. She always has track of it.

Denise has hitchhiked in the past. Denise has been living with me for about nine months. We have lived at the Graham address for about four months.

It takes quite a bit to get Denise mad. She has argued with me on previous occasions and she has never walked out on me. I don't consider my comments about the dog as even an argument between us.

Both of us were in a tired grumpy mood. We had stayed late at a card game and I told her we had to leave and she was a little upset about that.

Denise doesn't drink much. She might have had half a beer at the park but that was all. She had not had any drugs. She was not the type to contemplate suicide.

Denise feels real responsible about her ITT Peterson School as a computer programmer. She would want to get back for her exam.

Denise has two rings on each hand plus a watch. Two rings have blue stones. The one ring is a big blue stone in platinum. The other is a diamond shaped onyx, very large, black. She has a band on her little finger. She wears the watch on the left hand. The watch is gold with a chain clasp. When she left, she took a pack of Camel filter cigarettes.

She had very short blue jean cutoffs with a black belt. Has ornamental piece of leather on each side of brass buckle. Buckle sticks through the leather to fasten. The cutoffs were frayed on the ends. She did not have all the belt loops. It had one belt loop in the back and one on each side. They were made from "leg" jeans. There is a leg tag on the back pocket. The cutoffs were faded and worn, no holes, pockets were intact. She had on a navy-blue halter top. It had a loop around the neck and tied in the back. It was a fine, silky texture. It was a dull blue.

Normally she wears bikini underpants. She has pierced ears. She had good teeth, no fillings or color showing; no painted toe nails. Her finger nails were painted blue the day before. She had asked me what color I liked the best. I said blue.

She would go either to her mother's, grandmother's house, her father's, Robin's house, or back to our house.

During the time we were at the park, Denise was with me until I fell asleep. Her swimming suit was left with us as well as her sandals and towel. She would not go anywhere without sandals on her feet. She did not have any money on her.

During the time when we were first at the park about 1300 hrs., Denise had four valium, five milligrams each, little yellow tablets. She smoked part of a joint. She is a friendly girl and if someone would offer her a joint she would take a toke. I'm sure she had complete control of her senses. She last had taken four valium Friday night. I don't think she took anything (in addition) to that.* *Author's note: this is somewhat unclear.

She has been under a doctor's care for (redacted).

Just before we dozed off, we had eaten some hot dogs and chips.

I have read the above statement and it is true and correct to the best of my knowledge.

We searched the park until 8:30 p.m. on Sunday. Bob and Nancy took Denise's car to get their car at about 8:00 p.m. and then they returned to the park.

Taken by DETECTIVE RANDY S. HERGESHEIMER

Statement of ROBERT J. SARGENT

July 18, 1974

On Sunday morning, July 14, 1974, my girlfriend, Nancy Battema and I called Ken Little and Denise Naslund and invited them to go to Lake Sammamish State Park. The four of us met at a tavern called Charley's East in Eastgate. We had a beer in the tavern and left for the park about 1:00 p.m. in Denise's tan Chevrolet. We got ice en route for the case of beer we had with the four of us. We got to the park about 1:30 and parked. En route to the park, Denise, Ken and myself each ate four valiums. We parked and walked to the main picnic area and took up a spot halfway between the bathroom and the Rainier bandstand. At the parking lot we had met Don Cook and two girls who were friends of mine and Nancy's. They joined us at our picnic spot. The seven of us shared a marijuana joint. We sat and talked and drank beer and listened to the band. Then Denise, Ken, Nancy, and I went over and watched the keg toss until it was over. We returned to our picnic area. We ran into Steve Campbell, a friend of mine, and talked to him for a while and he left. Don and the two girls were off somewhere else. The four of us then walked down to the lake to the end of the little peninsula where the boats were tied up. We watched the action there for a while and the four of us walked back to the concession stand. I got some snacks and the four of us returned to our picnic area where our towels and ice chest were. We talked and drank beer. Later I went to the restroom at the concession stand and after that I got hot dogs and hamburgers for the four of us. The four of us then ate the food at our picnic area after Denise awoke from a nap beside Ken. We sat and talked and drank beer. Around 4:15 p.m., Ken dozed off. About 4:40 p.m., Denise got up from where we were sitting and walked away without saying anything to me; that was not unusual, because I assumed she was going to the restroom or to find her dog that we had taken to the picnic. She never returned and we began searching for her. We looked all afternoon and evening without finding her. Before this day, I had only met Denise three times and I do not know her well, nor do I have any idea of where she might have gone or why.

This statement is true and correct to the best of my knowledge.

Taken by ROBERT D. KEPPEL

Statement of NANCY R. BATTEMA

July 18, 1974, 4:30 p.m.

I have known Denise Naslund for about five months. Periodically, we used to go out and when we would play pool in a tavern, she would ask to go to a separate table so someone would ask her to dance.

On July 14, 1974, Bob Sargent and I met Ken Little and Denise Naslund at Charlie's East tavern in Eastgate at about 12:45 p.m. We all went to Lake Sammamish State Park in Denise's car. We got to the park at 1 p.m. While we were coming to the park, Denise complained about the car needing fixing and Ken said he would do it.

We parked on a grassy field before the main parking lot. We walked along the grass and sat about two hundred feet in front of the restroom near the end of the parking area. I saw several motorcycle people in the area. Later in the afternoon, there (were) quite a few in the parking area near the restroom we were sitting in front of.

Denise had taken three or four downers at the park. Denise fell asleep about four o'clock. Prior to falling asleep, Denise mentioned that she was feeling high. At about 4 p.m., Bob returned with hot dogs. Ken tried to wake Denise up. But she did not want to wake up at first. We ate the hot dogs. Ken dozed off. I asked Denise what time it was. Denise said twenty after 4, or 4:30. We sat for a few minutes. Denise got up without saying anything and walked straight towards the restroom.

Denise watched out for her dog quite a bit and locked her purse in the car. If she did not have all her stuff, it would not surprise me if she picked up with some other guy. But, in this case, she probably would have only been gone for twenty to thirty minutes. She is not the type who talks a lot. She doesn't seem to be overly impressed by any guy. She wouldn't go out of her way to talk to anybody, nor would she go out of her way to avoid anyone

Denise always had drugs when we would go out. I don't know that she always used them. She always had the same downers.

I have read the above statement and it is true and correct to the best of my knowledge.

Taken by ROGER E. DUNN

Statement of ELEANORE M. ROSE

I am the natural mother of Brock Naslund, and Denise Marie Naslund, who was born October 10, 1955. Denise graduated from Chief Sealth High School in January 1973. Denise was really thick with Patty White, while they were in high school and then she dropped Patty and took up with Robin Woods. Robin and Denise got arrested in Tukwila for shoplifting just before she turned eighteen, and she has told me she smokes marijuana, but I don't think she has been involved with drugs or pills.

Denise ran away for three days when she was twelve, but she had been very considerate of me because of my nervous condition. I feel that if she was able to, she would have contacted me since she disappeared on Sunday.

The first I knew that something was wrong with Denise was when her boyfriend, Ken Little, drove up in her car around 9:00 p.m. on Sunday, July 14, 1974. Ken told me that, "Denise is missing." He said he searched Lake Sammamish State Park for four hours but he couldn't find her. He said they had been fighting all afternoon while at the park. He said he was asleep and Denise walked off. He really did look concerned. He didn't appear to be messed up, and I didn't notice any marks or scratches on him. She told me she left her car but she left her sandals and purse locked in the trunk.

Sometimes Denise would drive, and sometimes Ken would drive the car when they would go out somewhere. He said that maybe Denise had just taken off for a few hours because he would do that to her on occasions. Denise first met Ken last October while she was living with Robin and they moved in together at 4522 S.W. Graham in March 1974. He drove off with Denise's car and purse and has stopped by on two different mornings, once he took Brock over to Lake Sammamish and they looked for Denise.

Since Denise has been missing, I haven't heard anything from her, and no one has contacted me with ransom demands about her disappearance.

Denise has spoken of going with Robin to the Flame Tavern. Ken and Denise said they usually went to the Fire Dog Inn and Digby's Tavern to play pool and drink beer. Denise called me at noon on Sunday and said they were going to the park with Bob Sargent and that was the last time I heard from her. Denise said that Ken had never struck her during their arguments.

Denise was going to school at I.T.T. Peterson, studying computer systems on Monday, Tuesday, and Thursday nights from 6:00 – 10:30 p.m. She worked on a part-time basis of about twenty-four hours a week through Dean Tops Agency in downtown Seattle. Denise is very loving, and would often pick me up a gift for no special occasion, and I have always felt very close to her. When she walks into my house, it's just like sunshine coming through the door.

This three-page statement is true to the best of my knowledge.

CHAPTER SEVEN

The following report was created by King County Washington detectives for detectives at the Leon County (Florida) Sheriff's Office who had requested it. Because the Leon County cops were in investigative darkness as to who Bundy was and the crimes he was suspected of committing, they were looking to be brought up to speed on every aspect of what had by then developed into homicide cases in multiple jurisdictions. As such, when King County responded, they did so with much information and data for not just the murders that occurred in Washington State, but some of the murders that happened in Utah and Colorado as well. It also contains some very unusual—and not often seen—information on Ted Bundy, such Bundy crashing a car into a police cruiser in Seattle! It is important to note too, that you'll be reading about certain victims that we've already touched upon in this book. However, these reports are detailed, and do contain new information not touched on earlier in this book, but provide an interesting narrative as well. It begins with a brief synopsis of the Washington murder victims, and next discusses the dump sites where they were found, and continues in order from there.

January 4, 1974

KAREN L. SPARKS, WF, 21 years

4325 8th NE, Seattle, Washington – near University of Washington

Seattle P.D. Case # 74 – 755

Went to sleep in her basement apartment. Roommates found her assaulted and unconscious in her bed at 1930 hrs. on 1 -4 – 74. She had been beaten in the head and a probe was shoved into her vagina. She was left for dead but has recovered. She has undergone hypnosis but memory cells were destroyed. The basement doors were commonly left unlocked and no suspects have ever been developed.

LYNDA ANN HEALY, WF, 21 years, 5'7" 115 #, long brown hair parted in the middle, blue eyes, pierced ears.

5517 12th NE

Seattle, Washington

Disappeared January 31, 1974, 2400 hrs. Thursday, from her basement apartment 16 blocks from where Sparks was assaulted. Evidence at scene: Blood was found on her pillow and her bloody nightgown was hung in the closet. She had apparently been dressed by her assailant and taken from her apartment.

Found: March 3, 1975, with Rancourt, Ball, and Parks.

Location: Taylor Mountain, 34 miles from her apartment near Hwy # 18, 4 miles south of I – 90.

DONNA GAIL MANSON, WF, 19 years, 6/9/1954, 5'0", 100 #, long brown hair parted in the middle, blue eyes. Ears were not pierced.

Evergreen State College - 60 miles south of Seattle on Interstate # 5.

Disappeared: March 12, 1974, 1900 hrs. Tuesday,
Activity: walking from dormitory to a jazz concert 300
yards across campus.

Found: Still missing.

SUSAN ELAINE RANCOURT, WF, 18 years,
10/12/1955, 5'2", 125 #, blond hair parted in the
middle. Blue eyes, pierced ears.

Central Washington State College, Ellensburg,
Washington, 100 miles east of Seattle on I-90.

Disappeared: April 17, 1974, 2200 hrs. Wednesday, as
she walked across campus for a distance of 4 blocks.

Found: March 3, 1075, with Healy, Ball, and Parks at
Taylor Mountain which was 87 miles from where she
disappeared.

ROBERTA KATHLEEN PARKS, WF, 20 years,
2/27/1954, 5'7", 120 #. Long blond hair parted in the
middle, blue-green eyes, pierced ears. 280 miles south
of Seattle on Interstate # 5

Disappeared: May 6, 1974, 2300 hrs. Monday, as
she was walking across the campus at Oregon State
University.

Found: with Healy, Rancourt, and Ball at Taylor
Mountain 262 miles from where she disappeared.

BRENDA CAROL BALL, WF, 22 years, 11/8/1951,
5'3", 112 #, Long brown hair parted in the middle,
brown eyes, did not have pierced ears. 2323 S.W.
172nd, Seattle, Washington. 20 miles south of
University of Washington campus.

Last seen: June 1, 1974, 0200, Sat., at a tavern in south Seattle.

Activity: She was dancing and was seen leaving the tavern with a "TED" lookalike with his left arm in a sling.

Found: March 3, 1975, with Rancourt, Healy, and Parks at Taylor Mountain which was 30 miles from where she was last seen.

GEORGANN HAWKINS, WF, 18 years, 8/20/1955, long brown hair parted in the middle, brown eyes, pierced ears, 4521 17th NW, Seattle Washington.

Near the University of Washington campus. 14 blocks from where Healy disappeared. 11 blocks from where Sparks was assaulted.

Disappeared: June 11, 1974, 0100 hrs. Tues.

Location: Alley west of her sorority house.

Activity: Spoke to a friend in an upstairs window and walked toward her sorority house 40' away and vanishes without a sound.

JANICE ANN OTT, WF, 23 years, 2/14/1951, 5'10", long blond hair parted in the middle, green eyes. Ears not pierced. 75 Front St. S. Issaquah, Washington, 20 miles east of the University of Washington.

Last seen: 7 – 14 – 74 1230 hrs. Sunday.

Location: Lake Sammamish State Park at Issaquah, Washington on Interstate 90.

Activity: Sunning herself on the beach among 40,000 people when approached by "TED." She was last seen pushing her bike toward the parking lot with him to help load his 'sailboat' and go 'sailing.'

Found: September 7, 1975, with Naslund and an unidentified female.

Location: 4 miles east of the park, north of I-90 and near an abandoned railroad line.

DENISE MARIE NASLUND, WF, 18 years, 10/10/1955, 5'4", 120 #, long black hair worn with bangs, brown eyes, pierced ears. 4522 S.W, Graham St. Seattle, Washington.

Last seen: July 14, 1974, 1630 hrs. Sunday.

Location: Lake Sammamish State Park.

Activity: In the same area that Ott disappeared four hours before.

Found: September 7, 1975, with Ott and an unidentified female.

Location: 4 miles east of the State Park.

King County Department of Public Safety

Issaquah Dump Site

The location where Ott and Naslund were found is four miles east of Lake Sammamish State Park on Interstate 90. It is on the north side and access to the north side is by the old abandoned Sunset Highway; a median prevents a left turn when eastbound. The corridor along the highway has been condemned for highway expansion and all homes near the site were vacant. There is a small gravel road which leads north uphill from "Old Sunset Highway" and across an abandoned railroad line.

When they were dumped, the stinging nettles and underbrush were very thick, but a vehicle could drive back into the brush to within forty feet of where the characteristic grease spots were found. There was a third set of bones found at the site but no skull or mandible was found which could provide identification. There were two grease spots within driving (Author's note: be advised, the writer must have meant 'walking distance') *distance with blond hair nearby. There was another grease spot a little farther uphill near Naslund's skull and mandible.*

The skeletons were badly scattered by animals and no evidence of trauma, dismemberment, or assault could be detected. There were no clothing, jewelry, or other personal effects near the scene. In a mile radius of the site several articles of women's undergarments were found but none belonged to any of the known victims. No occult or witchcraft symbols were found near the scene.

The victims were probably killed elsewhere and dumped at this location shortly after their disappearance. They were found thirty-five days after their disappearance. An extensive search was made in the area but the skull of Ott is still missing as are the skull and mandible of the third person.

The two possible victims for the third set of bones would be Georgann Hawkins and Donna Manson.

A large quantity of immature elk bones was found ¼ mile east of the scene on "Sunset Highway." These bones were bagged in burlap gunny sacks and bound with twine. On October 16, 1974, a citizen found a porno book near the scene. It described an incident of "Ted" luring "teaser" type girls to his parent's house on the hill so he could seduce them. These victims were short with long hair parted in the middle and wearing tight Levis or ski pants.

The following report describes the 'dump site' on Taylor Mountain.

The Taylor Mountain site is four miles south on Interstate 90 on the south side of Highway 18. It is remote and the property is adjacent to a power transmission tower line.

The skulls and/or mandibles of Healy, Rancourt, Parks, and Ball were found at this location. There were several other bones found at this location but they were all non-human. This gave rise to the theory that the girls had been decapitated, however, no cervical vertebra was found in the search. Animals in the area include coyotes, bears, and rodents, but the possibility of their consuming all bones of the body is slim.

The area at all times of the year is very brushy and would be extremely dense during June when Ball disappeared. The killer could have dumped the bodies in an area of evergreens nearby where there is less underbrush but no grease spots were found in this area either. No clothing, weapons, jewelry, or occult symbols were found at the scene.

The nearest homes to this site are five miles away but trailbike riders and hunters are usually in the vicinity on weekends. This site is 7.7 miles S.E. of the Issaquah site and eleven road miles.

What follows concerns the abduction and murder of Caryn Eileen Campbell who was abducted by Ted Bundy while she was staying at the Wildwood Inn in Snowmass, Colorado, in January of 1975. The King County report continues.

Recent Background of the Aspen Victim and the Case

Caryn Eileen Campbell, age twenty-three years, a registered nurse from Farmington, Michigan, came to

Snowmass at Aspen, Colorado, on January 11, 1975, at approximately 4:30 p.m., accompanied by her fiancé, Dr. Raymond Gadowski and Gadowski's two children from a former marriage.

Caryn Campbell and the three Gadowskis registered in room #210 at the Wildwood Inn, Snowmass, at Aspen, Colorado.

Caryn Campbell, during the duration of January 11 and up to approximately 7:30 – 8:00 p.m. January 12, 1975, was in the company of other persons known to her personally.

At approximately 6:00 p.m., January 12, 1975, Caryn Campbell, Dr. Gadowski, his two children, and Dr. Rosenthall, ate dinner at the Stew Pot Restaurant in the mall area, adjacent to the Wildwood Inn. Caryn Campbell ate beef stew and milk.

Dinner was finished between 6:30 and 6:45 p.m. and the same party, intact, walked around the mall area, window shopping for approximately thirty minutes. The group, still intact, stopped at a Walgreen Drug Store to look over magazines. Campbell and Rosenthall began looking at a Viva magazine. Campbell remarked that she had the current issue of Viva in her room and would trade Rosenthall the Playboy for the Viva.

The party, still intact, then went to the lobby of the Wildwood Inn. Upon entering the lobby, Campbell requested Gadowski go to room # 210 to get the Viva magazine to trade with Dr. Rosenthall. Gadowski declined, stating he wanted to stay by the fire in the lobby.

Caryn Campbell then went to the elevator with the Gadowski children between 7:30 p.m. and 8:00 p.m. When the elevator arrived in the lobby, Campbell instructed the Gadowski children to stay with their father and entered the elevator alone, intending to retrieve the Viva magazine from room # 210.

Caryn Campbell arrived on the second floor of the Wildwood Inn and was met by six persons who knew her personally. She was still alone in the elevator. Campbell spoke briefly with the people she met on the second-floor landing, stating she was going to her room to get a magazine and would be returning to the lobby in a few minutes. Campbell exited the elevator and the party of six entered the elevator to go to the lobby.

Between 8:00 p.m. and 8:20 p.m., Dr. Gadowski became curious as to why Campbell had not returned from room # 210. Gathering his children, he used the elevator to the second floor. Arriving at room # 210 he knocked several times – there was no answer. Remembering that Campbell had the key for the room and not knowing where Campbell could have gone, Gadowski and his children returned and took the elevator to the lobby and obtained a key for room #210.

Gadowski made several telephone calls to various friends who were also staying at the lodge, inquiring if they had seen Campbell and no one had.

Gadowski searched for Campbell himself until approximately 11:30 p.m. when he reported Campbell missing to the Pitkin County Sheriff's Office. Two Pitkin County Sheriff's Deputies were dispatched to the scene and interviewed Dr. Gadowski and made a missing person's report.

The two deputies examined all possible entrances to the room but could not find any signs of forced entry. Further search of the room revealed that Caryn Campbell's purse, wallet, and identification were still present. Nothing was missing from the room. All valuables were accounted for. There were no signs of a struggle, nor any blood or hair in the room.

Both deputies made an extensive search of the Wildwood Inn that night, including the entire Snowmass at Aspen Village area; no sign of Caryn Campbell was located.

On January 13, 1975, uniformed deputies and investigators made an extensive search of the Wildwood Inn elevator shafts, laundry rooms, garbage cans, and all rooms of the hotel. The search failed to reveal any sign of a crime scene or trace of Caryn Campbell.

The photograph of Caryn Campbell depicted on her Michigan state driver's license was copied and charged (sic) *and the Wildwood Inn guests were then contacted for possible witness information and/or leads into Campbell's disappearance. No witnesses were found.*

Background information was obtained on all the employees of the Wildwood Inn. All were checked against the NCIC network for reported criminal records locally and out of state. No leads were developed.

A complete guest list was obtained for all hotels, ski lodges, and condominiums for the weekend of January 10 – through January (????) in the Aspen, Snowmass at Aspen, Basalt, and Glenwood Springs, Colorado areas.

All the passenger manifests for all flights from Denver to Aspen and Aspen to Denver, from January 10 through January 15 on Rocky Mountain Airways and Aspen Airways (the only commercial air-carriers serving the Aspen, Colorado area) were obtained.

Extensive background investigations were conducted, most specifically on Dr. Gadowski and Dr. Rosenthall in the Detroit area of Michigan.

Past boyfriends, male acquaintances, and fellow employees who worked with Campbell were identified and the whereabouts of these individuals on January 12, 1975, were determined and verified without any leads being developed.

The night of January 12, 1975, and during the following two weeks, snow fell continuously accompanied by sub-zero temperatures in the area. By January 15, 1975, investigators were sure that Campbell had not left the Aspen area by any commercial source of transportation, nor had a similarly described female been treated by any hospital, nor had any similarly described female checked into any ski resort, hotels, motels, etc. in the Aspen, Basalt, Snowmass at Aspen, and Glenwood Springs areas.

Caryn Campbell had not contacted her mother or father in Detroit whom she contacted telephonically normally on a daily basis (????) her brother, sister, and friends.

No trace of Caryn Campbell could be found.

No witnesses were ever found that saw Caryn Campbell after she got off the elevator on the second floor of the Wildwood Inn on January 12, 1975, enroute to her room.

The investigation continued uninterrupted without finding Campbell, or developing any substantial leads or suspects, other than those in close proximity to Campbell at the time of her disappearance, i.e. Drs. Gadowski and Rosenthall.

Dr. Gadowski was availed of the opportunity of a polygraph examination, results indicated that he had been truthful with the investigators in that he had not killed Campbell, nor conspired with Campbell or others to arrange her abduction.

Monday, February 17, 1975, a nude female body was discovered on the Owl Creek Road, in Pitkin County between Aspen and Snowmass at Aspen, Colorado.

Examination of the Scene

The nude female body was lying face down approximately fifteen feet from the south shoulder of the Owl Creek road, perpendicular to the road, head pointing south in an open field of crusted snow.

It was apparent that the body had suffered a great deal of animal destruction by coyotes. The entire head was skeletal and upper shoulder and torso in front to just above the breast. (Author's note: meaning, the flesh had been almost completely removed from these areas of Caryn's body)

No human footprints or depressions were noted in the crusted snow anywhere near the body or along Owl Creek Road. Tire tracks were also lacking.

Animal and bird tracks were noted, specifically coyotes and magpies.

A 360-degree view of the scene was taken, accompanied by close-ups of the position of the body.

Approximately three and one-half feet from the south shoulder of the road was a deep depression which perfectly matched that of a body, which had laid on its side, head pointing west. It was also apparent that the body laid facing the open field. (????) both earrings, small gold earrings for pierced ears were found where the head would have been positioned. Surrounding the depression were several coyote tracks. Leading from the depression (head position) were drag marks.

The 17th of February 1975 had been the fourth day of an extreme warming period. The body had thawed from under the snow. Losing its human scent, coyotes had eaten the body as it lay on its right side, then dragged the body in view of passing motorists.

The Owl Creek Road where the body was found is parallel bordered(??) by small oak brush undergrowth approximately four feet high with a high snowbank produced by regular plowing of the road at night.

An extensive search of the Owl Creek Road area failed to produce Campbell's clothing, or any clothing, for that matter.

The body was located 2.8 miles from the Wildwood Inn, Snowmass at Aspen, Colorado. The pathologist's examination of dental charts and (????) points of individual characteristics identified the body as that of Caryn E. Campbell.

The pathologist's examination determined that death was caused by three blows to the rear of the head consistent with a blunt object. The examiner could not determine if any signs of strangulation were evident due to the animal destruction of the upper torso. Sexual assault could not be verified as phoserus (phosphorus) *was present, however, Dr. Gadowski and Campbell had engaged in intercourse on the night of January 11, 1975, the night before her disappearance. Based upon the fact that Campbell's stomach was full and the conditions of its contents, which were consistent with the stew she had consumed, the examiner concluded that Campbell had died approximately two hours after eating dinner the night of January 12, 1975.*

During the months of February and March of 1975, investigators went to the Detroit area and began investigations into the backgrounds of Drs. Gadowski and Rosenthal.

Neighborhood canvassing was done to determine if Rosenthall and Campbell had been seeing one another at their respective places of residence. All former boyfriends were re-interviewed and cleared. Both Rosenthall and Gadowski were again availed of the opportunity to have a polygraph examination. The results indicated that both parties had been truthful with investigators throughout the investigation and neither had planned or schemed with others or Campbell herself, to disappear. Both Drs. Gadowski and Rosenthall were cleared.

During the winter, spring, and summer of 1975, the investigation into Campbell's death continued uninterrupted. Many suspects continued to be developed and were all later cleared.

Investigators from the states of Washington, Oregon, Utah, and Colorado were now in agreement that they now had a shared suspect(??). Authorities in Seattle, Washington had developed a suspect named Theodore Robert Bundy. Bundy was believed to be in the Salt Lake, Utah area, but could not be found.

Bundy was known to have departed the Seattle, Washington area sometime in September 1974; Seattle activity then stopped. Bundy arrived in Salt Lake City, Utah, in September of 1974, for the purpose of XXX or something to remind the reader why he was there. In October 1974, activity in the Salt Lake area began, continuing until November 1974, and then stopped. Activity in Colorado began in January of 1975 and continued until April 1975. Investigators did not locate Bundy's name on any motel registrations or airline passenger manifests relative to the Aspen area.

I need to suspend the narrative of the King County report, so that I can include a very interesting and revealing postscript to the Caryn Campbell abduction and murder.

This came forth in a news conference given by Colorado investigator Mike Fisher on the morning of January 25, 1989, the day after Ted Bundy was executed, and after Mike had returned to Aspen. While a great deal of information (much of it new and obtained from Mike Fisher) about this murder appears in my book, *The Bundy Murders*, what you're about to read does not. Despite the many conversations I had with the retired Colorado investigator, both by phone and by email, we never touched upon this small, but extremely significant, piece of information. What follows are excerpts from an article published in *The Aspen Times*, dated January 25, 1989, and it explains what Bundy was doing while in Aspen, and gives clues as to how he gained control of Caryn Campbell at the Wildwood Inn:

> *Bundy told Fisher that he drove around Aspen several hours before the murder and then headed up to Snowmass Village to find a victim. Bundy hobbled on crutches amongst the lodges in Snowmass carrying ski boots... Bundy told Fisher he stopped at the edge of the Wildwood's pool and was hoping a woman nearby would help him carry his ski boots to his car. But the woman ignored Bundy and he waited for several minutes until Campbell – his second choice – walked across a balcony and asked Bundy if he needed some help.*

The article goes on to say that Caryn Campbell carried Bundy's ski boots to his car. Bundy states he then hit her with the boots and "stuffed her into his vehicle." He didn't say how this was accomplished, but most likely it would have been very similar to how he accomplished this with other abductions: Georgann Hawkins was waylaid as she was putting his briefcase into his VW, and Julie Cunningham was also struck as she was placing Bundy's crutches in the car. So, in the case of Caryn Campbell (because Bundy struck her with the boots), she was (perhaps exactly as Julie Cunningham had done), placing the crutches into Bundy's VW when she was knocked unconscious. However, the striking of Campbell with the boots did not kill her. Once inside the Volkswagen, Bundy also hit Campbell at least once in the head with his crowbar.

Lastly, Fisher was asked by reporters if Bundy had admitted to sexually assaulting Caryn Campbell, but he hedged here (desiring, no doubt, to protect the victim's family) and did not convey the truth of the matter until many years later when I was working closely with him during the writing of my book, *The Bundy Murders*. At that time, Mike told me that Bundy admitted to hitting Caryn with the crowbar "just once" before adding, "I did my thing right there in the car."

On August 16, 1975, a Utah State Trooper noticed a suspicious Volkswagen late at night. The trooper attempted to stop the Volkswagen, but the driver attempted to elude the trooper. The vehicle finally stopped and the driver of the Volkswagen was identified as Theodore Robert Bundy. He was arrested for eluding and booked into the Salt Lake County jail.

At the time Bundy's vehicle was stopped, the police narrative reports a small brown satchel was found in the car. Its contents were listed as: one flashlight, one ice pick, one short crowbar, one pair of handcuffs, one black pullover face ski mask *(Author's note: this is incorrect. Bundy's ski mask was tan or light brown, with a darker brown stripe around the top)*, one full face mask made from panty hose, white nylon rope, and several torn strips of a white sheet.

The following information comes from a hand-written notation on a form the police used in Washington State to handle telephone calls, sometimes anonymous, coming into the precinct. This particular sheet—pertaining to the Bundy case—also contains numerous notes about Bundy or the victims. What makes this interesting is that it comes from a former teaching assistant to Dr. Erwin Sarasen, mentioned elsewhere in the record. The assistant was providing additional info on Bundy, as he believed Bundy might be involved in the missing and murdered women.

Rec'd a call from U of W professor Joel Kestenbaum, 525-0153, who formerly was a teaching assistant to Ted Bundy, 24-25, 5'8", 160, light parted hair, good student, personable, possible accent, class of Abnormal Psychology, couple years ago, instructor was Erwin Sarasen. Kestenbaum moving to Ohio on August 1.

Theodore Robert Bundy 11-24-46 Burlington, VT. B/S on June 10, 1972. Parents' address 3214 N. 20th Tacoma (1968).

The below police report contains the interview of David Knutson, about Leslie Knutson, (David Knutson's ex-wife) describing her relationship with Ted Bundy. Bundy had met Leslie in June 1975 at a party given by Paul Van Dam, a Salt Lake County prosecutor. They hit it off from the beginning, and this was the beginning of a relationship that would last for a number of months.

Follow up Report

Homicides – Missing Girls

SUSPECT: BUNDY, THEODORE R. W-M-29

GENERAL: 3-8-76 1000 hrs. Talked to David W. Knutson, who is staying with Fred Abrams at 1218 6th Ave. W. Mr. Knutson is just up from Salt Lake City, and will be staying with Mr. Abrams for about two weeks, while Mr. Knutson attempts to find a radio reporting job and a place to live in the Seattle area. Mr. Knutson drives a 1974 brown Datsun 240Z.

Mr. Knutson's ex-wife, Leslie Knutson (W–F–33, blond hair), who remains on good terms with Mr. Knutson, had Bundy visiting her and staying with her at her place on Redondo Street in Salt Lake City just prior to Bundy's arrest for murder, kidnapping, etc. Leslie met Bundy at a party thrown by Salt Lake Prosecutor Paul Van Dam in Salt Lake City, and was courted by Bundy for six -eight weeks, up to the time of his arrest. This was around August and July 1975. Bundy was apparently attending the University of Utah Law School during this time. Mr. Knutson saw Bundy at Leslie's place twice, both times when he (Knutson) was visiting his six-year-old son, Joshua, of whom Leslie has custody. The first time Bundy took Joshua and a few neighborhood children swimming ("He was always doing things like that"). The second time Mr. Knutson saw Bundy vacuuming the inside of Bundy's tan Volkswagen Bug, with the seats out. Mr. Knutson stated to me that this struck him as being a little strange, even at the time, because he had called Leslie earlier (unknown interval of time) and she had told Mr. Knutson that Bundy was out cleaning his car. And Mr. Knutson thought to himself, on seeing Bundy cleaning his VW, "Why would anyone clean a ratty Volkswagen so often?"

Mr. Knutson stated that he had no other contact with Bundy. Leslie talked to Prosecutor Paul Van Dam and the Salt Lake City Police about Bundy after his arrest. She told them that Bundy became depressed and took to drinking more beer after a certain point in their courtship. She came to know later that this point in time coincided with Bundy's original arrest for speeding, etc. Bundy did not even tell Leslie about this arrest. She learned about it from the newspapers, after Bundy's felony arrest.

Mr. Knutson's brother is some kind of reporter in Salt Lake City, who is married to the dean of admissions at the University of Utah Law School. Salt Lake City authorities have had no contact with Mr. Knutson.

What follows is the original Utah police report of the Carol DaRonch abduction from November 8, 1974, and is included in the King County report for Leon County. Those familiar with this case will know that Carol ultimately was able to escape from Bundy while the abduction was still in progress. This in turn caused Bundy, who was at that time in an altered state of blood-lust and seeking to murder, to go and seek a victim elsewhere. That victim, Debra Kent, would be overpowered by Bundy about two hours later in the darkened parking lot of Viewmont High School in Bountiful, Utah, and ultimately murdered.

For those who are not familiar with the Ted Bundy/Carol DaRonch encounter, a little background info is in order:

It was a Friday evening, and Carol DaRonch had gotten off work at Mountain Bell at 5:00 p.m. and headed home. She wasn't going to be home very long, as she had a Christmas present to buy, and her decision to shop at the Fashion Place Mall in Murray, Utah, would change the course and tempo of her life forever. Ted Bundy, who had already changed the course of his life forever when he made the decision to be a destroyer of women, would find this night pivotal as well. Things would not go well for him, and the ramifications of this night would eventually catch up with him.

Bundy, having come to Utah to attend law school, although he rarely attended classes that first fall semester of 1974, had plans to abduct his next victim from the popular mall on State Street in the greater Salt Lake City area. While it is unknown what time he arrived at the Fashion Place Mall, it's almost certain that he spotted Carol driving her Camaro and parking it in the lot near the entrance to Sears.

Without Carol's knowledge, Bundy followed her into the mall—a mall that was teeming with people, many of them young people who were part of the regular Friday night crowd. Also unknown to Carol, Bundy was watching her as she stopped and spoke with her cousins. Not long after this, as she stood looking into a window display of a Waldenbooks store, Bundy walked up to the very good-looking young woman with long brown hair parted in the middle and the ruse began. After he gained her attention, he introduced himself as a Murray Police officer by the name of Roseland, but he did not show her a badge. Bundy figured his words would provide all the authority he'd need for the somewhat timid eighteen-year-old girl, and for a time he was correct.

Bundy asked Carol if she had a car in the parking lot and she admitted that was true. Bundy then informed her that a man had attempted to break into her car and that she needed to walk with him out to her car. As Bundy led the way, Carol followed him to her car. Bundy had already explained to her that his "partner" was holding the man inside the mall. Once they reached her car, Carol looked inside and commented that everything looked fine to her. At this point Bundy suggested she unlock the driver's side door and she did so, acknowledging that opening the door did not reveal anything was wrong or missing either, as it presented the same view to her as when she looked through the window.

And then, in what must have seemed like a strange request to Carol, "Officer Roseland" asked her to unlock the passenger door as well. Carol immediately refused to do so, and with that, she and Bundy returned inside the mall to locate his partner and the man he had allegedly arrested. Not finding them, Bundy claimed he needed to check out the police substation situated across the street that runs alongside the mall, and the two headed off in that direction. Carol watched as he attempted to open a side door on a building that was operating as a cleaner and laundromat. The door, marked 139, was locked, and given Bundy's proclivity for planning murder, he must have already known that it would not open. It was at this time that he informed Carol that he needed her to go with him to the Murray Police Department to file a formal complaint. He then led her to his tan weather-beaten VW parked some twenty to thirty feet away. This raised a bit of a red flag with Carol and she asked to see his badge, and Bundy produced one but he did not allow her to get a very good look at it.

Once inside the vehicle, Carol expected him to drive straight to State Street and head for the police station. But instead of doing this, Bundy did a U-turn, drove to the main road running behind the mall, turned left, and within a minute, he stopped in front of the McMillan Elementary School and attacked her. Carol now knew she was in a fight for her life.

Murray Police Department

Victim: Carol DaRonch

Location of occurrence: Sears Lot FPM (Fashion Place Mall)

Victim 1: Carol DaRonch, Age 18, Works for Mt. Bell, 205 East 200 So.

Victim's car: 1974 black/red Camaro KAD 032

Suspect 1: WM, 25–30 years, brown hair, medium length, approx. 6'0, thin to medium build, mustache neatly trimmed. Wearing green pants and sports jacket, color unknown. Patent leather, shiny black shoes. Very polite, opened doors for victim. Gave victim name of Officer Roseland, and seems to victim that first name started with a "D" however, cannot remember the first name.

Suspect vehicle: Light blue or white Volkswagen, older model in fairly beat up condition. Victim did not see license plate. Victim stated that the rear seat, the top is ripped and the stuffing is coming out. Victim does not remember seeing any stickers or emblems on the vehicle. Can remember nothing else about the vehicle.

Weapon used: Small handgun, type and caliber unknown. Handgun described as being a little larger than a starter pistol. Is not known by victim if the handgun was a revolver or an automatic. Suspect had handgun in his jacket pocket and believed that suspect held handgun in the right hand. Victim was shown pictures of revolvers and automatics and different type weapons and still unable to determine exact type model weapon used. (Author's note: during my research for my first book, I was told by a member of the prosecutor's team that they had doubts that Bundy used a handgun, despite Carol's insistence he did. I did not ask him why they felt this way, but perhaps it stems from her apparent confusion described above.)

Another weapon used was described as a crowbar, approx. 1 ½ ft. long. This was held by the suspect in his left hand.

Evidence obtained: One pair of handcuffs. They are Gerocal A brand, made in Taiwan. Have no serial number and identifying marks on the handcuffs. Detective Joel Riet dusted the handcuffs for prints, obtained some. Also, Detective Riet attempted to obtain prints from the door knob of the laundromat, which will be explained later in the body of the report, with negative results, and will make contact with complainant tomorrow to try to obtain fingerprints off the right-side door of the victim's vehicle. Door was wet from rain this evening. Victim's father was going to place the vehicle in his garage, keep it until tomorrow until Detective Riet can make contact and obtain prints.

Missing items: One brown leather purse, has a zipper top, medium-sized purse, had a shoulder strap. Also, being brown leather, which is held by two gold rings. Inside the purse was one woman's gold wallet. This was fold over brushed leather. Value $5.00. Wallet contained approx. $20.00 cash. This will be one five, one ten, and some ones and change. Identification in the purse will be victim's Mountain Bell tag, has her name and social security on it. Also, her house keys and car keys. Also, two layaway slips that would have had victim's name and address on them. One is from the Nobby and one is from Rafters which is uptown. There is no other identification in the wallet. No checks or credit cards. Victim was advised to have the locks on her vehicle and also locks on her home changed.

Witnesses: Victim was picked up on approx. 5800 South 300 East by a Mr. T Walsh, 144 5600 South. Mr. Walsh and some of his family picked victim up and brought her into our office. At the time of this report (????) conversation with Mr. Walsh, however, dispatcher did talk to him. Mr. Walsh stated they did not see anyone else in the area besides victim. Detective Riet was given this information for follow up.

SUPPLEMENTARY REPORT

I had just come 1024 from case 10180 when I was informed by Officer Hoffman that there had been a kidnapping, that the victim was presently in our office. I was given a description of the suspect vehicle by Officer Hoffman that the vehicle was last seen in the area of McMillan School which is 5900 South 300 East. I then proceeded to this area and started checking the area. I asked the dispatcher to have Officer Peterson who was in the office to get a description of the suspect and vehicle and put it out to our officers and all other agencies as quickly as possible. Myself and Officer Hoffman checked the area for a few minutes.

I then came into our office where I talked to the victim, Carol DaRonch. In talking to the victim, she stated at approx. 7:00 p.m. this date she went to the Fashion Place Mall and parked her vehicle on the west side of Sears and walked into Sears. This being through southwest doors. She then proceeded into the mall through Sears, walked down towards Castleton's and down toward Auerbach's. While in the mall she stopped and talked to some cousins for a few minutes. She then turned around and was proceeding back when she was approached by suspect near Walden's bookstore. At this time, she had been in the mall approx. 10 or 15 minutes.

Suspect approached victim and asked her if she had a car in the parking lot on the west side of Sears. She told him yes, he then asked for her license number. At this time she told him. He then told her he was a police officer and a suspect had been caught breaking into her car with a pry wire and that he wanted to accompany her back to her vehicle to see if anything was missing; also to see if she could identify the suspect. The victim walked back through the mall into Sears and out the Sears doors into the parking lot with suspect. At this time she checked her vehicle by unlocking driver's side and looking in and could see that everything appeared to be O.K. There was no damage to her vehicle. Nothing missing. At this time suspect asked her to open up the passenger side door, that he wanted to check inside. She told him no, it would not be necessary, she could see that everything was there, however, suspect did, she believes, touch the door handle and try and open the vehicle.

At this time suspect stated that he would like her to accompany him to the other side of the mall where he believes the car prowl suspect would be located, that she could identify him and sign a complaint. At this time, she proceeded with suspect back through Sears and out into the east parking lot. Suspect looked around, stated that the burglary suspect must have been taken to the Murray Police substation. At this time suspect asked her to accompany him to the Murray Police substation. They then walked through the parking lot, went back into the mall through the main doors on the east side of the parking lot, just north of Castleton's. Proceeded through the mall. Proceeded out into the mall parking lot and across 6100 South to a laundromat which is on the north side of 6100 South, the address of the laundromat is 139 East 6100 South.

At this time suspect told victim that this was the Murray substation at the mall and he believed the burglary suspect would be located there and she could sign a complaint. He then (Author's note: left off report, but probably "tried") *the door. This door is on the southeast corner of the laundromat. Appears to be a door to a maintenance room. Has the number 139 just above the door. The door was locked. The suspect did touch the door. Detective Riet tried to obtain prints with negative results.*

At this time suspect told victim that they would have to go to the main Murray Police Department, victim asked suspect for some identification, she had asked him once before in the mall. He just kind of laughed. While walking over she did look at a wallet badge which he produced. Badge is described as similar to Murray Police in shape. This was a miniature size badge, approx. half the size of our wallet badge.

It appeared to be solid gold. The victim cannot remember engravings, or names or designs on the badge. She later picked out a similar type badge, out of the George F. Cake Company book for Detective Riet. See his supplement report.

After trying the door of the laundromat, both parties then walked to the suspect's vehicle. Suspect then opened the door and let the victim in. Suspect then went into driver's seat and put on his seatbelt, told the victim to be sure to put on her seatbelt that it might make him nervous if people didn't while he was driving. At this time, she said no she would not. He also made sure she locked her door. He then made a U-turn and proceeded up 6100 South to 300 East where he made a left turn and then proceeded north on 300 East to the area of approx. 5800 South 300 East in front of McMillan School. Suspect then pulled his vehicle over. This would be on the east side of the road.

The assault that then took place approx. 25 paces from the northwest corner of McMillan School/ 300 East. Location of assault was determined later by finding victim's shoe laying in the gutter at this location. Victim stated that while in the vehicle, she could smell the odor of alcoholic beverage about the suspect. As the suspect pulled up and parked the vehicle, the victim tried to get out, at which time suspect reached over and grabbed her, started a scuffle. Suspect got out a pair of handcuffs, grabbed her by the right wrist, put the handcuff on her right wrist. At this time, she started fighting. The suspect was trying to handcuff both hands, however, ended up putting both handcuffs on right wrist. Victim kept fighting with suspect. At this time, suspect reached into his coat pocket. Pulled out a pistol which was described above, pointing the pistol at victim and told her if she did not stop struggling, he would shoot her. At this time, she struggled harder. Got the door open and managed to get outside. (Author's note: the writer of this report must mean that Carol was attempting to get outside, but had NOT actually cleared the vehicle; making it a fight both partially within the VW and partially outside the vehicle, because once Carol was out of the car she immediately began running toward the approaching car lights, and she wouldn't have been standing around waiting for Bundy to exit the VW and then grab the crowbar.)

At this time suspect also got out of the vehicle and approached her. At this time, he picked up a crowbar, had the crowbar in his left hand and was raising it as though to strike, at this time victim grabbed a hold of the crowbar and started pushing and shoving with suspect. Victim believed that she scratched suspect, probably on either the hands or arms, that she did notice some blood on her hands that must have come from suspect, that she was not injured herself. However, she does not remember actually hurting the suspect. Victim struggled with suspect, finally breaking and running and running out into the middle of the road where she flagged down witnesses described above who brought her to our office. Witnesses did not remember seeing anybody else in the area. Victim came to our office where Officer Peterson removed handcuffs from her wrist. Stated both handcuffs were in place when victim arrived.

In talking to victim, she states she believes she could identify suspect if she saw him again, that she spent approx. 20 to 30 minutes with him in the mall and walking through the parking lot and in the vehicle. Victim last saw suspect going eastbound on 5900 South. Victim believes her purse was still in the suspect's car.

I later returned to the area with victim where we did locate her shoe in the gutter described in the above report. Victim states that suspect did not make any sexual advances toward her, did not indicate any of his intentions. Also stated that (he) had no unusual features and had no accent. The voice, nothing unusual about the voice, suspect did identify himself as a Murray Police Officer. Victim was questioned by Detective Joel Riet – see his supplement report. Also, was shown pictures from the sex transcript with negative results. Detective Riet will do a follow up. A search of the area of McMillan School on 5900 South was done by all officers and reserve officers on foot. Looking for possible evidence or victim's purse with negative results.

Victim's father was going to talk to cousins who victim talked to in the mall to see if they remember possibly any men loitering around her or following her, that he would call back if there was any information and give us their names and addresses, however, we have not heard from him. Appears this would be negative. This case can be considered open.

DO NOT RELEASE THE VICTIM'S NAME UNDER ANY CIRCUMSTANCES!!!!

Again, from the King County report prepared for the Leon County Sheriff's Office, what follows is a report that is titled: CHILDHOOD, and it contains some interesting names, places, and other facts pertaining to Bundy's childhood and continuing into his adult years:

BORN: 11-24-46   at   Burlington   Vermont   as THEODORE ROBERT COWELL

PARENTS (Unwed): ELEANOR LOUISE COWELL and JACK WORTHINGTON

Surname changed on 10-6-50 to: NELSON in Philadelphia

ELEANORE and "TED" moved to Tacoma and lived with JOHN COWELL

FAMILY 3-19-51:

ELEANOR LOUISE NELSON and JOHN CULPEPPER BUNDY (Married) in Tacoma (Washington)

Stepbrothers: Glen – age 20, Richard – age 13

Stepsisters: Linda – age 22, Sandy – age 18

ADDRESS: 3214 North 20th, Tacoma

SCHOOLS: Graduated from Wilson H.S. – 1965, Attended Hunt Jr. High, Attended Geiger Elem. (Res. 658 N. Skyline Dr.), Attended Stanley Elem. (Res. 1620 South Sheridan)

COLLEGE: Started at University of Puget Sound September 1965

EMPLOYMENT: Tacoma City Light – June / September

BEHAVIOR: Students in Jr. and Sr. High Gym classes found him masturbating and threw water on him. Age 13 – he was naïve about sex and had a violent temper. Left-handed, left-eyed. Babyish actions in 5th grade. Mischievous. Liked to do superior work. Didn't like to be singled out for discipline.

ACCIDENT: 3-29-65- reported being in a car wreck the previous Friday might and had headache; scratches on face.

Later in life, Bundy would again be noticed for having scratches on his face; scratches caused by a female fighting for her life. As such, these 'scratches' may not, in my mind, be connected to an auto accident.

COLLEGE:

At University of Puget Sound - Jan. – June.

Living with parents.

Summer Job: (Author's note: job missing here)

COLLEGE:

At U of W. Sept. – Dec.

Living – McMahon Hall.

FRIENDS:

DIANE EDWARDS

MARLEIGH STEWART

LARRY

EMPLOYMENT:

Tacoma City Light June – Sept.

COLLEGE:

At University of Washington Jan. to June.

COLLEGE:

Stanford University – June to August.

Res. Palo Alto.

COLLEGE:

At U. of W. Sept. to Dec.

RESIDENCE:

5015 16th N.E.

FRIENDS:

DIANE EDWARDS – broke off relationship.

EMPLOYMENT:

Started 9/67 at Seattle Yacht Club and left 1-13-68.

1-20-67 Sent transcript to University of Colorado.

7-8-67 Had dinner in San Francisco with DIANE.

1-20-67 U.W. transcripts sent to Stanford and Colorado.

1-31-67 Transcript sent to University of Michigan.

COLLEGE:

Registered for winter quarter but withdrew on 1-18-68.

ADDRESS:

873 N. 16th on Reg. card at U of W. (B.O.)

Also lived in apt. on 17th N.E. per Mrs. Ferris.

EMPLOYMENT:

Worked at Seattle Yacht Club till 1-13-68 and one or two dinners during November.

Safeway: 4-12 to 7-26 (Queen Anne)

REPUBLICAN PARTY:

Campaign worker Aug. – Nov.

And active with ART FLETCHER.

3/68 worked at Olympic Hotel as a bus boy – let go for theft from lockers.

Practiced British accent for MRS. FERRIS and borrowed her car.

Also had access to Beater V.W., grey.

10-30-68 Transcript sent to Temple University.

1968: DIANE EDWARDS: moved to San Francisco in March.

COLLEGE: Spring quarter at Temple University, Philadelphia, Pennsylvania.

RESIDENCE: 4039 South Warner St.

RESIDENCE: Lafayette Hill, P.A. December 1969, Delaware County

Aunt Aude _____?

FRIENDS:

Showed up in San Francisco in spring with DIANE EDWARDS stayed in Mendocino, California in motel.

Sept. 69: Met LIZ KLOEPFER.

EMPLOYMENT:

Started at Legal Messengers, Inc. 9/69 to 5/70.

RESIDENCE:

4143 12th N.E. – ROGERS' House.

Fractured right ankle in Philadelphia.

OUT – OF – STATE:

Christmas 1969 – to Ogdon, Utah with friends of MARY CHINO, stayed with LIZ's parents. On way to Temple he visited COWELL's parents in Arkansas. Went to Ogdon/MRS. FERRIS – winter time.

FALL:

Goes to traffic school for bad driving record.

SUMMER:

Borrowed LIZ's car to go to Richmond with SUSAN REED, SUSAN REED says they never went there.

9-24-70 Changed major from Far East to Psychology.

COLLEGE:

Reentered U of W June to Dec.

RESIDENCE:

4143 12th N.E.

FRIENDS:

LIZ KLOEPFER

EMPLOYMENT:

Jan. to May with Legal Messengers, Inc.

June 5 to 12-31-71 – Pedline – U District.

OUT–OF-STATE:

8-20-70 Citation in Marin County, California.

8-29 to 9-4-70 – Trip to Ogden, Utah with LIZ.

Drove through Yakima – Baker, Oregon and to Utah.

Didn't go through Portland or Vancouver.

COLLEGE:

At U of W. Jan through Dec including summer quarter.

RESIDENCE:

4143 12th N.E.

EMPLOYMENT:

1-10-71 to 12-3-71 Pedline in U District.

1972:

COLLEGE:

Jan. – 6-10-72 at U of W.

Graduated with B.S. in Psychology.

RESIDENCE:

4143 12th N.E.

EMPLOYMENT:

June – September – Counselor at H.V.H. – Mental Health Center.

REPUBLICAN:

Sept. – Nov. – employed by Citizens for Evans/ Governor.

Seattle Crime Commission - November – 4/73

Law & Justice Planning – Sept. – Dec. in Seattle.

SPRING:

LIZ has abortion.

Registered in same (1) research class as LYNDA HEALY.

Registered in (2) research class as LYNDA HEALY.

SUMMER:

Bike rides at Green Lake with SANDY GWINN.

Goes sailing on Lake Washington with SANDY GWINN.

Went to Lake Sammamish State Park with SANDY GWINN.

Goes to Alpental Condominium with SANDY GWINN (her parents).

KAREN COVACH met BUNDY.

FRIENDS:

SANDY GWINN – met him – 4-22 at H.V.H. Mental Health. Her car was stolen in 6-72.

2/25/72 DR. SCOTT FRASER wrote letter of recommendation.

4/3/72 Letter from Utah Law School to BUNDY telling him of an indecisive area of qualifications for admission.

2/22/72 Sent application to Utah Law School.

4/12/72 BUNDY wrote letter to Utah Law School responding to his indecisive area.

5/12/72 Rejection letter from Utah Law School to BUNDY.

6/? /72 Recommended for Seattle Crime Commission by PATRICIA LUNNEBORG.

6/72 EDNA COWELL visited HEALY's roommate, KAREN COVACH.

6/72 – 9/74 EDNA lived at 903 N.E. 43rd.

SUMMER '72 – Summer '73 took frequent trips around Preston and North Bend areas, drove in country looking at old barns.

12/72 Had dinner with LIZ at KEIGH DEARBORN's house and he was upset about being rejected at U of W Law School.

5/16/72 UW transcript sent to U of Cal at Berkeley; UW transcript sent to Hastings College; UW transcript sent to Univ. of Oregon; UW transcript sent to Utah; UW transcript sent to Univ. of Southern Calif.

BEHAVIOR:

LIZ threatens suicide.

BUNDY belittles himself and says he's inferior.

At Crime Commission he was meticulous, aloof, tardy. Wore wig and moustache during Rossellini campaign.

1973:

JANUARY:

Law & Justice Planning. Lived at 4143 12th N.E.

1-9-73 King County Program Planning; signed contract.

1/31 $400 invoice.

1/26 Report of Recidivism.

FEBRUARY:

Employed King County Program Planning.

2-15 Application to Utah Law School.

2-15 Got $400 invoice.

2-27 Governor Evans sends letter to Utah Law School.

2-28 Got $400 invoice.

MARCH:

Employed by King County Program Planning.

3-16 Recidivism Progress Report.

3-19 Recidivism Summary Report.

3-2 Letter of Recommend from DR. EZRA STOTLAND.

LIZ saw TED's 4" bladed knife in her glovebox (given to him by VORTMAN).

S.P.D. detained for outstanding warrants.

Her car was stolen and she thought he took it.

3-30 Had VW key made at FREEWAY in at 1630, checked clutch, and added transmission oil.

3-21 $400 for work.

APRIL:

Republic Central Comm. at Olympia and Tukwila.

4-5 Accepted to Utah Law School.

4-16 Final invoice $400 – Corrections Consultant.

4-2 Received $400 for consulting work.

Employed 4-15 to 4-30 King County Program Planning.

JUNE:

6/14 – His application received at U.P.S. Law School.

6/13 – 15 Stayed at MARK HOPKINS' motel in San Francisco.

6/28 TOM SWAYZE wrote letter of recommendation.

6/21 UW transcript sent to University of Puget Sound.

6/21 UW transcript sent to University of Utah.

AUGUST:

8/3 Received letter from Utah of first acceptance to Law School

8/24 Wrecked LIZ's car in U District.

Sent letter to Utah Law School saying he was in auto accident and couldn't start Law School

8 – 20 – Freeway VW – 0915 – 1630 – Clutch repaired, parts furnished

8/31 to 9/4 DIANE in town

SEPTEMBER:

9/17 DIANE in town early Sept. and they stayed at Alpental. Had dinner at ROSS DAVIS' home. Ted using party car, she using TED's.

Got treatment for sprained right ankle.

Law School at U.P.S. Monday, Wednesday, Friday nights – commuted with 3 others.

Letter from Utah Law expressing sorrow that he wouldn't be able to attend school there. BUNDY had a beard and shaved it off.

OCTOBER: During fall sometime – LIZ saw sack of women's clothes in his room, bra was large and she thought it was Freda Rogers'.

Involved in campaign of BOB SANTOS and JIM MATTINGLY.

Had car accident with SPD Officer STEVE BUTLER at 45th and Cherry. (Author's note: throughout Bundy's adult life, he showed himself to be a lousy driver, and most individuals who follow the Bundy case have at least an inkling about it – but very few individuals are aware that he crashed one day into one of Seattle's finest!)

NOVEMBER:

11/20 $5 check to MOLLY KLEOPFER.

11/25 Had beard and moustache.

DECEMBER:

12/2 – Car repaired at Freeway VW. Set points and fix gas leak. In at 12:30 out at 1630.

Around Christmas he was injured skiing at Crystal Mountain.

Ski mask/hat seen in car by CHRIS SHARPE.

Has access to MARLIN VORTMAN's VW Bug.

12/6 Check to U. Bookstore.

12/6 ERNST ROGER (check).

12/8 University Auto Parts (check.)

12/19 Safeway (check).

12/28 Safeway (check).

Fidelity Ticket Office (check).

12/31 Tai Tungus (check).

12/31 Thriftway (check).

12/31 Shaga's Imports Chess Set for Marlin Vortman (check).

12/24 to 1/1/74 DIANE in town. (Author's note: this was three days before he attacked Karen Sparks, identified in *The Bundy Murders* as Terri Caldwell.)

Sparks: Assaulted 1-4-74 – Friday

4325 8th N.E.

This ends the package of King County information sent to the Leon County Sheriff's Office.

CHAPTER EIGHT

SEATTLE REPORTS AND ARTICLES

This is the Seattle Police report containing notes of the interview of Steve Burnham, who witnessed a man (Ted Bundy) in a leg cast and hobbling on crutches along the front of Greek Row at the University of Washington, only minutes before Bundy would encounter Georgann Hawkins as she was returning to her sorority house.

Seattle Police Report

DATE: August 8, 1974, Rec. call 1900 Hours

STEVE BURNHAM, Phi Kappa Sigma

DETAILS: Saw man described in PI article that continually dropped his brief case. Man had leg cast & crutches. Was helped by girl matching Hawkins description. Will be at frat house 1400 hours

INTERVIEW: STEVE BURNHAM W-M-21 Lives at 4711 17th NE., Seattle, Wash.

His girlfriend is Pamela Joan Meade. Pamela lived at Kappa Delta, 4500 Block on east side of 17th NE.

On Tuesday night, June 11. 1974 ay approximately 1130 PM to June 12, 1974 at approximately 1230 Am (close to midnight) Steve took his girlfriend "Pamela" to Kappa Delta. As he was returning, he was walking northbound on the east side of 17th NE in the 4500 Block as he observed a white male 20 to 22 5'11 to 6" tall, narrow face, med. build 170 to 175 # dark brown hair down over ears hanging in a regular manner. He had no mustache, no beard, and no sideburns. His clothing was Levis (bleached), light colored shirt (short sleeves) and he had a slit in his pants up the left leg. He had a wrapping or bandage (cast maybe) on his left leg and just the toes stuck out and it appeared to be up to his knee. He was dropping his briefcase as he was crossing the street from the southwest corner of NE 47th & 17th to the southeast corner of NE 47th & 17th NE going eastbound.

As Steve cut towards the center strip of 17th NE and was about up to the suspect a white female came from the east sidewalk and assisted the white male. (Note the white male was on crutches of the wood type). He kept dropping a black or dark brown briefcase that had a handle on top. Since the female was going to help him Steve kept on going and crossed over to the west side of 17th NE and continued home to 4711 17th NE.

The female that helped the suspect was 5'3" med. build, dressed in pants and shirt (it was a warm night). Steve looked at the Hawkins photo and he says it was not her that helped him. The last time Steve observed the suspect was when the suspect was on the southeast corner of NE 47th and 17th NE and he was handling the briefcase. Steve Burnham seemed to be accurate with his descriptions and information. Note also that as Steve observed suspect on corner he also observed the female then going westbound on NE 47th from 17th NE alone.

Det. Dennis Falk

The below excerpts are from an article from *The Seattle Times* describing a young girl who was murdered and decapitated in December 1974. This crime, of course, may not be the work of Ted Bundy, but the similarities with decapitation and the body not being recovered, should give one pause. If this wasn't one of Bundy's unknown murders, it clearly shows the work of someone just as diabolical.

The Seattle Times (Special to The Times), Tuesday, August 5, 1975, B16

EVERETT. A skull found under a tree near Paradise Lake Road Saturday night has been identified as Janna Marie Hanson, 13, of Montlake Terrace, who disappeared last December 26. Snohomish County Sheriff's detectives were to return to a farm today where the skull was found. Police believed the girl to be a runaway. Mrs. Doreen Hanson, the girl's mother, declared at the time of Janna's disappearance that she would not have run away.

What follows are excerpts from the *Seattle Post Intelligencer*, dated Wednesday, August 6, 1975, which continues the search for answers into the murder of the Hanson girl.

Seattle Post-Intelligencer, A 4F

Snohomish County Sheriff's officers, aided by King County search and rescue teams, yesterday continued to search a 150-acre farm south of Snohomish. Meanwhile, yesterday, Capt. Nick Mackie of the King County Police who heads the investigation into the deaths of six Seattle-area women whose skeletal remains have been found, said his unit is not involved in the search near Snohomish. "At this point there is nothing that binds them (the cases)," Mackie said. Snohomish County Sheriff's Officer Glenn Mann said the "only thing" in common between the Snohomish County case and the Seattle-area cases is that skulls have been found.

CHAPTER NINE

DON PATCHEN REPORTS AND INVESTIGATIVE NOTES

In the summer of 2008, when I was nearing completion of my book, *The Bundy Murders: A Comprehensive History*, I traveled to Florida to interview retired detective Don Patchen about his role in the Chi Omega investigation. He graciously brought me into his home where we spent a good number of hours discussing his role in the case and going over his case files, in some cases including the original documents, that were housed in a large clear plastic container. Most of the material consisted of copies of the police reports and what you'd expect to find in such a collection of investigative material.

But when I came to a number of pages that contained what appeared to be hastily scribbled quotes that were placed in no particular order on the page – some centered on the pages, while others were tilted along the edges. Don told me this was from a time when Bundy had asked them to turn off the tape recorder, believing he could speak more freely to them in this manner. Unknown to Bundy, these notes and the information contained therein, would ultimately become part of the case the authorities would present to the court to bring Bundy to justice. What is exceedingly interesting about this is that Bundy actually believed these statements were "between them," as it were and, because of this, he started speaking truthfully about his internal issues, albeit for a brief time.

Here are the statements Bundy made to investigators while the tape recorder was turned off. I have italicized Bundy's statements and left the detective's notes or questions in normal font so as to differentiate between the two.

I want you to understand me so you can understand my problem.

Fantasies equal problems. Started out: What turns you on? *It has to do with fantasies.*

He would never tell what they were. *It has to do with voyeurism.*

Y'all want modus operandi – I'm not going to give it to you.

He never enjoyed the act – but he had to do it to keep the fantasies up.

The act is a downer. What was the act – I'm not going to tell you modus operandi.

He would drink beer and start driving; he was having personal problems.

He counseled people. He had a greater problem he couldn't take care of himself.

Sometimes I feel like a vampire; I never hurt anybody I knew.

Psychological block to never tell anybody, he wanted them to break him.

Girl on bicycle: *I had to have her at any cost.*

He talked about defense mechanisms. *In order to live with myself. I have made defense mechanisms. The person you're talking to could never hurt anybody.* He convinced himself it was another person who committed these crimes.

What turns you on, hard pornography? *No, soft pornography.*

You're going to have to help me break these barriers down.

He was a law student at U. of Wash. While everybody else was in class, he was a voyeur.

You don't understand significance of Lee catching me & Utah case – you will when it all comes out.

Detective Don Patchen was lead investigator for the Tallahassee Police Department in the Chi Omega case. This deposition of him, taken at 2:00 p.m. on February 26, 1979, was at the insistence of Ted Bundy and was conducted by lead defense attorney, Michael Minerva. It is of interest to note that the Q&A goes into some detail pertaining to the above statements Bundy made, as well as additional damning statements he'd made that were now being used against him. We will begin at page sixteen and continue from there.

STATE OF FLORIDA vs. THEODORE ROBERT BUNDY

Deposition of: DONALD PATCHEN

Q: In any event you did talk to Mr. Bundy beginning at 1:20 a.m. on the 17th?

A: Right.

Q: And that was the first time that you interviewed him other than those contacts when his lawyer was there since the early morning of the 16th?

A: Right.

Q: All right, sir. How long did the session take that began on the 17th at 1:20 a.m.?

A: It went throughout the night; it was after 10:00 in the morning I believe.

Q: Who was present?

A: Myself, Chapman, and Steve Bodiford

Q: Did Captain Pottinger come to Pensacola?

A: Yes, he did.

Q: During the time of that interview?

A: As far as I know, he wasn't there when we started the interview. It was, I believe, the next day when we arrived.

Q: Was any of that session tape recorded?

A: Yes.

Q: Was that session recorded with the bugged tape?

A: No.

Q: And there would have been periods of time when the tape recorder was turned off, is that right?

A: At the request of Ted Bundy.

Q: Yes, sir, I understand that. Did you start out tape recording the session?

A: Yes.

Q: Maybe you can help me here. I have this massive transcript here. Let's go off the record.

(Thereupon, an off-the-record discussion was held.)

By Mr. Minerva:

Q: Now, in the course of talking with Mr. Bundy there on the 17th, he told you some things that were not tape recorded; is that right?

A: Right.

Q: Is there any way you can explain those to me in a narrative form, the essence of what he was talking about?

A: I'll try.

Q: All right.

A: If I may see that again for just a minute?

Q: Sure.

A: I want to see where we left off without re-telling parts of it.

Q: All right. You can hang on to that if you want to.

A: Okay. He had – I believe most of that was that he had talked about a few of his other adventures in some of these other states, as far as to some other cases, as far as his escapes and what have you. He went into telling about his voyeurism.

Q: Did he use that word?

A: Yes, he did. He went into telling us about some of his girlfriends, his past girlfriends and problems that he had. He went into – let's see - he talked about when he was working for some representative, or someone that was running for office that he had worked with, and some of the dirty tricks played there. He went into talking to us about that he had wanted to tell us of the things that happened to him, but that he had had a mental block that pretty much restrained himself or brought himself to never be able to tell anybody. Uh – do you follow what I am trying to say?

Q: Somewhat.

A: Okay. He kept telling us to keep talking to him, that this in essence helped him to come across with what he wanted to tell us. He at one point uh – I had asked him whether or not directly he had killed the girls at the Chi Omega house in Tallahassee, and he stated that if he was pressured into giving an answer that that answer would be no. And in that context of saying that, he would tell us that he didn't want to lie to us. But again, if he was pressured into answering, he would have to say, no. Of course, he explained to us the facts that he had built up in his mind never to reveal certain information that he wanted to tell us but he couldn't. He talked about, in his words, his VW that he had in Colorado, I believe it was. He used the word cargo, carrying cargo. He recalled an incident where he was riding down the street on a bicycle and he saw a girl, but that on this particular occasion he didn't do anything to the girl, or anything at that point, but that uh – I don't know exactly how to explain how he explained it. He stated that he had some feelings of the type that, you know, that he was controlling it at that time. In going over these feelings that he had, he stated that when he escaped from Colorado, that he felt that uh – this last escape that he had, when he came to Florida, that he felt that he could control his problem. And that having his psychology background, that he could be able to control his problems on the outside. And that he found out that he couldn't control his problems, and in essence, you know, that more or less, scared him.

He told us during that time that in the previous day and that night that there were several times when he could have escaped; he was relating to the windows and the make-up of the Pensacola Police Department. And we took him to the bathroom one time, I believe, and there was an open window right to the outside, and a few other things that, you know, we discussed with him at this time. He didn't want to escape, and that he felt that this was the time in his – the time in his life that maybe he could tell somebody what he had done in the past.

Q: What was the closest he ever got in telling you what his problem was?

A: I believe it was this night. I would have to, of course, listen to all the tapes to make sure. I believe it was this night that he talked about at one time he had restrained one of his girlfriends, or something to that effect. Or restrained her in a manner, you know, of tying up her arm, her hands, or something.

Q: Did he talk about harming females?

A: In what way?

Q: Well, I mean did he use that terminology?

A: I don't believe he ever pinpointed specifics. He would always more or less go around the bush.

Q: You say he talked about voyeurism, is that how you got involved in this discussion to start with? Is that – what does he – let me see if I can get you to a jumping off place. Did he start out by talking about his life as a young boy, and then as going to college, and –

A: Pretty much so.

Q: All right. As briefly as you can cover the subject, what did he tell you about that part of his life and that –

A: Well, it's kind of hard to bunch it all together. He would start out, you know, talking about his life, the whole story of his life, and then he would talk about certain aspects of it, and then he would jump back. Because he wanted to, you know, more or less give us an outlook to understand him. That's what he told us, he wanted us to understand him.

Q: Well, try to consolidate it then. Maybe not in the sequence that he told you, but give me the substance of what he told you even though you might put it in a different order than what he said. If you took it from a chronological viewpoint of what he told you from when he first began to describe his life, you know, and leading up to the part where he got into trouble with the law.

A: Okay. He talked about uh – I believe that night he talked about a police officer that had stopped him, I believe we talked about it more than one time too. We talked about as far as where a police officer stopped him in a neighborhood. He in his possession had some handcuffs and –

Q: Was this in the DaRonch – was this when he was arrested in the DaRonch case in Utah?

A: The girl that was kidnapped from the shopping center?

Q: Right.

A: I believe uh – we talked about so many things, you know. I'm trying to remember whether or not he connected that at the time. He had some pantyhose or stockings, a bag of sorts, in his VW.

Q: All right. Well, I'm familiar with that. That was in Utah, and that was several months after the DaRonch kidnapping; does that sound right?

A: Yes.

Q: He was in his car in the neighborhood and a police officer pulled him over?

A: Right.

Q: All right. Did he go back and tell you about his college days in Washington?

A: Yes, he did. He talked about the college atmosphere, as far as him liking – well, why he came to Tallahassee in fact; him liking the college atmosphere and that he could get in among the crowd of people could obtain a new identity. He is used to, you know, the surroundings of a college, the college people, and what have you.

Q: What did he tell you about voyeurism?

A: Let's see. The best I can recall is that he – after he mentioned voyeurism, we – I believe we asked him if this was the start of his problem. He uh – I don't think he gave us specific cases where he would go around, you know, looking in the windows or, you know, that. But he did use -- you know, he stated, you know, that he was a voyeur.

Q: Did he tell you that he obtained any sexual gratification from doing that?

A: I don't believe so.

Q: Did he ever tell you anything about actions that he almost took?

A: Pardon me?

Q: Well, if he would have gotten maybe inspired to do something but then was able to restrain himself, to keep himself from doing anything.

A: I told you about the incident with the bicycle.

Q: Okay. Did he become emotional at all during these times?

A: Yes, he did.

Q: Did he cry at times?

A: Yes.

Q: How frequently was that?

A: Very infrequent.

Q: Did he seem to have remorse for something at that time?

A: It was usually at the point where he was explaining to us that he wanted to tell us, he wanted to get this off his chest. I believe he stated that the previous day, I believe it was, that he asked to see a minister, and he had seen him. He thought he could get everything off his chest by telling someone; and this didn't give him the relief that he thought he would get.

Q: Did you keep coming back to the Chi Omega case to try to get some specific information from him on that?

A; I didn't harp at it, or neither did the other two. Because he more or less wanted us to understand him. Every time we started to talk about Tallahassee specifically, he did not want to answer any questions concerning Tallahassee or the murders.

Q; Did he seem to be somewhat concerned with control or lack of control?

A: Control of what?

Q: Over what he was doing, or whatever general problem it was that he had?

A: Lack of control.

Q: Did he talk to you about efforts he had made to try to bring his problem under control?

A: Other than having a degree uh – I guess he has a degree. I don't know if it is in psychology or uh – when he was incarcerated, he did not have the problem, that the problem dissipated. When he was out the problem became greater to him.

Q: Did he associate anything with the heightening of the problem, any kind of stimulus?

A: I believe alcohol was mentioned.

Q: Was there anything about pornography?

A; I believe we asked him about pornography, but uh – I can't remember exactly whether or not he denied if that gave him any great stimulus or not.

Q: The word problem became sort of shorthand as a reference to something else?

A: Yes, I would say so.

Q: How specific did he get into defining that term? I mean obviously if you all were talking about a problem you had to have some understanding of what it stood for, didn't you?

A; In what realm?

Q: Well, I mean that all through these transcripts there's references to, Ted, you have a problem; we have talked about problems. What is it that you all meant by the problem – the term, the problem?

A: I think there was a certain understanding to everybody that Ted had a problem that he could not control, and that he wanted to tell us about. He kept asking us to talk with him and help him because, as I said before, that he had blocked from telling anybody.

Q: Well, was this a problem that had any criminal aspect to it?

A: We assumed the problem was from the alleged murders.

Q: What made you assume that?

A: From lengthy discussions with him as far as all of his life and uh – of course, you know, as far as the idea of a problem, I guess that would be more of my personal, you know, opinion.

Q: Well, did he ever say anything that a reasonable person would assume would be an admission that there was a criminal problem?

A: Well, he stated, you know, to us that the evidence was there, you know, to find it.

It's clear from this portion of the deposition that defense attorney, Mike Minerva, was trying to back Bundy out of the incriminating statements he'd made to the investigators when the interrogations began soon after his capture. It was an uphill battle for the defense, and in the end, would be unsuccessful.

Q: The evidence of what?

A: Talking about the Chi Omega murders.

Q: When was that statement made?

A: I believe it was that night. I would have to go through those other transcripts and see if it was said in any of the other reports.

Q: Is it on the transcript?

A: It may be, I don't know.

At this portion of the transcript, there is much back and forth with little revelation coming forth concerning the case, so from this point forward, I will be leaving out what I deem are unimportant or redundant statements, adding only those portions that I believe will be of interest to the readers.

Q: Was Mr. Bundy being asked about cases other than the Chi Omega case when he got over here to Tallahassee?

A: Yes, sir.

Q: What other cases?

A: The Lake City case.

Q: Did you ever hear him make any statements about that case?

A: Bundy?

Q: Yes, sir.

A: Yes.

Q: What did you hear?

A: Okay. We had talked with him as far as – I don't – we were talking with him in relation to Lake City. The little girl that was murdered over there was not found at the time, but there was a search going on. A photograph was brought to us over there from Lake City of the little girl, and it was showed to Mr. Bundy. He said something to the effect that, you know, uh – the best that I can recall it was something to the effect that, you know, we wanted to find the little girl and uh – 'you don't want this' – I am trying to put it in his exact words; I can't remember exactly how it was. At one point we got out of talking about Lake City and were talking about, you know, the number of people that he might have or might not have had this problem with, you know, the matter of figures. We sort of wanted to know how many people we were talking about. And of course, at this point we had the information from Colorado.

Q: And what did he say?

A: As to what?

Q: As to the number of people? I mean did he make any response?

A: Yes, he did. He made a response to the fact that I understood that it was over 100. Now, whether he was, you know, dead serious about it; I don't know.

Q: Was that statement made over in Tallahassee or in Pensacola?

A: Here.

Q: During some of this time there were some efforts being made to work on a deal, or work out some kind of agreement that he was trying to get, and you all were talking about; and there is mention of it here in these tapes.

A: Right.

Q: What did Mr. Bundy say that could reasonably be interpreted as an admission or an acknowledgment that he had some responsibility for these murders? I could read, of course, what is in the transcript itself; but I'm speaking of things that are not written down here. I'm merely asking for your recollection of it.

A: I get the feeling that you're asking me for an assumption on my part.

Q: Well, somewhat I guess I am. As you know from reading this there is a lot of interpretation that goes into it. But I also know that I don't have the full conversation because they were not all recorded. So what I am asking you is for things outside of these transcripts, that you remember, that could be termed some sort of admission that he made. It is very difficult to ask specifically because I wasn't there and I don't know what the questions were. But you were there.

The deposition continues, and the remainder is an attempt by the defense to discredit the detectives, because Bundy had never actually admitted to the murders and, as such, they had no evidence against him based on the statements he'd made to them during the interrogations. Without question, Bundy had alluded to his guilt at certain points in these interviews, and the defense would gain little ground here.

What follows are statements Ted Bundy made to Detective Donald Patchen and other Florida investigators during the same interview. After Bundy was arrested in Pensacola, Florida, he did not reveal his real name for a time, therefore, the police identified him as "Doe" for the first question or two, but then Doe disappears and he's identified as Bundy. Why there was an abrupt change in the same Q & A is not explained.

Bundy Statements

1. Bundy admits being in Sherrod's:

Patchen: Do you recall stealing cards out of Sherrod's; it's a bar they have around FSU?

Doe: Yes, I recall being there. Yeah.

2. Voluntariness of Bundy's confession:

Chapman: Okay. And uh, after talking with these people, uh, I believe during this time that they were here you told me that later on when uh, they had left and (you) desired to talk to us, in relation to any incident or whatever you wanted to talk to us uh, without these individuals present, is this correct?

Bundy: Yes, I approached you and said that I wanted to talk to you later.

3. Lived at the Oak and used – used Chris Hagen name and Washington Street address.

Bodiford: When you registered, when you rented that room in Tallahassee, did you use the name and address in Ann Arbor?

Bundy: Mmm ...

Bodiford: Did you pick somebody's I.D. in Ann Arbor?

Bundy: Didn't do a thing in Ann Arbor, didn't pick up an I.D. that was, the name and address that I gave to the Tallahassee apartment was just grasped out of thin air except ...

Bodiford: Made it up?

Bundy: Except for the (mumble) I recall the Washington Street in Ann Arbor.

Bundy: So that's all there is for right now as far as that name. I don't know where Chris Hagen came from. I don't know a Chris Hagen, and I didn't pick up an I.D. of any kind.

4. Why he picked Tallahassee:

Bundy: See, I didn't plan on staying in Atlanta. I knew I was coming south. Now, let me get back to Michigan, we wanted to find out how I got to Tallahassee.

Chapman: Yeah.

Bundy: Now, why, what was I gonna do. Ok. See, I, I knew I was gonna come to a place in Florida that had a college campus. A large college campus. Now I didn't know anything about Tallahassee. I didn't know Tallahassee from...

Patchen: You knew that you were ... can you ... you said you knew you were gonna come to a campus in Tallahassee.

Bundy: Well yeah, sure because I know how to operate in and around college campuses. I knew I would pick up an I.D. I know how to be a student, I know how to look like a student, I know how to act like a student.

Patchen: Oh, I see.

Bundy: I blend in.

Bundy: Yeah, right. So it's just, all this is just almost random in a way. Superstitious. And so then I came to the catalog for Florida State University. And looked at it and it says there's a place called Tallahassee. Tallahassee was where it's at. I looked at it and said well it's not too far from the ocean, um, it looked right. Why it looked right I don't know.

5. Got to Tallahassee – went to "The Oaks":

Bundy: The bookstore was open that day 'cause it was the early part of the quarter. It was a Sunday, but it was open on Sunday. So I put some of my stuff in one of those lockers in the bookstore on campus. And I started walking up and down the streets in the neighborhood or in the area surrounding Tallahassee, the university. Looking for a "For Rent" sign. Anything. And uh, I had misfortune finally of, the only place that had a sign out, which was a room for rent, which is all I could afford at the time. And I wanted to get a place quick 'cause I didn't want to, I didn't know where I'd stay. There was no Y in the area. So there was The Oaks or whatever they call it. And it's really a rat hole.

6.   Bundy says he never went into Sherrod's until first week of February. Admits knowing band at The Oaks.

Patchen: Did you spend a lot of time there, you know, where you stole this credit card in Sherrod's, with people or anything like that?

Bundy: I never went into Sherrod's.

Patchen: You know where I'm talking about?

Bundy: Um hum.   I never went into Sherrod's until maybe a week and a half ago.

Patchen: A week and a half ago?

Bundy: That, and you'll find as you look back over some of the stolen cards you'll be able to verify that I can't tell you the exact date but it wasn't you know, more than a week or two ago at the most.

Patchen: You've got to have credit cards on Jo Ann Hale, on the 3rd and the 4th, she can't remember.

Bundy: Oh, what, in February?

Patchen: Yeah.

Bundy: Yeah, well, what is that, about two weeks ago?

Patchen: Yeah, I guess it would be, yeah, do they have bands in there? I haven't ever been in there.

Bundy: No, it's just a discotheque kind of thing.

Patchen: Disco?

Bundy: It's too crowded and noisy, normally the sound is just unbearable. You know how those places are.

Patchen: Did you make any friends in Tallahassee or talk to them or make acquaintances?

Bundy: The only I made, the only acquaintances that I made were in the house that I lived in and those were only passing. I was kind of surprised they had a band that lived on the floor I lived on, unemployed band.

Patchen: (Laugh)

Bundy: And uh, you know, they were always trying to get it together you know, they're trying to get it together. They kind of kept to themselves, as you know. They didn't let me into their little circle (indiscernible) uh, but I made a passing. I was developing a relationship with them, uh, then there was no one that I had to, you know, that I saw regular that you could call a friend or anything.

7. Denied being on streets at night.

Patchen: Did you ever, you know, like in the middle of the night, just couldn't sleep and just wander around, walk around wherever you know uh, we had of course policeman around there checking people.

Bundy: Yeah.

Patchen: All the time, it's a regular routine, weren't you ever checked out or anything if you walked around? You know, get out in the early hours.

Bundy: I didn't walk around at night, that, I'm ... again, I made it a point as much as possible to stay off the streets late at night, if I was out at night I rode my bicycle for the very fact that uh, people don't stop.

8. Admits signing lease on January 7, and statement reference license plate number 13D11300* on January 13, 1978.

*That tag number was on the white FSU media van that Bundy was driving when he murdered Kimberly Leach in Lake City, Florida. It was also written down by witness Danny Parmenter when he came upon Bundy talking with his younger sister Leslie, as she was waiting for Danny to pick her up from a K-Mart parking lot in Jacksonville, Florida.

Bodiford: That tag that was in the floorboard of that Toyota that our deputy stopped you in the other night and you ran from him, do you know which one I'm talking about? That was in the floorboard that he asked you about?

Bundy: Yeah.

Bodiford: Do you remember where you came by that?

Bundy: No, I really don't.

Bodiford: Do you remember how soon after you got to Tallahassee it was?

Bundy: I don't imagine it was until sometime after I was in Tallahassee. You know, I can't say exactly when. You sparked my memory because I had forgotten completely about any tag that was on there that (This statement not fully thought out by the detective) *origin of the tag that was on the floorboard.*

Bodiford: Your rental agreement, under the name Chris Hagen, was dated the 7th.

Bundy: Um hum.

Bodiford: Did you get that tag off of a vehicle?

Bundy: I may well have, I probably did.

Bodiford: It was reported stolen on the 13th.

Bundy: Thirteenth of?

Bodiford: January.

Bundy: Thirteenth of January. Well, it doesn't ring a bell exactly.

Bodiford: Okay. I was just wondering. I mean it's only six days after you rented the room.

Bundy: Um.

Bodiford: I wondered if you know, if somebody else ripped it off before you got to it and then you got...

Patchen: It was you know, was it taken off?

Bodiford: Want some more coffee, Ted?

Bundy: Um, sure.

Patchen: It was listed as being taken off a van, do you, does that spark any memories, a white van?

Bodiford: Orange.

Patchen: Was it an orange van?

Bodiford: Orange, orange, brilliant orange, you can't miss it.

The FSU media van was white only. Bodiford must have been momentarily confused and thinking about the stolen orange VW Bundy was driving at the time of his arrest in Pensacola, Florida.

Bodiford: Brilliant orange and white van, does that spur any memories?

Bundy: I remember one truck that I took a tag off of.

Bodiford: Was it a pickup?

Bundy: I – yeah, a pickup truck.

Patchen: Was it a normal type?

CHAPTER TEN

SUMMARY REPORT ON THE CHI OMEGA MURDERS

What follows is a summary report on the Chi Omega murders:

LEON COUNTY SHERIFF'S DEPARTMENT

Criminal Investigations Bureau

DATE: Sunday, 15 January 1978

TIME: 0300 hours

LOCATION:

Chi Omega Sorority House (F.S.U.)

661 West Jefferson Street

Tallahassee, Florida

VICTIMS: Margaret Bowman and Lisa Levy

SUMMARY

At 0300 hours, Sunday, 15 January 1978, Nita Neary (member of Chi Omega Sorority) returned from a date, and entered the sorority through a rear door off the patio. As she entered the house, she walked through the living room and to the front steps leading to the bedrooms on the second floor. As she approached the lobby (location of the main steps), she heard someone running down the steps. The subject then went directly to the front door and exited. The subject was described by Ms. Neary as a white male, early twenties, brown short, straight hair, 5'8" to 5'9", 160 – 170 pounds. The subject was further described as wearing a black or dark snow cap, black or dark waist-length coat, and light pants. He was carrying a 2 ½ – 3 foot stick or club in his right hand. The subject apparently never saw Ms. Neary.

Ms. Neary, at this time, thought the subject was probably a prowler, so she immediately went upstairs to see if anyone was awake, and possibly saw the intruder also. She walked to the top of the stairs and found another sorority sister awake. While the two were discussing the subject that Ms. Neary saw, a bedroom door opened a short distance away and another sorority sister, Karen Chandler, staggered into the hall. Ms. Chandler was bleeding severely from wounds about the head. Discovered at the same time was Kathy Kleiner (Chandler's roommate). Kleiner was bleeding from the head also. In addition to head wounds, her teeth had been knocked out. A quick check was made of the other rooms on the floor by other sorority sisters, and the body of Lisa Levy was found in the room next to Chandler and Kleiner. By this time the first law enforcement officers arrived. All of the sorority sisters were moved downstairs to the living room, and the officers discovered the body of Margaret Bowman, directly across from Levy's room.

SUMMARY OF INJURIES
(1) MARGARET BOWMAN
a. Death by strangulation.
b. Severe blows to the head.
c. No evidence of sexual assault.

(2) *LISA LEVY*
a. *Death by strangulation.*
b. *Bite marks on body.*
c. *Evidence of sexual assault.*

(3) *KAREN CHANDLER*
a.*Severe blows about the head area.*
b.*Bruises about the neck and shoulders.*

(4) *KATHY KLEINER*
a. *Severe blows about the head area.*
b. *Teeth knocked out (top and bottom).*

There was no evidence of sexual assault on Chandler, Kleiner, or Bowman. Only Levy was sexually assaulted.

Approximately 1 ½ hours later (0430 hours) two females living at 431 Dunwoody Street were awakened by noises coming from the other side of their duplex. This location is almost four blocks away (west) from the Chi Omega House. The two females became alarmed and called the next door apartment. As the phone rang, the noises subsided, however, no one answered the call. They then called law enforcement. When officers arrived on the scene, Cheryl Thomas was found in her room with severe wounds about the head. Thomas was unconscious and bleeding severely. Entrance and exit to the apartment had been made through a kitchen window. There was no evidence of sexual assault.

Between 15 January and 11 February 1978, investigators from the Leon County Sheriff's department, Tallahassee Police Department, Florida State University Department of Public Safety, State Attorney's Office, and Florida Department of Criminal

Law Enforcement interviewed approximately 3,500 individuals. A central command post was set up for all agencies, with approximately forty investigators assigned.

On 9 February, surveillance units were set up in various locations surrounding the Florida State University campus for the purpose of checking prowlers and suspicious persons. On 11 February, at 0147 hours, a deputy stopped a subject for a routine check near campus. The subject was locking the door of a green Toyota. While the Deputy was attempting to check identification, the subject ran and got away. A license plate (13D-11300, Florida) was found in the front floor-board of the Toyota. A check of the license plate revealed that it was stolen on 13th January (2 days before the homicides and assaults) from a location approximately 150 yards from the assault on Dunwoody Street. Further investigation revealed that the license plate was seen on a 1976 white Dodge van (stolen from Florida State University on 6 February) by a white male who attempted to "pick up" a young female as she was leaving school in Jacksonville on 8 February.

On 15 February, an officer with the Pensacola Police Department stopped a 1972 orange VW after a license check revealed the car to be stolen. The individual driving the VW identified himself to the officer as Kenneth Raymond Misner. Approximately 30 minutes after the arrest, the Leon County Sheriff's Department was notified that the VW had been recovered, and the driver arrested. The subject, at the time of his arrest, had several stolen credit cards belonging to students at Florida State University. These credit cards were stolen from various locations in Tallahassee on 3 – 4 February, however, the majority of the cards were *stolen from a lounge located next door to the Chi Omega Sorority House.*

It was later learned that the subject arrested was not Kenneth Raymond Misner, but was someone using Misner's identification.

The Leon County Sheriff's Department and the Tallahassee Police Department sent investigators to Pensacola to interview the subject. After approximately twenty-four hours, the subject identified himself as Theodore Robert Bundy. A further check revealed that Bundy was listed on the FBI's "Ten Most Wanted Fugitives" list, and it was further learned that Bundy had escaped from Aspen, Colorado on 31 December 1977. (Author's note: Bundy actually escaped from the jail in Glenwood Springs on this date, He escaped from Aspen (his first escape) on June 7, 1977 and was recaptured on June 13, 1977. Bundy had already been convicted in Utah for the kidnapping of Carol DaRonch, and was on trial in Colorado for the murder of Caryn Campbell who had disappeared from the Wildwood Inn in Snowmass, Colorado on January 12, 1975.

Through the use of a photograph lineup (and before his photograph appeared in the news media) the young girl in Jacksonville identified Bundy as the one trying to pick her up on 8 February. The Deputy in Leon County also identified Bundy as the subject that ran from him near the FSU campus on 11 February.

By tracing the stolen credit cards, the whereabouts of Bundy between 21 January and 15 February are well documented. In addition, Bundy made credit card charges in Jacksonville on the same date that he attempted to pick up the young girl (Name), *and in*

Lake City, the same date, (9 February) that a young girl (Name) *was reported missing.*

Shortly after his arrest, Bundy agreed to talk with investigators, and a total of approximately forty hours of interviews were conducted before Bundy decided to quit talking.

Bundy was incarcerated in Colorado from August 1976 to December 1977. To escape, he lost approximately sixty pounds (Author's note: this number is absurdly incorrect. He didn't lose 60 pounds. He wouldn't have been able to walk had this been true. No other source, including Det. Mike Fisher, has stated something so ridiculous. This is just a mistake in the record that needed addressing.) *to enable him to crawl through a small electrical opening in the ceiling of his cell. Once on the outside, he stole a car and was going to drive to Vail, Colorado, however, the engine blew up and the car was abandoned on the side of the highway. He then caught a bus to Denver, Colorado, and from there a TWA flight to Chicago, Illinois. He spent one to two days in Chicago and then went to Ann Arbor, Michigan. While at this location, he visited the University of Michigan Library to look up information about colleges in the South. He initially picked Gainesville, however, he wanted to be closer to the coast, so he chose Tallahassee and FSU.*

On 2 January, Bundy was sitting in a lounge in Ann Arbor, and was watching the Rose Bowl game. He stayed in Ann Arbor for two days, and then stole a car and drove to Atlanta, Georgia. In Atlanta, he left the keys in the car and abandoned it in a black residential neighborhood. He then caught a Trailways Bus to Tallahassee – arriving in the early morning of 7 January.

Shortly after his arrival in Tallahassee, Bundy walked around the FSU campus, and located an apartment approximately two blocks from the university. At this location he leased a room using the name of Chris M. Hagen, 2445 Washington Street, Ann Arbor, Michigan. (The name and address proved to be false, however the lounge he frequented in Ann Arbor was on Washington Street.)

Currently, Bundy has been charged with approximately forty felony charges including, burglary, auto theft, and forgery, however, evidence available has not been able to tie him to the Chi Omega case, and the investigation is still open.

Any agency wishing to obtain additional information on Bundy should forward the request in writing to ... (Author's note: the report ends here.)

CHAPTER ELEVEN

REPORTS, REVELATIONS, AND SUSPECTED BUNDY MURDERS

Seattle police sent Bundy's Utah attorney, John O'Connell, a letter concerning the whereabouts of his client, Ted Bundy, during the rash of homicides the state had suffered for most of 1974.

October 17, 1975

Mr. John O'Connell

12 Exchange Place

Salt Lake City, Utah 84111

Re: Ted Bundy

Here are the dates, times, and locations where female homicide victims were last seen. Please have Ted Bundy determine his whereabouts on the dates concerned. We have not been able to eliminate Ted through his employment records, school attendance records, or close friends.

01-04-74   02:00 a.m. University District, Seattle, WA.

01-31-74   11:00 p.m. University District, Seattle, WA.

03-12-74   07:00 p.m.   Evergreen State College, Olympia, WA.

04-17-74   09:30 p.m.   Central Wash. St. College, Ellensburg, WA.

05-06-74   11:00 p.m.   Oregon St. Univ., Corvallis, Oregon

06-01-74 02:00 a.m.   Flame Tavern, Seattle, WA.

06-11-74 01:00 a.m.   University District, Seattle, WA.

07-14-74 12:30-4:30 p.m. Lake Sammamish St. Park, Issaquah, WA.

08-02-74 11:00 a.m.   Vancouver, WA.

If you wish additional information in this matter please contact Detective Robert D. Keppel, Homicide Task Force.

Thank you for your cooperation in this case.

LAWRENCE G. WALDT, SHERIFF-DIRECTOR

J. Nick Mackie, Captain

Criminal Investigation Division

Multiple strange vanishings and homicides of women and girls occurred in the states where Bundy was known to have operated or had traveled to or through and, as such, could not be ruled out as a possible suspect during those investigative years. Because of the advancement of DNA testing, some individuals (like Melanie Cooley) have been ruled out as Bundy victims. Some of these murder cases have presented evidence, however, that match Bundy's modus operandi, at least in part, while others do not. What makes these particular missing and/or murdered female reports important and interesting enough to mention here, is that they were all a part of the Bundy investigation at one time or another.

When writing The Bundy Murders, I gathered case files from all the states where Bundy was known to have murdered women. What I found during this time of research, was that the detectives who were hunting this elusive killer of women were also communicating with law enforcement officials in surrounding jurisdictions and receiving information about their missing and murdered women and young girls. Of course, we may never know if Bundy is responsible for any of these crimes, but it's clear he can't be completely ruled out from a number of them. One thing is certain: no matter how many murders Ted Bundy committed during the time of his murder sprees, he was not alone in such activities, as each state had killers operating during the same time as Bundy.

I will first present materials that were sent between detectives and other officials pertaining to the California homicides, and then add information about the murder of Leslie Maria Perlov, and Washington Detective Bob Keppel's response to their inquiries, before delving into the abductions and murders in Rawlins, Wyoming.

DISTRICT ATTORNEY

COUNTY OF SANTA CRUZ

August 7, 1974

Mr. Robert D. Keppel, Detective

Homicide – Robbery Division

King County Police

Court House

Seattle, Washington

Dear Bob,

In reference to our telephone conversation this date, enclosed are copies of our case summaries concerning Rosa Linda Cantu Zuniga, Deborah Lee Shelton, and Terry Kay Pfitzer.

I have also attached a copy of my letter to Carlstedt which is self-explanatory. Let me know if we can be of any assistance.

Sincerely,

R. F. VERBRUGGE
INSPECTOR

DISTRICT ATTORNEY COUNTY OF SANTA CRUZ
E. Carlstedt, Detective Sergeant
Sonoma County Sheriff's Office
2555 Mendocino Avenue
Santa Rosa, California 95401

Dear Butch:

In reference to our conversation and your subsequent letter on June 13, 1974, attached are case summaries on our two unsolved female murders, the victims being, Deborah Lee Shelton and Rosa Linda Cantu Zuniga. Also, the missing person's information on Terry Kay Pfitzer.

I have also enclosed copies of the following, Dianne Uhlig, summary of San Mateo County, 187 P.C. Case number 72-2632, by Sheriff's Inspector Rudy Siemessen who may have additional similars.

May I also suggest that you get in touch with the following investigators who all have similar unsolved cases:

Sgt. Tom Sheppard, Monterey County Sheriff's Office, 408-424-0352

Sgt. Bob Malone, Santa Clara Sheriff's Department, 408-299-2211

Sgt. Duane Gull, Alameda Sheriff's Department, 415-483-6520

Let me know when you want the information on our unsolved males, we've still got a couple of those laying around.

Sincerely,

R. F. VERBRUGGE

A portion of the left side of the following report was copied incorrectly, leaving a small portion of these words missing. I have attempted to fill in the blanks, and where I have been unable to confirm a particular word, I will denote it by a question mark.

INTER–OFFICE MEMO

TO: SHERIFF STRIEPEKE

FROM: DETECTIVE SERGEANT CARLSTEDT

SUBJECT: Meeting at CII, Sacramento on 6/26/74 with Dave Struve of the Special Projects Office

On June 26, 1974, RO and Captain John Hess met with Criminal Specialist Dave Struve at CII to discuss the information this department has developed concerning unsolved female homicides in seventeen surrounding jurisdictions with similarities to the six female homicides our county has experienced over the past two years. The other 17 jurisdictions have 22 unsolved female homicides. When Dave Struve received this information from this department, he checked the CII files back to 1970 and came up with 56 more female homicides that were similar to our cases but covering a larger area of Northern California for a total of 84 unsolved homicides.

This meeting was held to determine the following:

1. *What criteria or similarities did each case have to meet for us to keep them as similar cases in the homicides we are investigating.*

2. *To ascertain if a suspect profile or victim profile can be developed with the information available from these cases.*

3. *The ultimate goal of having a seminar with all departments concerned with the information pieced together to come up with a suspect or suspects and the apprehension of those responsible in these numerous motiveless killings which at this time outnumber the Muslim or Zebra assassinations.*

Santa Clara County (California) Sheriff's Office wrote a letter to Detective Robert Keppel of the King County Police seeking possible connections between murders in California and Washington State, and Ted Bundy's whereabouts at the time of these California homicides.

May 27, 1981

Der Bob,

We have recently read the article in Reader's Digest about Ted Bundy. We have noticed several similarities in two homicide cases from our area that are unsolved and feel that Bundy would be considered a possible suspect.

The first case was the strangulation death of a twenty-one-year-old white female, whose body was discovered on February 16, 1973, in a wooded rural area near Palo Alto, California. The locater of a victim was on property owned by Stanford University. The victim, Leslie Marie Perlov, was last seen talking to a young man at the law library of the Palo Alto Municipal Court. The composite of the young man seen talking to Perlov at the law library closely resembles the composite of Bundy which appeared in Reader's Digest.

The second case is similar in M.O. in so far as the victim, Janet Ann Taylor, was discovered March 25,

1974, in a rural area not far from Palo Alto. The cause of death was also strangulation.

If possible, could you provide us with any information concerning Ted Bundy's whereabouts on or about February 13, 1973, and March 25, 1974?

We have enclosed a flyer and a photo copy of the composite from the Perlov case.

We appreciate your efforts to assist us on this matter. Please send your reply to Sgt. Ken Kahn, Santa Clara County Sheriff's Office, 180 West Hedding Street in San Jose, California 95110

Text from the Santa Clara Sheriff's Office bulletin concerning Leslie Perlov:

COUNTY OF SANTA CLARA

Office of the Sheriff

Your SHERIFF'S DEPARTMENT needs help in finding the person who murdered LESLIE MARIE PERLOV after 3:00 p.m. on Tuesday, February 13. Anyone seeing persons or vehicles in the vicinity of the QUARRY GATE ON OLD PAGE MILL ROAD should contact the SHERIFF'S DEPARTMENT at 299-3844 between 8 A.M. and 5 P.M. or 229-3902 after 5 P.M.

Don't hesitate in calling with any piece of information even if it seems minor to you, as it just might fit in with the information developed in the past week by 995 hours of investigation. Your efforts in helping solve this brutal murder will be greatly appreciated by not only the Sheriff's Department but the entire community.

Thank you,

SHERIFF JAMES M. GEARY

King County's response to Santa Clara County's request for additional information regarding Bundy's whereabouts and time frame.

KING COUNTY, STATE OF WASHINGTON

Department of Public Safety

June 1, 1981

Sgt. Ken Kahn, Detective Division

County of Santa Clara

Office of Sheriff

180 - West Hedding Street

San Jose, California 95110

Dear Ken:

Ted Bundy's contacts in your jurisdiction were numerous from 1967 to 1974. The account of his activities is as follows:

June – August 1967: Attended Stanford University and lived in Palo Alto.

July 8, 1967: Had dinner in San Francisco with his girlfriend.

1969: Late Spring was in San Francisco with girlfriend. Stayed in Mendocino.

August 20, 1970: Bundy received traffic citation in Marin County.

May 16, 1972: Bundy sent Univ. of Wash. transcript to U of C, Berkeley.

June 13, 1973: Bundy stayed at Mark Hopkins Motel in San Francisco.

Information regarding Bundy's whereabouts on February 13, 1973, are sketchy at best. Our records *indicate Bundy sent an application to the University of Utah Law School on February 15, 1973; Bundy received a $400 invoice for consultation services on February 15, 1973; Bundy received a $400 invoice for consultation services on February 28, 1973.*

Information on Bundy's whereabouts on March 24, 1974, is as follows:

(1)Checking account:

03/23/74	*Safeway Foods, Seattle*
03/25/74	*PEMCO, Seattle*
03/25/74	*Standard Oil*
03/25/74	*Two (2) deposits*
03/26/74	*University Bookstore, Seattle*
03/25/74	*43rd and Roosevelt, Seattle*
03/26/74	*Olympic Hotel, Seattle*

The checks as well as credit card receipts possess Bundy's signature.

Bundy's lack of activity in February 1973 probably indicates he ran out of money or was imposing upon his Seattle girlfriend. Records for May 5, 1974, were also sparse and it turned out he was in Corvallis, Oregon – 265 miles from Seattle – killing Roberta Parks. (Author's note: this is incorrect. Bundy abducted Kathy Parks on May 6, 1974.)

Bundy did have a San Francisco girlfriend who was the major reason he went to California. This girl's identity has been kept quite confidential on our part. We wish to protect her from any press inquiries. However, if you see the need to contact her to further isolate Bundy's activities in California, please contact FBI Agent Kathy McChesney in the San Francisco office.

McChesney is my former partner who investigated Bundy with me and has also kept up a relationship with his (Bundy's) *girlfriend.*

By the way, Bundy did have a beard for various periods of 1973. Leslie Perlov certainly appears to fit the profile of Bundy's victims. Bundy was a frequent law library visitor throughout his prowling activities. (Author's note: Incorrect in that Bundy was a regular visitor of the main student libraries on college campuses when he was hunting, and not law libraries. Law libraries may have been a part of it on rare occasions, and were probably spur of the moment events.) *It may also interest you that Bundy used a sling and dropped books in front of a library as a scam to have girls lured to his parked VW Bug.*

If I can be of further assistance, don't hesitate to call (206) 344-2668.

Sincerely yours,

BERNARD G. WINCKOSKI

Det. ROBERT D. KEPPEL

Between July and August 1974, a female child of ten, a young girl of fifteen, and two nineteen-year-old women were murdered in Rawlins, Wyoming. The crimes remain unsolved to this day, and the remains of only one of the victims have been found. The authorities believe these murders were the work of one man. At one time they believed they had a promising suspect but because of the lack of evidence, no charges were ever filed against him, and that suspect died of a heart attack a number of years ago. This same individual they were looking at had previously been charged with the murders of two girls in another state, but the charges were dropped for a lack of evidence. Of course, Ted Bundy has been looked at concerning these murders, and it is true that he travelled through the state in March of 1975, and that he may have been within the boundaries (however briefly) of Wyoming on other occasions. That said, it seems unlikely he was in Wyoming that July/August of 1974, as July was a busy month for Bundy with the double abductions and murders from Lake Sammamish State Park on July 14, 1974, as well as other (and normal) activities he participated in.

The murders in Wyoming are often referred to as *The Wyoming Rodeo Murders* as many in local law enforcement believe they are related. Technically, however, they are listed as four different cases, and a brief synopsis of the cases is as follows:

On July 4, 1974, Carlene Brown and Christy Gross, both nineteen, attended the Little Britches Rodeo in Rawlins, Wyoming. Brown was a native of Rawlins, but Gross was from South Dakota, and according to information obtained by the police, the women had been living in hippie communes. Those who would tell the police that they had been seen at the rodeo had no answers as to how they may have gone missing. On October 27, 1983, the remains of Christy Gross were located in a field just outside Sinclair, Wyoming. Her skull had suffered fatal damage from two heavy blows to the head made by, authorities believed, a large rock. A ring she wore was also recovered at the site.

Exactly one month later, on August 4, 1974, Deborah Rae Meyer, fifteen, disappeared while walking to a movie theater in Rawlins and has never been seen again. On August 23, 1974, ten-year-old, Jayleen Banker, while attending the Carbon County Rodeo, became separated from friends and was never seen again.

Sheriff of Carbon County

Rawlins, Wyoming 82301

May 15, 1975

Detective Roger Dunn

King County

516 3rd Avenue

Seattle, Washington 98104

Dear Roger:

Enclosed are a few flyers on the missing females from this area that we are investigating.

Carlene Brown and Christy Rose have been known to live in hippie communes and are known pill poppers and smokers. Deborah Rae Meyer, as far as we can ascertain, is a pretty clean-cut girl and was a reliable employee at Gibson's Discount Store here in Rawlins at the time of her disappearance.

Very truly yours,

Ed M. Tierney

Deputy Sheriff

What follows is a profile of the Washington State killer which came forth after the abductions and murders Bundy committed at Lake Sammamish State Park on July 14, 1974. Some of these are right on target while others are wildly inaccurate. Accompanying this information sheet was one of the composite drawings that came forth after Lake Sammamish and was based on eye witnesses at the park:

7-24-74

"TED"

Predator

1. *Loner: see definition*
2. *Juvenile sex offense*
3. *Has a record – not the 1st time*
4. *Chronic sex-offender*

5. *Aggressive heterosexual offender*

6. *Might have girlfriends*

7. *Probably has been married*

8. *Peeper*

9. *M.O. on sex offenders*

10. *Sexual psychopath*

11. *Not a drugger*

12. *Usually steals an object from the victim*

13. *Sadomasochist*

14. *Combat duty in Vietnam*

Four % of sex offenders look like it! The rest are normal looking.

CHAPTER TWELVE

JERRY THOMPSON REPORTS

I received the investigative case file of the murder of Melissa Smith directly from Jerry Thompson, lead detective for the Bundy case in Utah. While I have drawn from this report for my previous books on the case (and duplicating much of it for *The Bundy Secrets: Hidden Files on America's Worst Serial Killer*), this single sheet was inadvertently left out as I believe it was shuffled into a stack of papers that had already been used, and therefore was mistakenly left out. What makes this single sheet so extremely important is that it includes an admission of guilt by Bundy to one of his housemates at 565 First Avenue in Salt Lake City. Also, I will be following it up with a file I will be using for the first time, and it contains many interesting tidbits about the investigation, interviews of witnesses, and case material from Utah.

On 11-26-75 a Chuck Shearer called County Attorney Dave Yocom and informed him that he was now residing at Scotty's Motel on North Temple in Unit # 52. He stated that he had lived across the hall from Mr. Bundy for a few months; then he left town and since has come back and learned that Mr. Bundy has been arrested and that he may have some information about him.

Contact was made with Charles Shearer and his wife, Rosemary, at this apartment on 11-26-75. Rosemary's mother and her 13-year-old sister were also present in the motel. A taped statement, which will be put in my case file, was taken from Mr. Shearer. It should be noted that an interview was made with both of these individuals some time ago, before Bundy was ever arrested at the apartment building at 565 First Avenue (Author's note: Det. Thompson is referring to the October 1975 arrest – Bundy's second incarceration – and not the August 16 arrest).

Since that time and since Mr. Bundy's arrest, it appears that Mr. Shearer has decided to come forth with a little bit more information than he originally did before. A brief summary of that tape is that Mr. Bundy was drinking one night and was fairly well plastered (drunk) with Charles Shearer. And Mr. Bundy made the comment to Mr. Shearer that the police were looking for him (Mr. Bundy) in regards to his car, that it was used in the kidnapping of three girls in the Utah area.

In fact, Chuck states that Ted told him that he had abducted the three girls, as near as he can recall. When Chuck asked him, "What did you say?" he stated that Mr. Bundy did not comment any further and got off the subject and would not answer him. His wife Rosemary also stated that as near as she could tell, that's exactly what he said.

Chuck Shearer also told of an incident between a girl and Bundy one night at 565 First Avenue:

One other item he mentioned is that they had a party or a get-together in his apartment one night. Ted just came walking in. A friend of theirs by the name of (Author's note: I'm redacting her name), *about 19-years-of age, living in the Kerns area (unknown exactly where), was lying on the bed. When Ted came in, he walked over to her and pinched her between the legs. She then got up and asked him what the hell was going on. She went back to Chuck and told him, "You sure have weird friends." He states there was no other pass made by Ted other than that, and he would do numerous things like this, which they thought was very, very strange. For further details of this interview see the full taped statement.*

Utah Detective Jerry Thompson interviewed individuals who knew Ted Bundy. Also of interest is a transcription of a recorded phone conversation that Jerry Thompson had with a sheriff's deputy in another jurisdiction concerning the escape of Ted Bundy. It is also presented on paper as a normal Q&A report. All of the information presented here can be considered excellent backstory info, and to my knowledge, most—if not all—of this information presented here will be new to readers.

On 1-29-76, after this detective received information from the FBI Laboratory, I contacted Bob Denning, the Undersheriff of Clear Creek county Sheriff's Office in Denver, Colorado. He was informed with our findings and he was also asked to submit his hair samples to the FBI Laboratory in regards to the homicide of Shelley Robertson, which occurred in July of 1975. He stated that he would have them in the mail immediately this date, 1-29-76, and would notify me of any information that he received from them or anything else and requested that he be kept posted. Detective Bob Keppel from King County Sheriff's Office in Seattle, Washington, was called by this officer and was also informed of our finding from the FBI Lab. He was also informed that they stated that they had not received his hair samples yet. He stated that he would apologize, that they had had a run around from a change in administration problems and that he guaranteed that they would be in the mail before the day was out. He also informed this officer that Mr. Bundy was in the Seattle area at this particular time and that he was under surveillance at different times. One time they would be on him and then they would back off a bit and go back and forth.

This same date, Mike Fisher from District Attorney's Office in Aspen, Colorado, was called at the FBI Academy in Quantico, Virginia, by this detective and informed (him) of the lab information from the FBI Lab, as he is back there on a school and is due back in Colorado Friday night, 1-30-76. Mr. Fisher informed this officer that he would be getting back into Aspen Friday night; that he would immediately get with his people, and that he would set up a meeting, they would go over the case, and that he would get back to me just as soon as they came up with any information letting me know if there would be a warrant or if there would not be.

On 1-31-76, Saturday morning, Dave Yocom from the County Attorney's Office contacted me and stated that he could not get ahold of Mike Fisher in Colorado. The information he got from the people in Colorado is that he did not get in on a flight Friday night and had not gotten in yet; that he had left word with them over there to have Fisher call as soon as he came in. At approximately 3:00 p.m. this same date I was called and contacted by Sheriff Whipple of Aspen, Colorado, who stated that he had not been able to get ahold of the District Attorney, Mr. Tucker, and that he would find out from them what their feelings were on the case; if they were going to issue on Mr. Bundy, he would get back to me no later than noon on 2-2-76, Sunday.

I informed him at that time our great concern for knowing was because on Monday morning at 9:00 o'clock Mr. Bundy had to appear in our District Court for arraignment for an evading a police officer charge, and at that time we would possibly like to bring up some more court orders requesting his pubic hairs and head hairs from him so that we can send them back to the FBI Lab and compare them with Melissa Smith's; but we did not want to do this and tip our hand if they were going to arrest him, we would rather wait till the arrest went and then we would make the order and get them; that if not, we were going to request this and of course this would tip our hand that we had something big going again, as we would have to reveal some of the information in order to get this court order.

There is no further information at this time.

Jerry Thompson, Detective

On 2-2-76, Lt. Ron Ballantine and this detective, Jerry Thompson, went down to the Salt Lake County garage complex on 8th South and again went through suspect Bundy's Volkswagen car. The car was re-vacuumed again with an evidence vacuum. The seat covers were taken off of both front and rear seats. All items were packaged in evidence bags and were sent to the FBI Laboratory to be compared with the rest of the evidence we had obtained. The evidence was sent back on 2-3-76. Along with this group was sent a known hair sample of Carol DaRonch, given to this detective by Sgt. Paul Forbes of the Murray Police Department.

Again on 2-11-76 this officer went over to the City-County Board of Health and picked up an envelope containing two blood samples of Mr. Ted Bundy. They were taken from the chemist, Lynn Davis, on recommendation of Dave Yocom of the County Attorney's Office. One vial of blood was taken from the envelope by this detective, from the bottom of the envelope, it was cut. The vial was removed, it was then signed by this detective and taped back over and returned back to the County Board of Health, locked in their refrigerator. The vial was initialed by this officer and given to Lt. Baldridge from Aspen, Colorado, to take back and have analyzed through the Colorado State Bureau in regards to a case out of Grand Junction, Colorado.

On 2-18-76, another package was sent off to the FBI Laboratory by this detective containing three items: (1) a vacuumed sample from a pair of brown type slacks; (2) the pants themselves that belonged to Debra Kent from Bountiful. They were given to Lt. Ron Ballantine, Bountiful Police Department, by Debra Kent's father, and then turned over to this officer in an attempt to find any pubic hairs of hers in this pair of pants and have them compared with the hairs out of Mr. Bundy's Volkswagen.

Also, on 2-18-76 a court order from Judge Stuart Hansen Jr., was presented to this officer by Dave Yocom of the County Attorney's Office which in turn was given to Capt. Hayward. The order requests that Capt. Hayward and Sheriff Larson, Chief Dean Anderson, Lt. Ron Ballantine of Bountiful Police Department, and Chief Cal Gillen of Murray Police Department, Sgt. Paul Forbes of the Murray Police Department, turn over any documents, papers, or anything that pertains to the Carol DaRonch case to Dave Yocom of the County Attorney's Office, or to have anyone under their orders working for them, etc., having any of this to turn it over. This order was brought about by defense attorney John O'Connell.

This officer then went back through his case file and in my opinion the only item I could find that I have not given Mr. Yocom was a copy of the phone numbers which had been subpoenaed earlier on Mr. Bundy, which a copy is now made and given to Dave Yocom. The other two departments involved in the subpoena stated that they have also researched their files and Lt. Ballantine came up with a few reports, brought them down and gave them to Dave Yocom, and Sgt. Forbes from Murray stated that he believed that all his information was already in Dave Yocom's hands. After going over my file again as of 2-18-76, I do not see any other items in there pertaining to the Carol DaRonch case that Mr. Yocom does not have or has not received the information from this officer.

The report below contains a very revealing interview with a friend of Ted Bundy's who lived not at the rooming house at 565 First Avenue in Salt Lake City, Utah, but next door to the rooming house at 563 First Avenue. This report has been sitting in my very large case file—consisting of many thousands of pages—for many years, and I can't account for how or why I missed it, but I did. Therefore, I am happy to present to you the very revealing interview that Detective Jerry Thompson conducted with James Harvey Dunn.

On 2-11-76 this detective, Jerry Thompson; Lt. Ballantine, Bountiful Police Department; and Lt. Bill Baldridge, Pitkin County Sheriff's Office, Aspen, Colorado, made contact with a JAMES HARVEY DUNN living at 553 First Avenue # 8, telephone 363-1328. He is a mathematics major at the University of Utah. Mr. Dunn was confronted at his door by the above officers and asked if we might come in and talk to him. He refused to let us in his apartment, stating that it was messy, nor that he would talk to us. When

I identified him, and told him who I was, he stated he wondered why I had not been there sooner. I told him that I understood that he was a close friend of Mr. Ted Bundy, and he stated that was correct.

He stated that he has known Mr. Bundy from approximately September or October of 1974, when Mr. Bundy moved in the apartment house next door to him. He stated that he is a good friend of Ted, in fact last Sunday, which would be 2-8-76, Mr. Bundy was over at his apartment and had supper with him and his wife.

He stated that he had nothing to hide and that he would try to answer our questions.   He did state that Mr. John O'Connell, the defense attorney, had also talked to him numerous times. I asked him if John was going to have him as a witness, and he stated, "I don't know, he hasn't said anything to me about it. I don't know what I could testify to, other than that Ted was a very close friend of mine and that from what I know of him, I don't feel he is the man capable of doing the things that the press indicate that he is possibly involved in."

Also he stated that the state must not have too good of a case, he started out with a $100,000.00 bail and it has since been dropped to $15,000.00 and that would be an indication to him that they had an over-zealous prosecutor and overcharged him. He feels that it may be possible that the girl made a bad identification and wished us luck, stating, "May the best man win."

He was asked if he could tell me if Mr. Bundy had been out of town at any time during the fall of 1974 and also during the winter of 1975. He stated he did not know that. He did know during that time that he was gone a lot, but he states he did not know if he was out of town or not. He was asked specifically if he knows if Ted had ever been in Colorado, and he stated, "I can't answer that, I don't really know." He was asked if in his opinion there was anything unusual or odd about Mr. Bundy. He stated, "Yes, he's an oral – anal fetish."

In regards to his apartment, he stated the individual is immaculately clean, that he keeps everything spotless, and he thought that was very unusual for an individual. He was asked what Mr. Bundy had told him after his first arrest. He stated that he had told him that he had been picked up for burglary tools, but he stated Mr. Bundy had never told him at that time, he learned later from his attorney, about the pantyhose and the handcuffs, etc. He was asked what his opinion of that was. He stated, "That's the only thing that troubles me and that does make me wonder, and is very suspicious to me why anyone would have pantyhose with the eyes and so forth cut out of them and a pair of handcuffs." He stated, however, "I still don't feel that he's involved in what they say he was, he may be involved in some other illegal actions, I can't say."

He was then asked to describe Mr. Bundy's dress, the way he dressed. He stated that Mr. Bundy dressed rather casually, like he was, in a pair of Levis and things like that, and that he did wear sport coats and dress pants when he went out occasionally, but he was a very casual dresser. He was asked anything about his shoes. He stated he wore a lot of loafers most of the time, and pointed down to what I was wearing, which was a pair of patent leather loafers. He stated, "He wears a lot like yours, but of course they weren't patent leather."

I then stated to him, "Mr. O'Connell's been talking to you, hasn't he?" He stated, "Yes, he has." (Author's note: this is classic Jerry Thompson - a really nice guy, but a no-nonsense cop who saw through the BS and always countered it with a proper response. To make his point that he's not letting it go, Detective Thompson continues asking questions about the shoes.) *I said, "Have you ever seen Ted wearing a pair of patent leather shoes?" He said, "I've never seen him wear a pair and to my knowledge, I don't know if he ever owned a pair. He did wear loafers like that but they weren't patent leather."*

This individual also stated that he recalled Mr. Bundy when he moved down in the light-colored Volkswagen and that he did recall the tear that was in the back seat of it, when he came down to Utah, which he assumed was caused by the sun going through the back window. He was asked if he knew why Ted sold his car or what the circumstances were, and he stated, "No, I just assumed that he sold it because he made the statement that he needed money for his attorney and that that was one way that he could get money for his attorney by selling his car and that he was going to move to a closer place to school. And that he could walk to school."

He was asked if he knew where Mr. Bundy was staying at this time, and he hesitated, he then stated, "Yes I do, however, I don't think that I should tell you at this time without conversing with Mr. O'Connell or him." It appears that the individual has definitely been heavily prompted by either Mr. Bundy or his attorney as to what information to give us. He did not refuse to answer anything other than the whereabouts of Mr. Bundy. But it is the opinion of this officer that the individual could possibly be holding back some information that could be pertinent to us, however, it is hard to say.

On Wednesday, 3-3-76, at approximately 3:00 p.m., James Harvey Dunn, living at 553 First Avenue # 8, was waiting in my office for me. He stated that he wanted to talk to me. Mr. Dunn was one of the individuals who testified on behalf of Mr. Bundy, who lived in the apartment building next to him and was his closest friend. In fact, Mr. Bundy was best man at Dunn's wedding. Mr. Dunn was very antagonistic when I first interviewed him on 2-11-76, and he was also the same way in court. His first comment to me this date was, "I want to apologize," or "I'm sorry, I was a little hard on you the first time that I talked to you. I hope you can understand my point of view. I have known Ted since about September of 1974 and he has been my closest and my best friend, I thought. It was very hard for me to believe that he could possibly be responsible for the things that he's convicted of. Now that he is convicted, I don't know which way to go and which way to think. I would like to ask you personally do you truly believe without a shadow of a doubt that Ted was guilty." He stated, "I did not mean it that way. I'm sorry." I told him there was no doubt in my mind that Ted was definitely guilty of this case.

He asked me, he started to think now of the missing girls around the same time that this happened, etc.; he wanted to know if I thought Ted was involved with them. I told him I could not answer his question. He asked me if I was still investigating Ted, and I told him yes, he was still under investigation. He stated, "You know, it's hard to believe. The guy was over to my apartment almost continually, would have dinner, was with me and my wife lots of times, and he just never appeared to be anything like this. However, I will have to admit and say that I thought he was unusual to the effect that as a law student Ted never studied. I don't *recall him ever cracking a book. He was home during the day a lot. He was out at night a lot."*

He stated that he went away on a couple of vacations during 1975 to Seattle. And that he went over and took care of Ted's plants that he had in his apartment and took care of things for him, but there were several times during the early part of 1975, which he states, "I cannot remember exactly, but Ted would leave for two or three days at a time and would never say anything to me." He stated, "I thought it was unusual because I would usually take care of his plants, pick up his mail, etc., but he would not tell me on these particular days. When he'd come back I'd ask him why he didn't let me know he was going and I would have watered his plants and taken care of things. I can't remember his comment. It was something like, 'Well, I didn't know I was going, or something.'" Dunn stated he did not know where Ted went, Ted never did tell him and he doesn't know if he really ever asked Ted where he had been.

He was curious to know what had gone on in the trial, as he wasn't able to be there. I informed him I wasn't in the trial either. He wanted to know if he could read the transcript of the trial. I told him the county clerk's office would have it, and when it was transcribed it was a public record, to my knowledge, and that if he went down there he could possibly read it. He stated he did not know which way to turn now, that if there was anything that he could help the police with he would be more than willing to do so. He asked if I would come out and talk to him and his wife some night when I had time, as they wanted to talk to me. There may be something that he could do that would help this officer. And maybe I could help him more in his mind as he is thoroughly confused now, that he is not too sure that he really knew Ted. He stated, "I thought I knew him very well. We never went out on parties or anything like that, but I was in his apartment or he was in mine and I truly thought he was a fine young man. But some of the things I think of now were a little bit strange." I informed him that I would be more than happy to talk to him at a later date, that I would make an appointment with him to talk to him and his wife.

The following report is written by Detective Jerry Thompson, and it details the circumstances of the escape of Ted Bundy from the Garfield County jail in Glenwood Springs, Colorado.

On 12-31-77, Saturday at about 1:00 p.m. in the afternoon, I was contacted by telephone in my office by Mike Fisher, from Aspen, Colorado, where he informed me that he had just received information from the Garfield County Jail, that Ted Bundy had escaped sometime during the night, 12-30-77 to Saturday, 12 noon, December the 31st of 1977, that Ted Bundy escaped from the Garfield County Jail, by putting a shirt, stuffing the sleeves with newspaper hanging out one sleeve to give the appearance that he was in his bed and apparently escaped through a ceiling light fixture, which he removed, which has been loose for the past two years, according to the sheriff, and has not been welded because they have been having trouble getting someone to come in and weld it.

He stated that once through the ceiling, he could go across and down through the jailer's apartment that lives right next door. Took several shirts, a cap and ball rifle and a cap and ball pistol and then apparently walked out the front door. They have no idea or any indication of what time he left during the night or during the day. Since that time, the Colorado authorities filled an unlawful flight to avoid prosecution with the FBI out of the Denver office.

I have been in almost daily contact with the Salt Lake FBI office, Kirt Jensen, and on Tuesday, 1-3-78, this detective, along with Detective Dick Judd, Kirt Jensen from the FBI and Jay Farrington from the FBI, went to Tooele County, south of there, to a small community of Oefer (sic) *where we made contact with all the people that were home in this community, checking and attempting to see if Ted Bundy had made it to this area, as the FBI had received information that he was familiar with the area and that he would possibly go to that area.*

Several small caverns or caves or old mines in the area were checked by this officer and we were unable to turn up anything in this area. Contact was made with Tooele County Sheriff Bill Pitt. The situation was explained to him and he stated he would patrol that area and get back to us if he had any additional information.

The FBI came up with a name of a girl that had been visiting Ted in the jail over there by the name of Carole P. (Author's note: Actually, it's Carol Ann) *Boon, who supposedly lives at 10405 3rd Avenue, NW, Seattle, Washington, phone is 783-6331. They claim that she was in the Glenwood Springs area, approximately five days, the second week of December, visiting Bundy on a regular basis and departed for Seattle on the 16th of December.*

She has maintained continuous telephone contact with Bundy. Since that time this individual has been contacted by the Bureau and Bob Keppel of the King County Sheriff's office. They state that they do not believe she has had contact with Ted since his escape, but that in their opinion they do believe that she is in love with the individual and that his ties would be fairly close to her.

They have also made contact with his ex-girlfriend Elizabeth Koffer (Author's note: incorrect spelling of last name is spelled Kloepfer), *and many other associates in the Seattle area and have been unable to come up with anything pertinent at this time.*

A Scott Nelson, a former associate of Bundy's, who was living in the Canada area, where Bundy has made a call to him, was attempted to be located in Canada. They checked up there and was informed that he was possibly in the Sun Valley, Idaho area.

After a search was made of the Sun Valley, Idaho area, it was found that the individual had moved from there to the Salt Lake area and was living with his mother at 785 11th Avenue in Salt Lake.

Kirt Jensen of the FBI made contact with Scott, he made contact with his mother, who refused to tell them where he was at first, but stated that when she got a hold of him, she would have him call.

He later called the Bureau that night, was very reluctant to talk to them, however they did have an interview with him on the phone. I attempted to make contact with the individual several times at his home, but was unable to.

I then obtained a subpoena for this individual from Dave Yocom, the county attorney's office, requesting the interview to be held on Friday the 13th at 2:00 p.m.

I finally made contact by telephone with Scott's mother, informed her who I was, and asked her if she would please have him call me. She seemed to be very upset but stated that she would get the message to him. This was on Thursday, January the 12th. Later on in the afternoon, the individual called my secretary and informed her that he was not going to talk with me, and that if I wanted any information, I should contact Mike Fisher in Colorado, as he had talked to him before and was tired of being harassed. I immediately called him back and after some persuading to the individual on the phone, he reluctantly agreed to come in at 2:30 p.m. this date and talk to myself and Captain Hayward.

The individual came into the office that afternoon. After a short while with him he seemed to settle down and he was not so upset as he was at first.

He did not want me to tape his conversation, however. He basically went over when he met Bundy, which was in October of 1974, when Bundy moved into the apartment with him at 565 1st Avenue. He knew him from then until March, the last part of March when he moved out.

Stated that they had gone drinking a couple of times, had double-dated once or twice. Other than that he did not know the individual too awfully well, as he was studying at the U and he assumed that Ted was also.

He stated that he was very shocked to find out that Ted had missed almost the entire fall quarter, because he always left every morning and he assumed that he was going to college.

Scott also stated that he himself also left on weekends a lot, and does not know if Bundy was home, if he traveled, or what he did. If he did travel, he states that the individual never confided in him. He stated that the only vehicles that he knew Ted to have was a light brown or tan VW bug, and that he had an older model blue pickup truck that ran off and on.

He stated that he had never observed any scratches or marks or anything on Ted's face at any time. Ted was a neat dresser and kept himself rather neat all the time. He stated that they did go with Margaret Maughan who lived in the apartment at one time down to the Sun Lounge, that he was not aware of Ted having any girls up to his apartment, other than maybe for an hour or two to eat during the evening, and that he assumed that he was probably his closest friend, and he states yet that he was not that close.

He stated that when he came back to Salt Lake after he had moved, he was shocked to find out that Ted had been arrested, that it didn't seem possible to him, and that it was during the December months, just after Ted had bailed out of jail, that he ran into him in downtown Salt Lake where he was window shopping, he asked Ted a little bit about it, and Ted told him he was not allowed to discuss the matter on orders of his attorneys, so he stated he did not go into the matter.

He states he never heard or saw him since, but while Ted was in jail, he called his mother and wanted Scott's number, and that Ted did call him in Canada to talk to him.

He stated that he basically wanted to talk to him about the Laura Ann Aime case in Utah County, stating that the police were trying to involve him in that and also Scott and he just wanted him to be aware of it.

Scott denies ever being down in Utah County, Lehi, or in a café with Ted Bundy, where he was supposedly seen by some witnesses in Utah County. He states that he told the Utah County authorities and also Colorado authorities that, he's still sticking with that story that he never went down there with Ted, doesn't even know where the place is.

He was asked if he observed anything wrong with the seat in Ted's VW. He stated I don't know if it's from people asking me, but it seems to me that something was wrong with the passenger seat, that it was broken or something, but he can't put his finger on it.

He was also asked if he ever observed Ted with a pair of handcuffs. He stated here again, "Yes, I believe he did have a pair, but I just cannot remember for sure, where and how I saw them. I believe at one time he was playing around with them, and it seems to me that he put them on Margaret Maughan and hooked them onto the door," but he says, "I may be wrong there."

He was asked if he was aware of a meat block in Ted's apartment, he states that "Yes, Ted had got that after he had moved there from a want ad in the Salt Lake Tribune, and just more or less had it for a conversation piece."

He was asked if he knew anything about Ted's background, if he ever talked about it. He stated very little, but he did observe from being around him, that Ted did not like blacks or Orientals, for some reason. Other than that, he never talked too much about his home life. He was asked if he ever mentioned Liz, he stated no. He was asked if Ted ever mentioned a girlfriend in Seattle, he stated no, he didn't know that he had one.

The individual towards the end of the interview seemed to be cooperative, he assured the captain and myself, that if he heard from Ted or had any information, that he did not want to get involved in it, he did not want to get his life ruined in publicity in regards to the matter, that he would certainly give us a call.

He stated that if we had any more questions that we could call him, and he could try and answer them, however he was tired of being bothered by other agencies and that he was not going to talk to any other police department or agency, and that he would refer them back to us.

Because as he stated, this has got to end somewhere, and I don't want to get involved, and my life ruined for Ted, as I only knew him for six months, I lived in the same apartment building, and I'm sorry I ever met him.

The interview lasted for approximately two hours. As of 1-17-78, I still am in contact with the Colorado authorities and the FBI, out of Salt Lake, where I am kept abreast of any new leads or information in regards to the whereabouts of Ted, however, as of this date, nothing has come up whatsoever. Many leads have been checked out and proven to be false. All the phone numbers that Ted called with his credit card have been and are being checked out by the FBI Office and nothing has come up from them.

At this time the FBI is considering putting Ted on the Ten Most Wanted Fugitives, but the decision has not come down from the Washington office.

Just before the escape, Ted had won a change of venue, from the Aspen County Courthouse for his trial to Colorado Springs, Colorado, and this tentatively scheduled for January the 9th, with the same judge, Judge Lore presiding.

However due to his escape, this was cancelled and who knows when a new trial date will ever be set.

The below transcription is of a telephone conversation between Detective Jerry Thompson and an Undersheriff Hart, concerning the escape of Ted Bundy, and it follows a normal Q&A pattern:

December 31, 1977

A: Hello.

Q: Sheriff?

A: Yeah.

Q: This is Jerry Thompson, Sheriff's Office in Salt Lake. Just talked to Mike Fisher a minute ago and we're trying to get a broadcast out on Bundy over here, but I didn't get a description if he's wearing a beard, mustache, or anything you could help us with.

A: Now, now you bet, his hair is not too short, of course it's dark brown, and he just has a mustache and sideburns about halfway down to his ears, they say he shaved off his whiskers again.

Q: Okay.

A: And to the best of my knowledge, he would have, if he, I don't find those boots that he brought over here from Point of the Mountain (Author's note: the nickname for the Utah State Prison).

Q: Um hum.

A: And of course they got them marked you know and he got a bunch of his shirts out of the apartment, he went over the top of the sales, and come down in the apartment and he got a bunch of short-sleeved shirts out of there, all different colors.

Q: Out of an apartment?

A; Yeah, the jailer's apartment.

Q: Oh, I see.

A: And when he did, now he didn't take any coats with him, and he's got on blue jeans, and he took a muzzle loading rifle and a muzzle loading Derringer.

Q: Okay.

A: He didn't take any ammunition but he just got them, of course he can hock them.

Q: Um hum.

A: But he had about $7 in change on him and that's all I can see that the guy took. (Author's note: Bundy had over $700 with him as he escaped. This was money that had been sent to him by family and friends and was to be used to pay his attorneys and other legal expenses, and Bundy apparently had access to it. But the particulars of why he was allowed access to this money, which turned out to be a major mistake, is unknown to this author.)

Q: We got a time limit on him at all, Sheriff?

A: I wish I could answer that one.

Q: (Chuckles)

A: No, they called me at 12:10, I was eating lunch at home and they called me at 12:10, and said that Bundy was missing, and come to find out no one has seen him since about seven last evening and he fixed his bunk you know so that it looked like he was in there. And he stuffed one of the sleeves of his shirt with paper and put it out from under the cover, you see, so it looked like he was laying on his side and his arm was out from under the cover.

Q: Um hum.

A: So it looked like his arm there, and fixed it up and left it that way, one of the oldest ruses there are.

Q: And how did he get out of the cell, sheriff?

A: Well, they tore a light fixture out of there years ago and we've never been able to get the damn welders in here, they don't like to come in (here) *and work.*

Q: Um hum.

A: And we can't get the welder in here to fix it up, well, he just went out through there, it's about a foot square.

Q: But then does that get him outside the jail, or just into another area?

A: No, it got him into the jailer's apartment, then they've got a front door on that apartment which leads out into the street and he just walked out that way.

Q: I see, okay, well, I don't know if there's any indication he'll come back here in the area, but we wanted to get a broadcast and everything out as soon as we could.

A: Well, I'll appreciate anything you can do.

Q: Okay, if there's anything...

A: And I don't, I don't want any layman cripples, you don't need to send him back.

Q: Ha, ha, ha, I know just what you mean, if there's anything we can do over here sheriff to help you, why, don't hesitate to give us a call.

A: I certainly will.

Q: Okay.

A: And I appreciate your help very much.

Q: Thank you very much, sheriff.

A: You bet.

Q: Bye.

A: Bye.

INFORMATION

Melissa Smith Criminal Homicide

Report by Detective Jerry Thompson

On 3-21-77, Mike Fisher from Aspen, Colorado, and Milton K. Blakey, who is Chief Deputy out of the District Attorney's Office in Colorado Springs, Colorado. His telephone number is (303) 475-8500. Arrived in Salt Lake City and a conference was held Monday, Tuesday, and half of Wednesday, with these individuals, this detective, Dave Yocom, from the Salt Lake County Attorney's Office, Sergeant Paul Forbes from Murray PD, and Brent Bullock from county attorney's office in Utah County. Numerous other officers and people were contacted during this time, as they are preparing for their case on Ted Bundy, which goes to court April 4, 1977.

They made contact with several of the witnesses in the Salt Lake area in regard to their case. They were unable to make contact with Rose Mary Shearer, which had been used as a witness in the Carol DaRonch case. They asked this detective if I would make contact with her. Contact was made with Rose Mary Shearer at her apartment, which is in the Stratford Hotel in Salt Lake City, 169 East 2nd South, Apartment 301. She's living there with her younger sister and her mother.

They requested that I show her some pictures of some coats out of a magazine that they had left me, to see if she could identify any one of them or any resemblance to them that Mr. Bundy had worn during the time that she had lived across the hall from him. She was shown the pictures and stated, "It's been so long ago, I just can't tell you. I do believe, and in fact I am sure, that he had several jackets like windbreakers, of the slick finish, nylon type." She says, "I believe they were dark blue, but they could have been a different color. They did zip up in the front." And she was just not sure if they looked like the ones in the photo, or in the picture *or not. She says, "They could have been." But it's been too long for her to really tell.*

Also, they requested if I could get them another driver's license photo of a Scott Wesley Nelson (Author's note: individual's date of birth redacted by me). That driver's license no. is: XXXXXXXX. Two photos were acquired of this individual and the one will be mailed back to them; and contact was made with our intelligence division in an attempt to come up with his telephone number that he had when he was living in Salt Lake in '74 and '75, so that a subpoena may be served on that number in an attempt to come up with any long-distance phone calls this individual made. He is currently residing in Ontario, Canada. I do not have the exact address, but Utah County does and they have had the Royal Mounties in Canada make contact with this individual. Checking with the University of Utah, the only thing they have on this individual is he did graduate from the U of U in 1975, and at that time the only address they had was 421 West 800 South in Bountiful, Utah. They have no other information on this individual at this time.

At this time, it is noted that Bret Bullock from the Utah County Attorney's Office states that they have come up with some pertinent information in regard to the Laura Aime homicide down there, where they can now positively put Bundy with Laura Aime. Details of that instance will be in their reports, and a copy will be obtained by this detective for my file. Also, they are going over some of the evidence that they have now come up with down there, and have requested that the tires from Bundy's Volkswagen be removed so that they can send them back to the lab and compare them with two tire casts that they have now found in their evidence room. This detective will be working with the Utah County Attorney's Office in regard to this new evidence that they have come up with in regard to Bundy. That information will be kept on additional follow-ups as it comes in.

The following report concerns the Intermountain Crime Conference, which was held at the Holiday Inn in Aspen, Colorado, on November 14 and 15 of 1975. The report was written by Detective Jerry Thompson of the Salt Lake County Sheriff's Office.

On 11-12-75, Capt. Hayward, Sgt. Paul Forbes of Murray PD and this detective left for Aspen, Colorado, for a conference being held there at the Holiday Inn in regard to suspect Ted Bundy and the missing girls in the Intermountain West. The conference was held on the 13th and 14th of November in Aspen. Represented from the state of Utah, other than the three mentioned above, were Chief Anderson of Bountiful PD, Detective Ira Beal of Bountiful PD, Jay Hunt of Davis County Sheriff's Office, Dave Yocom from the Salt Lake County Attorney's Office, and Chris W. Eskridge from the Utah County Sheriff's Office. There were representatives from the state of Washington, from the state of California, and several agencies in the state of Colorado. A list of every individual at the meeting is attached in my file.

Ted Bundy was discussed from his time of birth up until the present with all the background that has been done on him by all agencies involved, plus all the evidence and the cases of all agencies were discussed in general. It was a very beneficial meeting and it enlightened all agencies of just what everyone else had and what everyone is up against and what they have to look for. There was nothing that came out of the meeting that would help us or any other agencies file a case at this time. Tapes were made of the individuals making their presentations at this meeting and are contained in my case file. This meeting was hosted by the Pitkin County Sheriff's Office in Aspen, Colorado, and was concluded on 11-14-75.

On 11-20-75, Ted Bundy was released from the Salt Lake County Jail at approximately 5:00 p.m. on a cash bail apparently put up by his mother and father who were in town at the time. Also on this same day it was learned by Deputy County Attorney Dave Yocom that Mr. Bundy had two titles to his 1968 Volkswagen. One of them was given to Vince Walton, the bondsman, and the other one was given to the Severson boy whom he sold his Volkswagen to. He had applied for a duplicate title some time ago and had signed both of them over. In regard to this situation, a complaint was signed by Deputy County Attorney Dave Yocom for fraudulently obtaining a motor vehicle title, or something in regard to that phrase. The bail was currently set at $2,500.00 on it. The following morning, on 11-21-75, Mr. Bundy appeared in Judge Grant's Court for the preliminary hearing on the aggravated kidnapping charge. At this time the subject was arraigned on this count and was placed on his OR (own recognizance) in regard to that, the judge stating he was already out on bail for another case. The trial lasted the entire day of Friday, 11-21-75, at which time Mr. Bundy, during his recess, made press releases to the press; he was very jovial, very happy, very talkative to everyone.

The case was then continued over the weekend to Monday morning, 11-24-75. It was held in the judge's chambers between Dave Yocom, Mr. Bundy's attorney John O'Connell, and Mr. Bundy himself. The judge then took it under advisement until Wednesday, 11-26-75 at 1:30 p.m. and the judge gave his decision stating *that the subject was bound over to the district court on aggravated kidnapping and that the judge was dropping the attempted criminal homicide charge, as he saw no evidence representing this type of crime. The subject then sneaked out the back of the courtroom and took off on a rather hurried walk through the halls and across the parking lot, not speaking to any news media or to anyone attempting to talk to him. He appeared to have just the reverse as when he first went into the courtroom, as he was very happy and jovial at first and now he was completely reversed.*

On 11-25-75, the F.B.I. Laboratory called our office and talked to Detective Forbes, telling him that from the samples of stuff sent back to them from the Volkswagen, they had definitely come up with human hair samples and that if we could send them back any samples to compare then with, they would see what they could come up with. They also told him that they had come up with a plastic type substance in the vehicle which represented, as near as they could tell, something that buttons and clothing would come with or be made, and to send anything back to compare that with, if we could. A sample of Melissa Smith's hair, which was already sent back to the FBI lab once before, is being re-submitted to them. Also, Vern Harrington of Utah County Sheriff's Office was informed of this, and he stated he would send the slides of hair from Laura Aime back to the lab. Detective Keppel of King County Sheriff's Office in Seattle stated that he would send back the hair samples of his girls up there that he had. Contact has not been made yet with Lt. Baldridge of Aspen, Colorado, in regard to his girl. Contact will be made with him, and all samples of female hair which we do have throughout the three states should

*be mailed off to the FBI laboratory before the middle
of the first week in December.*

CHAPTER THIRTEEN

REPORT ON THE KIMBERLY DIANE LEACH MURDER

Ted Bundy's last murder was the slaying of twelve-year-old Kimberly Diane Leach. What follows is the report from Investigator, James L. Daugherty, of the Lake City Police, Florida. While the first portion of this document is heavily redacted (they even redacted the name of the victim, but I have replaced these redactions with her name), readers will easily be able to follow it, and it paints a good picture of what it was like during those days. The second part deals directly with Ted Bundy and those who interacted with him while he stayed at the Holiday Inn in Lake City, Florida. For those of you who've read my book, *The Bundy Murders: A Comprehensive History* (the main book in my Bundy series now consisting of four books), you may remember the names of these witnesses, as I wrote about them while telling the story of the Kimberly Leach murder. However, for this book, I wanted to present the "raw" reports.

On February 9, 1978, at 3:26 P.M. the Lake City Police Department received a call from Thomas Leach of (Redacted). Mr. Leach advised that his daughter, Kimberly Diane Leach, age 12, was missing from the junior high school where she was a seventh-grade student. He also advised that the last time she was seen was around 9:00 A.M. that morning. A BOLO (be on the lookout) *was put out to all our units and* with the Sheriff's Office. On February 10, in the early morning hours, I received a call from Frieda Leach, the mother of Kimberly Diane Leach, she called me and advised that Kimberly had not returned home and she was very upset and worried and was in fear of foul play.

I did respond to Morris Williams the assistant principal of the junior high school, who resided on McFarland Avenue, with a resident telephone number of XX. After talking with Mr. Williams it was ascertained that Kimberly Leach, had in fact been at school the morning before, during the ninth (9th), Thursday, and had attended homeroom class and from homeroom class had attended the first period class which was in this case PE (physical education). Physical education was being held in the auditorium that day due to the foul weather outside.

The first bell rings at 8:30 a.m. and then the bell rings again at 8:35 a.m. which is the tardy bell for homeroom. Homeroom is a session for ten (10) minutes. At 8:45 a.m. the bell rings allowing the students four (4) minutes to go from homeroom to first (1st) period, then the bell rings at 8:49 a.m. This bell indicates that first period is in session. Kimberly Diane Leach had already attended homeroom which was taught by John L. Bishop of XX Street. While being in first (1st) period which is taught by Mrs. Caldwell, who resides at the corner of Montana and Broadway Street, Lake City. The physical education teacher, Mrs. Caldwell, she received a note, at approximately 9:15 a.m. by (redacted), a student of John L. Bishop. John L. Bishop had sent (redacted) with a note to Mrs. Caldwell to advise that Kimberly Diane Leach should return to her homeroom class and retrieve her blue denim purse which she had left in the room while attending her homeroom. This note was received at approximately 9:15 a.m. Kimberly Diane Leach did leave the auditorium area where physical education was being held that day with (redacted).

They did traverse the area of approximately 100 yards from the auditorium across the basketball courts and entered the south side of central building. They did stop and get a drink of water just inside the door and walked to the second classroom on the left which was John L. Bishop's and both students did enter the room and Kimberly Leach did retrieve her purse. While retrieving her purse she did joke briefly one student (redacted

Kimberly Leach left the homeroom, walking south the same way she came into central and opened the double doors at the end of the central building and exited those doors, this was viewed by (redacted) and several of the other students in the class. They viewed her walking south down the hallway but it appears that (redacted) was in a position to observe Kimberly Leach open the double doors and exit the building, in fact the same way that entry was gained by (redacted) and (redacted). This being at approximately 9:17 a.m.

This was arrived by putting (redacted) under hypnosis and she did advise at 9:13 a.m. is when she left the room to get Kimberly Leach, she looked at the clock and figuring the time it would take to walk the hundred yards over and the hundred yards back. At the time of the disappearance of Kimberly Leach, she was wearing a brown coat, three-quarter length, trimmed in white fur, this coat having a hood also trimmed in white fur. The trimming being at the cuffs, at the tail of the coat, and around the hood. She had on a sky-blue perforated football jersey with the red numeral 83 over a pullover white blouse. Now this pullover type blouse *was underneath the blue football jersey. She had on a training bra, a regular pair of panties, the name brand unknown at this time, a pair of blue jeans, a brown pair of shoes, suede-type two-tone shoes with a smooth crepe sole. She had on a very small delicate choker-type gold chain necklace. She had a gold ring with a green oblong stone. She had on gold loop earrings, her ears were pierced.*

She was twelve (12) years of age, she was five (5) foot tall, weighed approximately one hundred (100) pounds, she had shoulder-length hair parted in the center, and she had pretty, well-formed teeth. She also had a scar on one of her knees, the mother could not advise which one it was that had the scar.

Several people that should have been or were near or around the campus, were interviewed, it was ascertained that one of the janitors, Eddie Goodbread, Route 49, Lake City, Florida, the janitor for approximately twelve (12) or fourteen (14) years and the driver of a 1978 white Buick Riviera with pinstripes and a red interior had just pulled up to the south side of Central as the two girls were entering central. It seems as though Mr. Goodbread got out of his car and walked into the south side of central behind the girls but not seeing the girls. The girls entered the room just before Mr. Goodbread entered the building. Mr. Goodbread had walked past the room and was preparing to exit the building on the other end as Kimberly Leach came back out of the room and was exiting the building behind Eddie Goodbread in the opposite end of the building and in the opposite direction.

I interviewed Mr. Goodbread at length by myself as well as patrolman Parrish and Tommy Trammel of the Second Circuit State Attorney's Office and it is ascertained that he did not see anything that he could recall. That he just simply drove up, got out of his car, walked through central and to the office of the main building without noting anything. He did advise that he would be hypnotized if we so desired to see if we could get any further information.

Subsequently after talking to Mr. Williams, the assistant principal, he advised that I should talk with one (redacted), *age 14, of* (redacted), *in reference to him seeing Kimberly being apparently abducted by a black male driving a blue 4 door Chevrolet at the northeast corner of the campus Thursday morning.* (Author's note: this false story of the abduction of Kimberly Leach goes on for a paragraph or two, and is followed by other perhaps well-meaning, but completely false, renderings of the abduction, and because these are not relevant to the actual case of her abduction, I will pass over them and pick up where the story gets back on track.)

Kimberly's parents were interviewed numerous times by myself and Patrolman Parrish, myself and Chief Philpot, myself and Tommy Trammel (of the Second Judicial Circuit State Attorney's Office). On every occasion questions were posed to them that they always answered and appeared to be truthful, appeared to be remorseful, or anyhow at a loss by the disappearance of Kimberly Leach. They at no time ever felt that Kimberly Leach had left home or was a runaway as she had never before ever skipped school, skipped classes, or even run-off from home before, that she had no problems at home, that she had never really wanted for anything that she didn't get, that is anything within reason, and that as a matter of fact that she had just been elected runner-up queen of the Valentine dance that was coming up on the eleventh (11th) of February. And that her mother Frieda Leach and (redacted) *had already picked out a dress that she was going to wear to that dance. That Kimberly was real elated about the dance and surprised that she fared as well in the contest and was looking forward to the dance with much anxiety.*

Sharon Morgan, a sister of Frieda Leach, who lived next door to the Leach's for over a year, at that same trailer park which the Leach's now reside in, described them as a normal family and that they never had any out of the way arguments or any problems and found them to be a very close family.

Interviews with Kimberly's teachers which was Mr. Opperman, the principal of the junior high school, Mrs. Newell, Mrs. Caldwell, the PE teacher, Mr. Bishop, Morris Williams the assistant principal, Mr. Bishop being her homeroom teacher. Talking with all these teachers, they all generally agreed that Kimberly was quiet, very studious, made good grades, never skipped school or very seldom was absent and was, all in all, a good average student.

On February 11, 1978, a news release and photograph of Kimberly Leach were released to channel 12, channel 4, and channel 17 of Jacksonville, channel 20 of Gainesville, the Florida Times Union, and the Lake City Reporter. Also, Agent King of the FBI in Jacksonville contacted this office and advised us that he had been contacted by several residents of the Lake City area and had been requested to enter the case of missing Kimberly Diane Leach. Of course, he informed them as well as myself that he had no jurisdiction in this case, that is the FBI had no jurisdiction, and that they would render any technical assistance or any professional advice that the Lake City Police department so desired in this case but until a kidnapping or an across state lines crime had been committed, that they would not enter into the case.

On February 12, 1978, being Sunday, members of the Lake City Police Department searched the school grounds and the school. Now this search was literally from top to bottom. We went underneath the school, checked the sand under the school, checked in the attic, on top of the roof, and in every nook and cranny throughout the entire school buildings and campus. The woods to the rear and south of the school were checked, walked out as they were on Saturday. The Lakes in the immediate area, being Lake DeSoto, Lake Isabell, and Alligator Lake, were checked by boat; and a search of the woods around the lake was conducted and lead by Chief Paul Philpot.

Searches were also conducted of the wooded area behind the Columbia High School North Campus, around the old country club area over to Country Club Road, the woods located to the rear and north of Ken's Bar-B-Que, South First Street, northward all the way to Ivy's Trailer park; all of the woods all the way over to the residential area west of that area.

The wooded areas behind Summers Elementary School from Grandview Avenue all the way around Brown Road including the entire area of the city limits of the southwest portion of the limits were searched.

The homeroom class of Mr. John L. Bishop was visited by myself and Patrolman Parrish. We addressed the entire class asking for that information would lead to the locating of Kimberly Diane Leach or any information in reference to the disappearance of Kimberly Diane Leach. None could be furnished and again on Monday morning, being the 13th, Patrolman Parrish and myself visited the first period class of Mr. Bishop's, which would have been the class that Kimberly Diane Leach retrieved her book from. We introduced ourselves to the entire class and asked for any information that may be beneficial to us in locating Kimberly Diane Leach or to her disappearance. (Redacted) *said that she saw Kimberly come into Mr. Bishop's room and pick up her purse but had no further information.* (Redacted), *a student, stated that Kimberly joked with him briefly when she came in to pick up her purse.* (Redacted) *stated that he saw Kimberly come into Mr. Bishop's room and pick up her purse and leave the room and he was also interviewed again on February 18, 1978, as were the other two and no new information or nothing different was gained from these three people.*

Parrish and myself also interviewed the first period class of PE, that being the class that Kimberly Diane Leach left from and never returned, with no one being able to furnish any information other than that she was seen at class and was also observed leaving with (redacted). *No one saw her return.*

The residences surrounding the two (2) blocks that the Junior High School is located on were all canvassed by myself and Patrolman Parrish, no one observed anything out of the ordinary or unusual and subsequently no information was gained or obtained that would have been any benefit in this investigation.

On February 14, 1978, in the a.m., Chief Paul Philpot advised me that he had requested that the FDCLE enter the case and he stated to me that the FDCLE's feelings were essentially the same as the FBI and that they did not wish to enter the case at this time until more evidence was obtained indicating that the girl had in fact been abducted.

The names and addresses and telephone numbers of Mr. Leach's family in Tennessee were provided to the FBI in hope that they would check up there for any information that may lead to the whereabouts of Kimberly Diane Leach. We were informed that they did not think it was necessary and would just advise that we hold on to them by Agent King and Agent Cooke of the FBI. Searches were held or conducted in all of the wooded areas of the city limits and immediately surrounding areas throughout the week and the school was repeatedly searched from top to bottom again and again daily for the remainder of the week. Various leads were checked by Patrolman Parrish and myself, leads which I've found to be of no benefit to this case or proved to be false information and subsequently won't be mentioned in this particular report.

A list of students that were tardy, absent, or dismissed early was obtained from the school in hopes it may reveal some light on this case, it did not. A list of all the CETA program workers that were working on the campus was obtained. Background investigations of all these individuals were checked with no bearing on this case. A background check of Mr. Williams, the assistant principal was also conducted in depth and revealed nothing detrimental or of no value to this case. Also Mr. Bishop was questioned at length and his background was also checked in depth with no bearing to this case. Lanny Crosier, a teacher with Niblack School was also interviewed with no value to this case. Ray Hart, a PE teacher, was also interviewed, he had nothing to render to this investigation and he was absent that day due to an illness in his family.

We obtained a list of all sex offenders throughout the entire third judicial circuit and a review of those revealed nothing pertinent to this investigation.

CHAPTER FOURTEEN

BUNDY FLORIDA ARREST REPORTS

The below report concerns the arrest of Ted Bundy, and the first of this report deals with the stolen credit cards Bundy had with him when he was apprehended. Because I have dealt with the credit cards sufficiently in two of my previous books in this series, I will skip this and avoid redundancy. However, the report continues with Bundy's appearance and strange actions during this period. While I have quoted from this report for my first book, I am presenting the full document here.

Lieutenant Boatwright, of the FHP had secured all these evidentiary items which were the vouchers and folios and the credit card receipts from the Holiday Inn and turned these items over to Tommy Trammel of the Second Judicial Circuit State Attorney's Office. I will attempt to relate the way these cards were used as according to an interview with Karen Elizabeth Tadlock, Rt. 5 Box 132, Lake City, Florida. The telephone number being a Branford Extension. She is the assistant innkeeper at the Holiday Inn at the Lake City exit at I-75 and US 90.

Evidence item #2 was a dining room charge voucher for the evening of February 8, 1978, which indicates that, two beers had been purchased and that the subject ate at the buffet. The check number was (redacted) *and it was charged to evidence item #1A, which was a charge voucher, which was in turn put in a folio which is evidence item #1 at the desk which was number* (redacted). *David Cane was the waiter and Doris Whitehead was the dining room cashier. The Evans subject* (Author's note: Bundy was using the credit card of a Mr. Evans) *checked in at 8:44 p.m., February 8,1978, Pearl Walker, Dale Sconyers, Randy Jones, and Denise Lee were the desk clerks. Evidence item #4 is a disco lounge voucher, a bar tab which indicated that he sat at the bar and not at a table. He charged four gins and one draft beer. The lounge is open from 8:00 p.m. to 12:00 p.m. February 8, 1978. The amount $6.40 was charged to his room. The subject did sign the voucher, he also changed the names.*

On February 19, 1978, at 10:55 p.m., I did talk with Sharon Colquitt, who was the bartender at the Holiday Inn on February 8, 1978, and did wait on Mr. Evans (Author's note: Bundy) *who showed her a room key and wrote "Miller" on the top of the ticket after he had signed Miller at the bottom. He advised that he was Evans at first. He was sitting with another man, it was on a Wednesday night and he sat on the third seat south of the curve in the bar and the bar running from east to west and then south and he was at the west end of the bar at the curve.*

Wednesday night was a very busy night at the bar and Mrs. Colquitt states that she was training a new bartender named Joe, the rest of his name in unknown as he never returned. A lot of loud music and dancing, she could not remember if the "Evans" subject got up at all. She stated that she couldn't remember anything about the other man and that they were standing together preparing to leave when Evans signed the ticket before he left.

On February 19, 1978, I talked to William Dale Sconyers, who was the desk clerk at the Holiday Inn

TED BUNDY'S MURDEROUS MYSTERIES | 269

on February 8, 1978. He checked in the subject, Ralph Miller (Author's note: this was Bundy using the stolen credit card of Ralph Miller) *on February 8, 1978. His hair appeared to be greasy, dark, and dirty, about collar length, a Fu Manchu-type mustache, about 12- or 13-day beard. He had a slender face, looked weird, high forehead, acted doped up, slow speaking, slow filling out forms, medium slow voice, eyes appeared to be dilated, he was slow answering questions posed him, such as when he was leaving and vehicle information. He had a green army jacket, sleeves appeared to be short or ¾ sleeves. He had a flat forehead. Mr., Sconyers stated that he may be able to identify this man in a live lineup.*

That same night I talked with Randy Alton Jones, who was also a desk clerk on February 8, 1978, at I-75 and US 90. He was present when the subject checked in. He observed a white male, a day or two old beard, hair dirty, not washed for a day or two, he looked either drunk or spaced out, he acted funny, slurred his words, his clothes were rough, may have had on Levis, the clothes went along with his shabby appearance. His hair was a little below his ears, dark hair. The desk was very busy at the time. Showing him a six-photo spread, he positively identified Bundy as the subject that checked in under the name Ralph Miller.

Joseph Rucinski is a porter at the Holiday Inn. Mr. Rucinski states that he was unloading a tour bus around 9:00 p.m. on February 8, 1978, at the Holiday Inn at I-75 and US 90, and noticed a white Dodge van with white bumpers and windows in the rear doors. He did not think it had hubcaps. The truck appeared to be brand new. He did not notice a tag. The next morning on February 9, 1978, he had to load the same tour bus between 7:30 and 8:00 a.m., and the truck or the van was still there. The reason for him noticing the van was because he was sort of into vans and wondered if the van had been bought for customizing. He notices all vans and imagines how he could fix them up by painting and customizing them, etc. He also had to walk around this van in order to get into the bus properly. This van was located on the northeast side of the parking area at the northeast corner of the Holiday Inn property, being very close to room 443, used by the person who we later identified to be Bundy.

In closing out Bundy's final murder, the killing of little Kimberly Leach, I would like to pass along some reflections of Robert J. Cook, a minister that was on staff at Parkview Baptist Church in Lake City at the time of the murder. Kimberly Leach was a member of the church, and her funeral was conducted at Parkview. Indeed, Bob told me when we first started communicating, that the murder of Kim Leach hit both the church and the city very hard. The funeral for Kim Leach was the second largest in attendance, being surpassed only after the death of a police officer. Indeed, the reverberations of her murder can still be felt today in this small Floridian city.

When I asked Bob about the mood of the church after Kim Leach went missing, he spoke of *"a mixture of fear, confusion, and hope for the best."* Of course, after her remains were discovered, the effect on the church was devastating. Speaking of it recently, he said, "There was great sadness, grief for the family and friends, shock and horror at the way she was treated, a general fear for personal safety, and a great hatred for Ted Bundy. The mood of the church and the entire city became very dark. Great fear and hatred gripped a town formerly known for its love and forgiveness."

CHAPTER FIFTEEN

A LETTER FROM BUNDY'S ROOMMATE

John E. Muller

This is the testimony of John E. Muller, a roommate of the Rogers rooming house in Seattle, Washington, who knew Ted Bundy and had some interactions with him. The following letter, which has been sitting deep within the official record, has never before (to my knowledge) been published in whole or in part, and is addressed to Detective Roger Dunn, King County Police, 516 3rd Avenue, Seattle, Washington, 98104.

Mr. Dunn,

I am writing this letter in regard to your investigation of Mr. Ted Bundy. I met Mr. Bundy when I moved into a rooming house at 4143 12th Street NE, Seattle, Washington. I moved in during the month of August 1973. I moved out of the house approximately June of 1974. During my stay there, I, on occasions, had conversations with Mr. Bundy as well as the other two roommates. Ted left the house late fall of 1973 (Author's note: this is incorrect. Bundy left for Utah on September 2, 1974) *heading for Utah to attend law school. Thus, I knew Ted for only five months, if that. Most of our conversations dealt with politics and courses we took at school. Recollecting my brief acquaintance with Ted, I do not feel that I'm a very good judge of his total character or personality.*

I was shocked to hear that Ted was being investigated as a suspect in the "Ted" murders. During the time I knew him, he was easy to get along with, very spirited, kind, and intelligent. In my opinion, he led a very normal life at that time, for a student. He studied hard and maintained a normal social life. Most of the time I lived in the house, Ted was very busy at school in Tacoma or visiting with his fiancée. Occasionally, once or twice a week, I had a chance to talk with him, and on rare occasions we played racket ball at the University's IMA building. That was the extent of my contact with Ted Bundy.

Ted left the house late fall of 1973 (incorrect) *and returned only once in 1974, five or six months later. He mentioned that he was transferring to a law school in Utah because it offered a better academic program and his fiancée's parents who resided in Utah recommended the school. He had mentioned too, that he might marry her after law school. Ted returned to the house on 12th in 1974 to clear up some long distance phone calls with Freda the land lady and to sell an old bicycle (broken down) that had been in the garage for several years. Mainly he stopped by just to visit. He got along well with everyone in the house. I only saw and spoke to him once, for a brief time, during his return to Seattle. He stayed with his fiancée or his folks during that stay. I haven't heard from Ted since.*

As far as characteristics go, he had none which seemed odd or abnormal. I recall he is left handed from the racket ball games we played. He was always well mannered and very friendly. At no time did Ted ever seem anything but a gentleman. He liked all

TED BUNDY'S MURDEROUS MYSTERIES | 273

sports, particularly, bicycling, snow skiing, and tennis. Socially, he liked to have a beer once in a while. Twice we went out for a beer. Once at the Northlake Tavern, another time at the Pipeline Tavern. He smoked once in a while but not heavily enough to classify him as a smoker. Ted almost always wore turtleneck shirts, they were his favorite style. Once during the time I knew him he grew a beard but shaved it off no sooner than he grew it. The events and facts above are all that I recall at this time. I am sorry I can't be more specific but it's been a while. I hope they can provide some help to you in this investigation. As I mentioned earlier, Mr. Bundy occupied most of his time studying or with his fiancée, and with my own schedule being very busy I could hardly say I know him well.

Mr. Dunn, again I am quite surprised to hear of Ted's arrest in this case. I would appreciate any information you could give me regarding his arrest and the progress of the investigation. If there is any way I could help you further in this investigation, please feel free to call. I would be very glad to help. Hope this letter will be of some help.

Sincerely,

John E. Muller

CHAPTER SIXTEEN

INTERVIEWS AND TESTIMONIES
OF OTHER WITNESSES

I. Kathy Kleiner

Kathy Kleiner was born Kathy Nordin, in Miami, Florida, on December 22, 1957. And while we know her life became quite tumultuous with her encounter with Ted Bundy in the early morning hours of January 15, 1978, her early years were tumultuous as well. From a young age, she was forced to face unpleasant and, in fact, life-changing events that young people should never have to experience. Her father, Jackson Nordin, passed away after experiencing his third heart attack when Kathy was only five years old. At the age of thirteen, she was diagnosed with Systemic Lupus Erythematosus; a life-long and sometimes debilitating disease.

Despite the death of her father and having to learn to cope with the unexpected disease, Kathy again found happiness when her mom married Harry Kleiner. As she explained to me in a recent phone call, Harry Kleiner was a good man, and their home became a very loving one. Life became good again for Kathy and her two siblings, and as the years stretched forth, the children grew into strong adults.

A native of Florida, Kathy enrolled at Florida State University in the fall of 1976, and almost immediately made it known that she wanted to become part of Chi Omega sorority. Living in the all-female Reynolds Hall at the start of school, she'd become a "Pledge" of Chi Omega by December of that year; and by the spring of 1977, had achieved her dream of becoming a full-fledged member of Chi Omega.

Although Kathy was busy with school activities and with Chi Omega, she also had a life outside of the university realm. A Christian, Kathy joined the Wesley Chapel as soon as she arrived in Tallahassee, and this church atmosphere provided friendships and fellowship seemingly at every turn. Kathy told this writer that she attended activities (such as pot-luck dinners) often and, in fact, found herself going to church-related functions a great deal. Indeed, in the afternoon of January 14, 1978 (and only hours before the attack), she attended a wedding at the Wesley Chapel before returning home sometime after 6:00 p.m. As she walked into Chi Omega that late afternoon, she had no idea that evil that would be visited upon them in the wee hours of the following morning. Kathy said she believes she got to bed between 10:00 and 11:00 p.m.

Ted Bundy, who'd been trying without success to abduct someone throughout the evening of the 14th, would soon decide on a course of action that finally brought him the results he was looking for. Records show he chased a woman down the street, only to have her outrun him. The woman, Cheryl Rafferty, an FSU student living in Reynold's Hall, gave a description that fit Bundy and identified the type of clothes he was wearing that night, which matched what Nita Neary, a Chi Omega sister, said the assailant was wearing when she saw him leaving Chi Omega. Rafferty also identified Bundy from photos after his arrest as the probable suspect who chased her that night.

Bundy also spent part of the evening at Sherrod's, the disco next door to Chi Omega, but came off weird to most of the women who, in turn, managed to avoid or rebuff him. The following is taken directly from the record and consists of an interview with a Ms. Black:

According to Ms. Black, at about 12:30 a.m. on January 15, 1978, she and a sorority sister of hers, Valerie Stone, went to Sherrod's. They entered into the premises and, eventually, after getting a drink, she was standing around the area in the northeast portion of the building, the area that has an exit directly adjacent to the Chi-O House. Ms. Black's attention was drawn to a subject who appeared out of place, that is, he did not fit the typical college crowd. His dress and age along with his appearance, i.e. greasy looking appearance, made him stand out to her. Moreover, this subject kept staring at her and she was afraid he was going to ask her to dance. Ms. Black states that he kept staring at her, along with many other persons, and that his mannerisms seemed to be more a "rude type of looking," "that he appeared to be smirking," or "that he felt superior," or a "I know something that you don't know attitude."

Given his state of mind, his current inability to abduct women as he once had, and his complete lack of concern about entering occupied homes at night, there wasn't any way the Chi Os were going to be left alone, and Kathy Kleiner's life, and the lives of others at the sorority that night, was about to change forever. It was approximately 3:00 a.m., and Bundy knew what he needed to do.

Before entering Chi Omega through an unlocked door, Bundy grabbed a log from a stack of logs and, barely able to contain the frenzied madness within, walked into the quiet of the sleeping sorority house and made his way upstairs.

In what would be the height of irony, given what was about to happen, Kathy had previously remarked to a Chi O sister that perhaps she should lock their bedroom doors at night. The young woman's response, purely rhetorical, was, "What do we need to do that for?" The bedroom doors stayed unlocked.

Bundy's attack upon the sleeping coeds of Chi Omega would kill two of them – Margaret Bowman and Lisa Levy—and seriously injure two—Kathy Kleiner and Karen Chandler. Kathy and Karen roomed together, and Margret Bowman was in the room next to them. Kathy and Karen's room faced the rear parking lot, and having their room situated here may have played a part in their survival. What follows is Kathy's version of the attack, both from her original recollection and then what came forth after the authorities brought in a hypnotist. It must also be noted that Kathy's attempted statements to police soon after the attack are disjointed, and because of the confusion, may include contradictory statements, which is not unusual given her head injury. However, as memory started to return, and with the aid of the hypnotist, a fairly clear picture of the attack in their room came to the fore:

Because Kathy was not in a deep state of sleep, she said she remembered hearing the door but did not open her eyes. However, when she heard what sounded like a foot kicking the footlocker that sat between Kathy and Karen's bed (her eyeglasses were sitting on top of this foot locker as well), she opened her eyes and saw what looked like a black shadow and a club coming down at her. After Bundy struck Kathy several times with the log he'd picked up outside the sorority, Karen woke up and Bundy attacked her as well. And then, out of nowhere, it abruptly stopped when Bundy saw the car lights of what turned out to be Nita Neary's boyfriend bringing her home. Still holding on to the log (which by now had lost most of its bark), he exited the bedroom and started down the steps. Unknown to Bundy, he was spotted by Neary as he left by way of the front door.

What follows is from my book *The Tail of Ted Bundy: Digging up the Untold Stories*:

EMTs Gary Mathews and Charles Norvell arrived in the ambulance called to the Chi Omega house. Met by a sea of cops and distraught coeds, they were quickly ushered upstairs. As they reached the top of the steps, Mathews broke off from Norvell and entered one of the bedrooms, where he found Kathy Kleiner and Karen Chandler. The light was on, and he saw immediately that both women were bloody and in a daze. There was blood on their faces and heads, as well as on the bed. What Gary Mathews couldn't see as he worked on the women and prepared them for transport to the hospital, were three of Kleiner's teeth that were left on the bed. Both women also had broken jaws. Kathy also suffered the loss of a number of her teeth which were found on her bed.

Kathy told this writer she remembers one of the EMTs telling her she'd been shot in the face. After placing her on a gurney, she was transported to an ambulance. She said she remembers hearing people talking, the crackling of a walkie-talkie, and how cold it was outside. Both her injuries and Karen Chandler's were severe.

Things were a bit of a haze for Kathy as doctors and nurses attended to her, and the pace of activity in and out of her room never seemed to slacken; at least at the beginning. Of course, all victims had twenty-four-hour police protection, and anyone entering her room, outside of hospital staff, had to be approved. Twelve days after entering Tallahassee Memorial Hospital, Kathy was released to her family. Soon she'd be heading home to Miami to be with family, but first she stopped by her room at Chi Omega. Once inside, she discovered her blood and Karen's blood was still present. It's very unlikely the university had already received the go ahead from the authorities to hire a crew to clean up the blood-spattered rooms. At this point, investigations were continuing and clean up probably occurred the week following Kathy's last visit. The reason for the visit was two-fold. Not only was she intending to pick up those things she needed, but the police had asked her to see if anything was missing, as killers will very often take items from a crime scene as one might pick up a souvenir, and only Kathy would know if something had been removed which might indicate such a thing had happened.

When she reached Miami, she settled in with her parents, and it must have felt very good to her to have made it through the madness and still be alive and on the road to recovery. As Kathy told this writer, she was "taken to see an oral surgeon to correct the misalignment of my wired jaw performed in Tallahassee. My jaw was rebroken, three pins were inserted into the jaw bone, and it was wired shut for an additional nine weeks."

To ensure her recovery continued without incident, two-man police teams were stationed at her house around the clock. Having survived the attack at Chi O, authorities were determined that whomever did this would not be able to get to her a second time. Kathy remembered one officer would often be seen sitting on the front porch, while the other patrolman sat in the car. Kathy said her mother would often give these men food and drink. During her recuperation, she received numerous cards and letters from around the world wishing her well. Rather surprisingly, she even received a marriage proposal from Saudi Arabia.

Kathy would see Ted Bundy face-to-face one more time. During the trial, she came to court to tell the jury and the court her account of what she had experienced. When I asked her if Bundy had avoided her eyes, she said no, he stared straight at her, and she stared right back at him.

Kathy also mentioned that she was angry each time Bundy was granted a stay of execution. She remembers thinking, when that day finally arrived on January 24, 1989, that she was glad he went away, "just as Margaret and Lisa were taken away."

II. Francine Bardole

In my book, *The Bundy Murders*, I cover the story of Bundy's relationship with Leslie Knutson, whom he had met at a party in Salt Lake City. When I was writing this section of the book, I did not have any contact with Leslie, but I did have the official record (Utah and Washington State records), and the police investigated this relationship and reported on it thoroughly; even so much as interviewing Leslie's ex-husband, David Knutson. Before bringing you up to speed with the new information, I must return to what the record states about that time, and about Leslie Knutson's relationship with Ted Bundy. What follows is information I originally obtained from Utah police reports which I previously included in *The Bundy Murders*:

Always on the lookout for a pretty young woman for his outer self (at one point he dated the daughter of a Utah Supreme Court judge who would actually have to recuse himself from one of his future appeals due to the killer's relationship with his daughter), Bundy had recently met yet another one. Her name was Leslie Knutson, recently divorced and with a seven-year-old son. They met at a party in June hosted by Paul Van Dam, the Salt Lake County prosecutor, and began dating soon afterwards. According to statements she would later make, they would spend time together in the mountains, at the drive-in, and in her apartment.

He never attempted to discourage Leslie from adding her son Joshua to the mix. Indeed, Bundy, who for a time that summer lived at Knutson's Redondo Street address, took Josh and a group of his friends to the local swimming pool on more than one occasion. In essence, Bundy was acting (as he had with Tina) as a surrogate father to Knutson's son. This may have seemed quite natural to him. But as with all relationships in which Bundy was involved, this one would die. Nothing he told Leslie or Josh was true, or had any real foundation to it.

Coming forward to 2018, I was recently contacted by Francine Bardole, and soon I was hearing the heretofore unpublished tales of Leslie Knutson and her son, Josh, and their connection with Francine Bardole and her son, Larry. And what is so great about Francine and Larry coming forward and, in fact, whenever anyone comes forward who has valid connections to this case, is that many holes and gaps are often filled in by the testimony of those coming forward. And so it was in the case of Francine and Larry Bardole.

I remember when writing about Leslie Knutson and Bundy's interactions with her and Josh, often including her son in their activities and even taking Josh and his friends places, I kept thinking, I wish I could locate these kids (now adults) to find out more about these experiences. And ten years down the road, I would, at least in part, finally get my wish.

Both Francine and Larry remember Ted Bundy as being exceedingly friendly. Francine told this writer that their first conversation consisted of small talk, and one aspect of it was Bundy talking about his time at the University of Utah School of Law. Bundy spoke of how difficult the work was for law school, and Francine said Bundy mentioned he was encouraging Leslie to go to law school too.

Leslie Knutson lived in a duplex at 1460 Redondo Avenue. Looking at the structure from the sidewalk, their door is on the left. Down the street (and on the opposite side) was 1409 Redondo, the home of Francine Bardole. Apparently, the connection with Bundy (and pretty much with Leslie) came from the friendship between Josh and Larry, which included those times when Ted took the boys places, and those occasions when Francine would agree to watch Josh for them so they could have some time of their own. As such, this information comes out of numerous interactions Francine and her son had with them, and, given what we now know about Bundy, they highlight and expand, if you will, an interesting picture of Bundy's dark and secretive world.

On at least two occasions, Bundy took the boys to the Redwood Drive-In, located at 3688 Redwood Road, and Larry freely admits it was fun, having gone with him. He also remembered the time when Ted told the boys to wait in the car, while he headed in the direction of the concession stand and restrooms. All of that seemed quite normal to them, of course. However, when he failed to return in what the boys believed was a reasonable amount of time, they went looking for him. Oddly, they found him standing close to the women's restroom, and he was watching the women who, one after another, were entering or exiting the restroom. This, of course, brings Denise Naslund to mind, and how Bundy stopped her as she was leaving the restroom at Lake Sammamish and he convinced her to go with him. What would Bundy have been thinking about at that moment? Killing one of them, perhaps, regretful that he had two kids with him. Bundy was not in control as to when that genie of murder began to rise, and what the boys saw that evening was most likely the beginning of that rising. The longer he stood at the restroom entrance watching his "prey" coming and going, the more forceful the desire and inclination became. However, the arrival of the boys brought any chance for him to act out on his murderous salivating to an abrupt end. One thing we don't know is, did Bundy take the boys home and then go back out into the night seeking a victim?

One of the things Leslie also mentioned to authorities is how Ted would take Josh and his friends to the pool, and while I had no knowledge as to what pool they frequented, Larry Bardole explained the pool was (and perhaps is) located within the grounds of old Fort Douglas. As such, it may well have been a private pool, and Larry believes one needed a special pass to get into it. If this is the case, Larry believed, Bundy's U of Utah student ID was probably all that was needed to gain entrance. And, as can be expected whenever Bundy was involved in something, it had its negative aspect as well.

One day after returning from swimming, Larry told his mother that he didn't want to go back to the pool with Ted. When she inquired as to why he would say this, Larry said Bundy liked playing a game called "shark" and that he didn't like it at all. Not only would Ted swim around the pool and pull them under (keep in mind, these were very young kids of eight or ten), but he would also "bite" them. Whatever emotion Bundy meant to elicit with the pulling of the kids under the water, and the mimicking of a shark bite, it's clear that he found it funny to frighten them; much like he had done with his girlfriend (and other women, as well) when he'd suddenly jump out from behind a bush and startle them. Whatever Bundy's true motivations might have been in playing "shark," Larry didn't like it at all.

Larry also related the story of a time when Josh asked Larry to come to his house one morning, and when he arrived, a very tired Bundy answered the door to let him in. With that, Bundy retreated back into the bedroom and shut the door. For the rest of the day, Bundy stayed in the room, and Larry noticed a food tray outside the bedroom door where Leslie had obviously brought him something to eat, and once he was finished, he simply placed the tray outside the door. Apparently, Bundy had been up all night, and then spent that day catching up on some much-needed sleep. This, of course, was nothing unusual, as Bundy the killer was a very nocturnal hunter of women. Sleeping during the day was very routine for him, and it was something that had been noticed by many others, including his girlfriend Liz.

One aspect that goes along with this has to do with the effects this sleeping pattern may have been having on Leslie and their relationship together. When I discussed this with Francine, she said the following:

"There were occasions where Leslie had arranged for me to care for Josh so she could do something with Ted. It was not unusual for her to cancel at the last minute because Ted did not want to or could not go. I could hear the frustration in her voice when she called to tell me the event was off. I highly doubt Leslie did not address the issue when she did see Ted. Ted would "hole up" in the dark during the day on occasion and like Larry said, want to be left alone. I can only imagine Leslie feeling like she was walking on eggshells during these moments."

Another interesting story is one that came from Leslie's duplex neighbor, Laurie Hulse. Hulse's son, Tom, was a friend of Josh's, and it's clear they all got along well together. However, Laurie remembers playing badminton in the backyard with her son one day, and Bundy, coming out into the backyard, angrily started complaining that her dog wouldn't stop barking and it was clear the pooch was really annoying him. Laurie said Bundy also blurted out that she needed to feed her dog more often. Perhaps he believed stuffing the animal with food would finally shut it up. Of course, no one who witnessed this rude behavior in the backyard that day had any idea what Bundy was really angry about, which was that his nocturnal hunting cycle of women was being interrupted by a dog, and that if he couldn't sleep in during the day, how could he effectively hunt at night? Laurie also mentioned there were times when Bundy was rude to Leslie, and overall, she just didn't like the way he treated her.

Despite the terrible things they would later learn about Ted Bundy, it's clear just how much Larry and Francine liked him. Larry still has good memories of Ted fixing his bike when the chain slipped. He told of the time when Bundy came and picked him up from the Kmart some seventeen blocks from his house, and after sticking his bicycle in the trunk of the VW, gave him a ride home. It was clear Bundy actually found time to be good to Josh and Larry, and it was no doubt the same type of kindness Bundy extended to Liz Kendall's daughter, Mollie. Even though he was without question a despicable, diabolical human, he still managed to show, at least to some degree, a genuine kindness to certain people. It may have been rare, and it may have been partly an act. But it was on display with Larry Bardole and Josh Knutson.

For many years now, Francine has been employed by the West Jordan, Utah Police Department as a forensic investigator. That she has spent a good portion of her life fighting crime and bringing criminals to justice, one has to wonder what Bundy would have thought of her profession.

III. "Maggie" of Tallahassee, Florida

Being a writer of books about Ted Bundy, I've grown quite comfortable with folks contacting me to tell me their stories about how remotely or closely they're connected to the Ted Bundy murders and, obviously, about what kind of impact it has had on their lives. Indeed, there is a passage in *The Bundy Murders* where I speak of the terrible effects Bundy's reign of terror caused the state of Washington. The ongoing fear experienced by many of its citizens was very real, and their reaction to the slaughter of a segment of its female citizens was nothing short of feeling terrorized. So, when Maggie (a pseudonym) contacted me and began telling me about her experiences and what it was like living in a city where a killer had boldly and viciously attacked four sleeping coeds in the Chi Omega sorority, killing two, and then almost immediately violently assaulting (and attempting to kill) another woman five or six blocks away, I was all ears.

What follows is the communication I've received from her, and I'll be presenting most of it verbatim. I will however (as I promised) edit out certain bits of information that will assure her desire to remain anonymous is fulfilled. You'll also notice two things: one, her very helpful guidance in sharing where Bundy roamed the city to either shop, or eat, or even steal; and two, how closely she might have been to the killer as he moved around Tallahassee. At the time of the Chi Omega attacks, Maggie was only thirteen years old. But unknown to her at that time, being thirteen was no guarantee of safety, as Bundy was both a killer of young women and young girls.

I was a thirteen-year-old resident of Tallahassee when Ted visited the Chi Omega house, and from the moment my family heard the announcement in church the morning after, the town was seized with terror and paranoia.

Back then the public only knew what the press decided to tell us, and they did not tell the public much back then about what Ted really did to the women he killed. It was only years later that I learned about the necrophilia, the choking, and other gory details.

When reading this book (Author's note: she's referring to my book, *The Bundy Murders*), *I had to put it down in horror quite a few times. For example, the credit card charges that Ted made fraudulently. The J. Byron's department store was in Northwood Mall, as was the Eckerd's he shopped at. That mall was right next door to the middle school I attended (Raa Middle School). I was in the 8th grade at that time, and after school my best friend and I would always walk to the mall to hang out for a few hours before our parents got off work to pick us up. That privilege was something we "earned" for being in our last year of middle school. It is terrifying to think that Ted might have been there when we were, both of us sporting our dark hair, parted in the middle, ambling through the large mall parking lot like we had all the time in the world.*

And the Tasty Pastry Bakery was in a shopping center adjacent to my old elementary school. It was called Timberline Elementary when I attended, but the name was later changed to Gilchrest Elementary after Principal Gilchrest retired (I think). The date of Ted's cookie-shopping visit to Tasty Pastry isn't in the book, but there is an exit/

entrance to I-10 a few blocks away, so maybe Ted got the munchies while he was driving to or from Jacksonville. That area is right on the edge of the upscale suburbs, so the fact that he was trolling around in there is truly chilling. Back then there wasn't much development, but now you can barely find a tree within a mile radius, there are so many shopping centers and places to eat. There is a McDonald's nearby that used to be the first sign of civilization as we made our way into town from where we lived.

Some of the other places Ted frequented were rather upscale, such as Andrew's 2nd Act and Clydes & Costellos, both places commonly frequented by politicians when legislature was in session, as they were just blocks away from the State Capitol.

And as an FSU student a few years later, I regularly visited The Phyrst, which was a campus bar that used to be Sherrod's, next door to the Chi Omega house. The description that Carla Jean Black gave of how Ted was staring at her in Sherrod's gave me chills, because the floor plan (and dark places) were easy to imagine as familiar locations inside The Phyrst. (The bar no longer exists after campus renovations.)

One of my friends was a member of Chi Omega, and during one holiday break when the sorority house was virtually empty, we went inside the house after leaving The Phyrst one night so she could give me a tour. I remember reading in the Tallahassee Democrat that on the night of Ted's murder spree, the club that he used to bludgeon the girls had been used to prop open the back door, so it was super eerie for me to walk in through that same door, which had been reinforced with a bolted-on metal strip to prevent someone from kicking it in.

The bedroom doors were all closed, but I remember the terror of walking past the rooms upstairs, before walking down the main staircase to the foyer. My friend didn't grow up in Tallahassee, so she wasn't that aware of the murders.

She said the sorority never discussed it. She seemed more nervous about pointing out the door to some sort of secret sorority room that they used in their meeting rituals, saying she could never let me even peek inside that room since I wasn't a member of the sorority. The house has been extensively renovated now, but it is still located just outside of the main gates of the university and Westcott fountain, a prime position for any Greek organization.

I don't think you discussed it in your books, but the FSU track club used to practice on campus, with bleachers next to the track where friends or onlookers would sit in the shade to study or eat lunch. That is where Ted did a bit of his thievery, because the track team would just leave their bookbags and belongings on the bleachers while they trained. When Ted was arrested in Pensacola, he was carrying the ID of a rather prominent track star who was about to graduate and start his career. When it was erroneously announced that he had been arrested for the Chi Omega murders, it ruined his life for quite some time.

As you know, it's not easy to find this information, since it happened before we even dreamed of the internet or cellphone cameras. Some people would think it is weird for me to say I enjoyed reading your books, but because it is a link to an experience I grew up with, I feel connected to the story and appreciate the information. I have had a few nightmares while reading this one, not gonna lie.

I remember reading in one of your books about Ted going to Chez Pierre with one of his neighbors a few times. That was also kind of a swanky place to eat. It's closed now. Tallahassee has changed so much, particularly the FSU campus. Roads that ran through campus have been closed or rerouted as the university grew.

IV. Andrew Valdez

I first came across the name, Andrew Valdez, when I was doing research for my book, *The Bundy Murders: A Comprehensive History*. At the time, I did not seek out Mr. Valdez for an interview, but I did quote some of his words from a Utah newspaper article. Here's that portion of my book that details Valdez's reaction upon seeing Bundy in class in January 1975. It is important to note as well, that Bundy started law school in Salt Lake City, Utah, in September of 1974, but because he was out committing murder, he attended classes only three times during that first semester, and this is what caused Valdez to believe Bundy was a transfer student:

Now that he was actually listening to the lectures, taking notes, and participating in class, his classmates weren't sure what to make of him. Andrew Valdez, also a beginning freshman law student in the fall of 1974, had this to say about him: "He first introduced himself to me in a contracts class. I thought he was a transfer student because I'd never seen him before." Valdez, who clearly liked Bundy (there were few who didn't), also gave Bundy high marks for whatever academic success he was able to maintain. "I remember him for his ability to pass tough classes when he rarely went to school."

For this book, my fourth in the Bundy series, I decided I wanted to reach out to Andrew Valdez to see what it was like for him dealing with Ted Bundy on a daily basis in that winter of 1975 during that second semester (as I mentioned above, Bundy actually began school there in September, but because he was out hunting women, he attended class only three times during that first semester), and I'm very glad that I did. When I first contacted Valdez, he was very agreeable to talking with me, which is always a good starting point. I must also give a word of thanks to Shirl Sipperley DiGugno, who has been helping me locate certain people, including Andrew Valdez.

During our phone conversation on November 12, 2018, Valdez told me he had at least two classes with Ted Bundy, one being contracts and the other, evidence. The first time he noticed Bundy was in January 1975, in his contracts class that was held in the afternoon, and he was sitting on the back row. When they spoke to each other, Valdez asked him if he was a transfer student, and Bundy said no. Bundy also mentioned he was from Seattle.

Valdez told me that Bundy looked like a "rich kid," and that he acted the part, as it were. He also mentioned that Bundy was a good dresser, but that often he would see Bundy wearing wrinkled clothes. Indeed, on that first day that they met, Valdez noticed that his turtleneck was wrinkled. When asked if his clothes ever appeared dirty, he said no, only wrinkled.

Although Bundy did begin coming to more classes that second semester, he still missed quite a few of them. Valdez said that Bundy came up to him one day and asked, "Do you mind if I look at your notes?" but he did one better and made copies for Bundy. Valdez said he made copies four or five times that winter for Bundy. He also mentioned that not only was law school "hard," but it was also very important for students to help each other as the school year progressed. However, he said, there was so much competition in school that help wasn't always forthcoming. So, when Bundy asked for the notes, he was only too happy to do it. Valdez also emphasized how friendly Bundy was to him. During our conversation, he was quick to add that Bundy could have been "playing him" as that's how sociopaths are. Even so, it's also quite possible Bundy liked him, and not just for what Valdez could do for him. That camaraderie would have limits, of course, but we can't rule out that some of that friendliness might have been partially genuine.

Of course, Bundy would continue to kill young women and girls throughout the remainder of the year, and on August 16, 1975, Bundy's life, as he knew it, was coming to a close forever, upon his arrest in Granger, Utah, in the wee hours of the morning. It was a routine traffic stop, but the results of this particular arrest were anything but routine.

When Bundy was pulled over by Sergeant Bob Hayward of the Utah Highway Patrol (Bob was brother to Captain Pete Hayward of the homicide squad of the Salt Lake County Sheriff's Office), he was arrested for attempting to elude a police officer, and for having implements in his car that were labeled by police as burglary tools. Valdez said the burglary tool charge was often used by police to arrest suspicious individuals in order to be able to hold them, in order that down the road, if need be, that burglary charge might be dropped or amended while additional charges could be added.

In Bundy's case, the bag he was carrying in his car that early morning was his murder kit; a kit consisting of a brown leather gym bag, with the following items inside: a ski mask, a pantyhose mask, two right-handed gloves, an ice pick, a box of large Glad trash bags, a rope for binding and perhaps choking a victim, an electrical cord that was used exclusively for strangulation, and strips of a bed sheet he'd use for the binding of his victims' hands and feet. Indeed, Salt Lake Detective Darryl Ondrak took one look at these things and knew it was far more than a bag used for burglaries. Some of these items, he correctly reasoned, were used for tying people up. These were the tools for abduction, and the astute detective knew it.

Valdez not only went to law school full time, but also worked for the Salt Lake County Jail, in the area of Pretrial Services. Essentially, Valdez was a "screener," and he would decide, through a point system, who could be released on his own recognizance, and those who, because of more serious crimes, would be held over in jail until they went before a judge; usually the following morning. Because Bundy was being charged with possession of burglary tools and eluding a police officer (both misdemeanors), he was eligible for being released on his own recognizance if he could meet the "point" system. The point system took into consideration several factors, such as, did he have any prior arrests (no); how long had he been living in the area (almost one year); what was his current status in the city (law student), and lastly, did he have good references (yes). Because Bundy had enough points, he easily met the criteria for immediate release. Obviously wanting to get out of confinement, Bundy asked Valdez if he was going to release him.

The moment of Bundy's arrival at the Salt Lake County Jail around 3:00 a.m. on August 16, 1975, is a surreal one for both of the men involved, which neither man understood at the time. For Ted Bundy, it was the beginning of his unveiling, when he was being pulled out of the dark cover of the shadows, and where his life would be changing forever.

But on this particular early morning, it was about two law students, who had already established a friendship, meeting at a time and place neither expected, and it would prove to be a line of demarcation for both men. When I asked Andrew Valdez about this odd moment, he said that after the initial greeting between the two men, he asked Bundy what had happened. Bundy initially told his law school buddy "I got lost," and would attempt to explain it a bit further over the next several minutes. Valdez noticed Bundy didn't appear nervous or concerned at all, and Bundy ultimately told Valdez what he'd already told arresting officer, Bob Hayward. Bundy said he'd been to see a movie at a drive-in and afterward he was just driving around; a story that didn't seem right to Valdez, who found it odd that Bundy had been driving around that area that late at night. Valdez also noted that his suspicion was not present solely because Bundy had been arrested, as he'd dealt with other law school friends who'd gotten arrested for one reason or another. His suspicion was based wholly on Bundy's less than credible explanation. Before the men separated, Bundy once again asked Valdez to "take good notes," while at the same time saying he'd soon see him back in class.

However, the world would grow much darker for Bundy by October of that year, as Salt Lake County Sheriff's Detective Jerry Thompson kept probing into the full extent of who or what Ted Bundy really was, as no one in law enforcement believed him to be a simple burglar, suspecting him of being involved in much more serious criminal activity, and they were determined to find out the truth. Their investigation produced results which culminated in an arrest warrant for Bundy for the abduction and attempted murder of eighteen-year-old Carol DaRonch, who escaped Bundy on November 8, 1974. The attempted murder charge was later dropped because they couldn't conclusively prove Bundy's intent was to kill her. When this arrest was executed, the entire state of Utah would hear of the charges against Bundy. Andrew Valdez was about to have his own epiphany during his second visit to the incarcerated law student.

Because of the seriousness of the crimes for which Bundy was charged, he was being held on the third floor of the Salt Lake County Jail, along with other inmates charged with serious and often violent offenses. Valdez visited Bundy three times while he was there just to see "if he needed anything." Bundy asked him to check on his locker at school, as he had his law books and perhaps other personal items in there as well, and Valdez assured him he'd take care of things for him.

Even though Valdez visited Bundy on three occasions while he was incarcerated on the jail's top floor, it was his first visit with Bundy that would forever change his opinion of his fellow law student. Because these visits with Bundy were not official visits being conducted while performing his duties in Pretrial Services, Valdez did not move Bundy from his jail cell into a private room where they could talk. Instead, they spoke through the iron bars of Bundy's cell. While they conversed, Valdez reminded him that these charges weren't like his first charges - these were felonies and very serious. And Bundy, instead of saying what most innocent people in similar circumstances might be saying, such as: "I'm innocent!" or "Can you make a call for me?" or "Who's a good lawyer in town?" Bundy simply said, "I don't think they have the evidence to convict me."

Valdez reacted like others reacted when confronted with these odd remarks from Bundy – it led him to conclude that Bundy may in fact be involved in the current situation the state was facing with their missing and murdered women. Each time before Valdez departed (he told me each of these visits were anywhere from five to ten minutes long), Bundy said, "Take good notes, I'll get out."

Valdez also told of an incident that occurred not long after Bundy's arrest on August 16, 1975. He wasn't certain of the exact date, but it was definitely somewhere in that relatively short period between Bundy's August arrest, when he was still under the radar of the media so that very few individuals were aware that he'd been arrested, and the October 1975 arrest that blew the lid off the investigation, rocketing the name Ted Bundy to the top of the nightly TV newscasts in all the states that had missing and murdered women.

Anyway, Valdez said that a very esteemed professor that taught one of the classes he and Bundy shared did something that surprised him. Bundy had gone down to speak with the professor after class, which has been a standard for students for as long as there have been classes and teachers. Sitting there, Valdez could see Bundy waiting patiently for several of the students to finish up with the professor. As the last one drifted away, Bundy approached the professor who, when he saw who was walking toward him, turned his back on Bundy and walked away. Bundy, who was no doubt stunned by this, may have called out an additional time, but the professor never turned around to address him. Speechless, Bundy walked away. Valdez believes that the professor, who had lots of connections in law enforcement, most likely was given inside information from the authorities as to what they were already believing Bundy to be: a killer of young women, causing him to reject Bundy's approach.

Ted Bundy was ultimately convicted in the abduction of Carol DaRonch, and received a one to fifteen-year prison sentence and was housed at the Utah State Prison. However, it wouldn't be long before Bundy was transferred to Colorado to stand trial in the murder of Caryn Campbell whom he abducted from the Wildwood Inn in Snowmass, Colorado, and subsequently murdered. Unbelievably, Bundy managed to escape twice from his keepers in the state, and the second time he managed to get all the way to Florida where he'd kill two more women and a twelve-year-old girl.

Of course, while Bundy was embroiled in the trial in Colorado, Valdez and the others were plowing ahead and preparing to take the bar exam. When word reached them in class that Bundy had escaped, Valdez said a number of the students started clapping and cheering. Apparently, a number of them still believed in his innocence and had Bundy known this, it's certain this would have caused him to smile.

V. A Friend of Kathy Parks and Lorraine Fargo

In August 2011, I received an email from a woman who knew both Lorraine Fargo and Kathy Parks, and was active in all the goings-on at Oregon State University when Kathy disappeared. I will not be naming her as I believe she'd rather remain anonymous, but she's in the record. It was good hearing from yet another person who knew and was friends with Kathy. Although the letter is slightly redacted, it's clear that, like Lorraine, she carries scars from that time, and that's understandable. And also like Lorraine, she wanted to finally face these negative feelings and deep fears by contacting me and reading my book. This email has been on file, as it were, for a number of years now, and has never been published in whole or in part prior to the publication of this book. I was, and I remain, appreciative for her contact.

Dear Kevin,

Please bear with me, this will take a bit of explanation.

I was (redacted) of Lorraine Fargo and attended Oregon State U during 1973-74. Kathy Parks was a friend of mine and I have something that you may want. (Lorraine was the last person to talk with Kathy before she disappeared.)

Lorraine and I lived on the same floor as Kathy at Sackett Hall. Lorraine and I went to the State Police offices in Eugene Oregon in the summer of 1974, in an effort to help. The detectives found some clothing and wanted to know if we recognized it, to see if it belonged to Kathy, it did not. I did not know Kathy well but counted her as a friend.

I have been searching for Lorraine for years on the internet; we lost contact in 1982 after I moved back to my hometown. I happened to run into a review she wrote about your book on Amazon and was very excited to think that I may finally have found her. When I searched for her on the internet, armed with her married name, I discovered that she passed away last March and I lost my opportunity, this saddened me immensely.

When I read her review of your book I decided that I wanted to learn more about the book. I have avoided reading most books about Ted Bundy over the years except for Ann Rule's book. Mostly it has been too painful and scary for me but I would like to read your book, it's time I faced the demon, so to speak.

The reason that I contacted you is that you seem like a genuine person that is interested in the case for the right reason and not because of morbid curiosity. I have kept over the years the missing person poster for Kathy Parks and if you have any interest in owning the poster, I think it would add to your understanding of the case. The poster depicts Kathy with the now famous portrait but also a full-length picture that I haven't seen on the net. (It may be in other books but I have not read them.) This poster will let you see that Kathy was a blond-haired person and did not have brown hair even though the picture is black and white. (Author's note: She did mail the poster, and it's now a part of my Bundy case files.)

Bundy's horrific actions are still causing pain, the ripples are still moving outward, like a rock thrown in a lake. It's been 37 years and I am still affected by all this, my kids and granddaughter are also feeling the consequences, they have been hammered constantly by me about strangers and trusting their gut about situations. I lost my innocence about the world in June of 1974, and I have a hard time trusting anyone to this day. I am sorry this is so long, no one that I know understands the pain that I carry and the survivor's guilt. I could have just as easily been in Kathy's place, we used to run around the campus of OSU at all hours of the day and night, believing the world was a safe place to play.

I know that Lorraine felt the same way, we had many conversations about these feelings over the years. I believe it is time for me to give up the poster. I used to show it to my daughter and try to impress upon her that the world is a dangerous place. I do not want to do the same thing with my seven-year-old granddaughter, she will be told about Bundy when she is older but the need to show the poster has diminished.

VI. The Escape of Leslie Parmenter

Leslie Parmenter was only fourteen years old when she encountered Ted Bundy in a K-Mart parking lot in Jacksonville, Florida. It was a brief meeting between the two that shouldn't have happened, and the encounter could have turned deadly very quickly (and in my opinion, was about to turn deadly) but it all suddenly evaporated before Bundy could make his move. What follows is from my book, *The Bundy Murders: A Comprehensive History*:

The next day he came close to literally grabbing what he wanted when he stopped the van in a K-Mart shopping center parking lot across from Jeb Stuart Junior High School, located at 4815 Wesconnett Blvd. in Jacksonville. He struck up a conversation with Leslie Ann Parmenter, age 14, the daughter of Lester Parmenter, a detective with the Jacksonville police. According to her report, an unkempt and agitated man (again, not the refined killer of 1974 and 1975) stopped his white van in front of her and got out, leaving his door open. He began making conversation with the apprehensive teenager. He was described as wearing "glasses, with heavy dark frames, multicolored colored plaid trousers, and a black or navy-blue jacket similar to a navy pea coat."' He had a plastic fireman's badge with the name Richard Burton pinned on the coat, which was probably little more than a cheap toy meant to entertain a child.

Suspicious of the odd man, Leslie admitted she just didn't know what he wanted. At this point, Leslie's older brother Danny pulled up in his truck and stuck his head out the window, asking Leslie what the man wanted. Danny's words and later testimony revealed what must have been going through the young man's mind as he saw this much older man talking to his sister. He knew something wasn't right as the man "wasn't a very clean-cut person ... kind of scrawny looking."

After telling Leslie to go over to the passenger side of the truck and get in, he approached Bundy, who was already nervous, and asked him what he wanted. Bundy was not stupid and he could see a physical confrontation on the horizon. He told Danny, "Nothing ... I just asked if she was somebody else and just asked who she was." Bundy got back inside the van, rolled up the window, and began driving away. Danny quickly scribbled down the license number and attempted to follow him, but lost sight of the vehicle in heavy traffic. He gave the license number-13D-11300-to his father. "He was very nervous," Danny Parmenter added. "Like he was almost shaking. His voice was even quivering." Theodore Bundy was facing somebody who could fight back, and he didn't like it.

Without question, it was a close call, a literal brush with death. Had Leslie entered that van (something she'd never willingly do) or been forced into it, her fate would have been sealed.

For this fourth and final book on the Ted Bundy murders, I very was fortunate to be able to interview Leslie by phone on January 28, 2019, and again on January 29, 2019. Like most folks, she's very busy, so I was very appreciative she took the time to speak with me from her Florida home. And what you'll hear from her will be more than just the facts of the case—facts that came out through her testimony—but also what was going through her mind as the infamous killer set his sights on her. Sometimes it only takes a matter of moments for things to go terribly wrong.

On February 8, 1978, as Jeb Stuart Middle School was letting out for the day, everything appeared to be normal, and everything pointed to it being just another routine day. Outside the school, Leslie Ann Parmenter's older brother, Danny, was waiting in his pickup truck for his little sister to come walking out the door. But Leslie was not moving as quickly as on other days, and to make matters worse, she had to pick up her books from her locker which made her late coming out. When she exited the front doors, her brother was nowhere to be found. Still holding the heavy books (she wasn't using a book bag or backpack), she returned to the office and called home. Danny, somewhat irritated by her absence, listened to her explanation about why she was late, and told her to start walking and he'd return to pick her up. Because the Parmenter home was only about six blocks away on Jammes Road, she figured it wouldn't be long before Danny would meet her.

On this day, Leslie had skipped her usual routine of wearing her Levis or otherwise comfortable clothes, and instead wore an off-white two-piece outfit (top and skirt) that her Mom had given her for Christmas. She's never worn it before today, and she topped it off with a pair of high heels. They might not have been the most comfortable shoes to walk home in, but she knew Danny was on his way. With the load of books in hand, Leslie set off for the K-Mart that was across Wesconnett Blvd and to the right a hundred or so yards away. As she crossed the street at the entrance way to the K-Mart, she was looking at the long stretch of road that ran along the side of the building and, as usual, she would be walking the strip of paved lot with the side wall of the store on her left, and a deep ditch (no longer there today) on her right which separated her from Wesconnett Blvd. As she walked, she could look directly to her right and across the street, to the softball field where many of her friends were playing on this otherwise normal day.

And then, out of nowhere, she saw a large white van coming toward her. During our conversation, Leslie said she wasn't sure if the van had been driving down Wesconnett

Blvd, spotted her, and turned left into the parking lot before heading in her direction, or if he entered the parking lot from the opposite end of the store from Blanding Blvd, drove along in front of the store until he came to the end of it and saw her walking up his way, which then would have caused him to turn right to meet her. But no matter the direction, as the van came her way, she found out very quickly what it was all about. Bundy, having seen the lone teenager, immediately drove down this little narrow road that runs parallel with the windowless side of K-Mart. As the van approached and slowed down, Leslie sensed something bad might happen. "I knew the second I had eyes on him he was up to something." It was Bundy's intention to stop alongside her, but as he did, Leslie kept walking, and by the time Bundy jumped out of the van, she was slightly past the rear of the van.

Upon jumping out, Bundy shouted, "Hey, hey, hey!" according to Leslie. "I'm Richard Burton, I'm from the fire department." Turning around to face him, Leslie said he kept repeating these words as if he had nothing else to say. She also said not only did he refuse to look her in the eyes (they were darting about), but she noticed how unshaven and dirty he was, and that his clothes were also dirty and wrinkled.

As they talked, Leslie said she contemplated hurling the heavy books at him if he tried anything, while at the same time, she was looking (and hoping) that some of her friends across the street on the softball field would notice her and, if something was going to happen, would be able to render aid. Bundy, obviously looking for the moment to attack if his cajoling to get her into the van didn't work, was about to be startled by the arrival of her well-built and soon to be very angry brother.

Bundy, never a brave one when confronting men, would soon make his exit after Danny quickly stopped, jumped out of his truck, and demanded of Bundy an answer as to why he was talking to his sister. After Bundy's mumbling answers to the incensed brother, he quickly drove off and believed that would be the last of them. But he had attempted to abduct the daughter of a homicide detective of the Jacksonville Police, and he wasn't going to get away so easily. As the derailed killer sped away, they wrote down the license number. Bundy quickly put distance between himself and Jacksonville, and would ultimately rent a room that night at the Holiday Inn in Lake City, Florida. Here, in this sleepy and peaceful Florida town, Bundy went on to kill twelve-year-old Kimberly Leach the following day. He didn't yet know it, but he had committed his last murder.

Danny and Leslie raced home to figure out what to do. Their dad, Detective James Lester Parmenter (not wild about his first name, he was always referred to as Lester Parmenter) was out of the state and, as this was an age before cell phones, they knew they couldn't reach him so they called and spoke to Detective John Bradley at the Jacksonville PD. Because the police had the ability to trace the license plate, they quickly determined that the van had come from Tallahassee. In the near future, that van would also be linked to the killing of Kim Leach, and ultimately, to Ted Bundy.

In the weeks that followed, Danny and Leslie assisted the police and even underwent hypnosis in the hope that they could remember additional facts about their encounter with the strange man in the K-Mart parking lot that February 8. Both assisted in making composite drawings of the individual. Once Bundy was arrested and they were shown photographs of men in a photograph line up, both picked Bundy out of the display. They also had a chance to sit across from Ted Bundy during a meeting with a Grand Jury judge. On one side of the table sat Danny and Leslie, along with their father, on the other was Bundy with his representation. Unlike that day in the parking lot, Bundy was neat, clean, and dressed in a nice suit. This time, those eyes that kept darting about as he tried to abduct the young girl, were now staring straight at her, unflinching, and it was clear to Leslie that he was being bolstered by the presence of his attorneys. Danny and Leslie Parmenter gave depositions in the case, and also testified at the murder trial of Kimberly Leach. It all must have been very annoying to Bundy, as he believed that on that day when he had fled from the angry brother, he'd never see them again.

In the years since, whenever the Parmenter family discussed the events of that day, the realization of what could have happened never left them. Being a homicide detective, and spending years seeing how far humans can descend to create destruction and havoc in the lives of innocent people, Lester Parmenter told a reporter, "I've felt that had my son not come up and picked up Leslie, I'd have never seen her alive again … I know Leslie would have been Bundy's next victim." It is a sentiment the retired detective repeats to this day.

VII. Dawn Kraut and Ted Bundy

In March of this year (2019), as I was putting the finishing touches on this book, I was contacted by yet another Ted Bundy contact; a lady by the name of Dawn Kraut. For a few seconds, I searched my mind as to who she was, as her named seemed familiar. And then, bam! I remembered: Dawn Kraut was an individual I'd written about in *The Bundy Murders: A Comprehensive History*. I remember when I came across her six-page statement to police, I needed to include most of the information about her encounter with Ted Bundy in the book. She spotted Bundy in the cafeteria at the University of Washington at Seattle. Bundy did not speak to her, although he had noticed the pretty young woman with long hair parted in the middle, and Dawn wasn't about to let him get away without confronting him; albeit in a gentle, non-threatening manner.

The story of their meeting is a fascinating one, and it's a well-written account of that day. Unknown to me (before she contacted me, that is), she has had a desire to see the report again for many years now, and once we began communicating, I had my wife scan and email the report to her. As I explained to her (with my usual splash of humor), it all began with her having a conversation with Ted Bundy, and after Dawn returned home and told her family, the police were notified. From this came a meeting at Dawn's home with Detective Kathy McChesney who, in turn, returned to her office and typed up the report. Once finished, Detective McChesney made an appointment to meet Dawn at the University of Washington so she could look over each page of the six-page report and initial it after determining its accuracy. Then, Dawn handed the report over to Detective McChesney so that she could turn it over to her boss, lead Detective Robert Keppel. Years later, I gathered her report along with dozens and dozens of other similar reports, during the research phase of my book. Now, several years later, I was able to send her a copy of the same report by way of a simple email. It was a "coming-full-circle" of something that was important to her, and it was a journey that would take some forty-four years to complete.

Because of the volume and type of information Dawn has provided, giving us an excellent "back story" to the event reflected in her report, I believe it's important to present the entire report as it will compliment this new information.

Date: 12-5-75

Statement of: Dawn Kraut:

On Thursday, December 4, 1975, I was at the Undergraduate Library Cafeteria at the University of Washington where I am a senior in psychology and anthropology. I had a class from 1:30 to 2:30 p.m. and then went to the cafeteria by myself. I sat alone at a table and was studying.

At about 3:00 o'clock I noticed a man I recognized as Ted Bundy from the newspapers, sitting about two tables away. I had never met Bundy. I wasn't really sure it was him as I thought he was in Salt Lake City.

The man I thought was Ted Bundy was talking with a hippy-type guy, he was about 25 years old and had long blond hair. Ted was eating a hamburger and laughing and smiling, although I could see under the table a kind of dichotomy – his legs and feet were moving as if he were very nervous. The blond man asked Ted what year he was in, in law school and said he had seen Ted's photograph in the paper. Ted appeared to know the blond man.

I wasn't able to hear much of their conversation and when they stopped talking the blond man and Ted got up from the table and parted. Ted was going near the door and I went toward the vending machine to get something to drink. I wasn't very far from Ted then and I quietly said, "Ted?" Ted turned around and said "Do I know you?" I said "No" and he nodded his head and asked my name. I frowned and he said, "Just your first name." I said Dawn. Ted said, "I saw you looking at me, it was more than just a double-take."

I said, "I never forget a face." Then I didn't want him to think I recognized him from seeing him in person before and I told him I had seen his picture in the papers. Ted said, "The mug shots." And I said I had seen an old newsreel. Ted said he was surprised that they had kept them.

At first Ted seemed nervous and then composed as we talked longer. He told me he was Ted Bundy. He was wearing nicely pressed old jeans, new reddish-brown loafers, a navy-blue turtleneck and a beige and brown striped sweater with a loose cloth belt. When he was eating his hamburger, he wasn't wearing gloves, but now he was. They were brown with leather stitching. We stood by the door and had a conversation for about 45 minutes.

I noticed Ted was carrying a clipboard, the kind that folds over. It was thin, like there weren't many papers in it and he had no books. I asked him how the case was going and he smiled and said, "Well," and then started talking about the sensationalism of the press. He also said, "It's something people will never forget." I told him I thought that people would forget. He disagreed with me about this, he seemed certain people would remember.

I asked him if it bothered him that I recognized him and he said it didn't and that he wished everyone would talk to him and then they'd realize that "I'm not that kind of guy."

We didn't talk about anything other than him. I asked him what he was doing in the library and he said he had come from the law school where he was told they didn't want him there using the facilities because of his reputation.

Ted told me that I was the first person to recognize him that didn't previously know him. He asked me if an attractive young woman like myself wasn't afraid to know that Theodore Bundy was around campus. I shrugged and didn't answer.

I told him I knew one of the girls who disappeared – Denise Naslund. Ted said, "Oh, that's a shame." "I feel sorry for the genuine friends and family of the people who disappeared." "I can really see why they'd be bitter and want the person or persons caught." "It must have been a terrifying nightmarish experience." I recalled that he only spoke about the incidents with the girls as disappearances.

Ted seemed talkative and I asked him if he had a sister. He said he had two and left it at that. He didn't talk about his family but mentioned he had a fiancé, a "wonderful woman." He talked about her when we were talking about the missing girls. He said he could understand how the families must feel because of his feelings for his fiancé and her daughter, whom he said was "the most beautiful 6-year-old girl." He said that he loved this little girl as if he were her father.

Then he talked about a real old girl or woman friend who was writing a book on this case. He said that he didn't know much about the evidence in this case but this older woman did and that she in fact knew more details than anyone and she "knows I wouldn't be responsible."

He talked about John D. O'Connell, his attorney from Utah. He said Mr. O'Connell wasn't from around here. He used slang in describing O'Connell as a "laid back" kind of person, a neat guy, a good lawyer, and young. Ted said it was nice to have a lawyer who you know believes you. He said he had a good feeling when O'Connell smiled at him.

Ted said that he had a lot of influential friends and was good friends with the prosecuting attorney but that he hasn't seen him since his arrest, thinking that would make things awkward for the prosecutor. He also mentioned that Seattle Police are putting pressure on to catch someone and get the case solved.

He said that he was staying at a friend's apartment and that his friends have given him money and taken him around or lent him their car, I don't recall which he said. *He said he had a lot of friends who had written him letters.*

He talked about the law system and the publicity in this case. He said the press had done a number on his case and had made him look guilty. He said when this was over he was going to get a lot of money suing people. I said, "That's only if you get acquitted." And I don't remember what he said.

He said he wanted to become a criminal defense attorney and that he will be able to get back into law school when this is all over, that he'd already talked to the school about that. I said, "Couldn't you be prevented from taking the bar exam?" He said he hadn't thought about that.

I asked him if it weren't the case that some young attorney might want to take his case to make a name for himself and Ted said Mr. O'Connell was not a status seeker.

Ted said that he used to want to be a prosecutor but now that he seen the other side and the amount of power the prosecutor has, he does not want to be one.

I asked him if he studied in jail and he said he had been in 8 to 12 weeks and was so upset he couldn't concentrate.

I remember that in referring to the woman he said that all the police had was coincidental information, and I said I thought that you could be convicted on circumstantial evidence. I mentioned the Eric Haga case and he didn't recall it. I told him a little about it and he said, "Isn't he out?" (of jail, referring to Haga) and I said I thought he was but that he had been convicted on circumstantial evidence.

I noticed Ted made quick glances and movements but he wasn't trying to hustle me. He appeared intellectual, articulate and careful about what he said although he responded quickly to my questions.

I asked him if he was afraid of being out and around, afraid that someone might shoot him? He said he didn't care what people thought, that he was going to do what he wanted to be happy. He said he was not bitter about anything and was being objective. He also mentioned the moral support of his friends and "donations."

He didn't talk much about money, he said he was 29 years old and I could see from his face he had wrinkles around his eyes, particularly when he smiled or laughed. He said he had gotten a B.S. at the University of Washington.

He said he had not pleaded guilty or not guilty yet in Salt Lake. He acted confident of being acquitted and seemed surprised that charges weren't dropped before.

He said he had been Christmas shopping. He didn't use slang expressions and looked in my eyes when we talked. He kept his head turned somewhat to the left. He didn't have a deep voice or accent that I noticed.

He said that he didn't know what the evidence was against him and that a witness at Lake Sammamish did not recognize him. I asked him if he thought he was being framed and he said it was too long and complicated of a case to be framed.

When we parted, he said he was going to get Christmas cards and thank you notes. Our parting was abrupt, he turned and went back across Red Square toward Montlake, and I went back to where I was sitting.

Dawn Kraut

What follows are some of Dawn's very insightful observations concerning her encounter with Bundy, as well as some very interesting information about another attack which, although it has not been greatly discussed, may very well have been committed by Bundy in northern Washington state. Keep in mind that Bundy admitted to killing eleven in Washington State, but only provided the names of eight victims. That said, there are not only a number of unknown victims out there, but there must also be a number of potential victims who did not fall victim to Ted Bundy, and so the following story might—and I stress might—be one of these.

Although I was a University of Washington student for years, in June of 1974, I enrolled for a brief summer quarter foray at Western Washington College in Bellingham, Washington, located near the Canadian border. (It is now Western Washington University.) It's a beautiful campus on the undulating hills overlooking the Puget Sound. I rented a small apartment in a converted old house that straddled the hillside. Although my apartment was on the upper floor, it was accessed from the house's backside via an alley and a wooden boardwalk. I had my 10-speed with me and initially biked the short distance to classes. But a couple of troubling things happened that summer. College coeds were disappearing like crazy in the Northwest. Everyone was really scared. My art class professor told us how upset he was about Susan Rancourt disappearing from Central Washington campus. Either he knew Susan, her family, or her professor, I forget, but he was very upset and his voice was cracking mentioning her. She disappeared April 1974, just 2 months prior. Then early that summer while I was at Western, rumors/news circulated that a coed on a bike was accosted in an alley by a guy,

she struggled with him and a fake moustache he was
wearing came loose. She got away & the assailant
took off. Women were warned to beware, avoid alleys,
avoid walking alone or at dark. My boyfriend came
up from Seattle and nailed shut all my windows & put
extra locks on my door. I was afraid to come and go.
And I was reticent to zip freely around campus on my
10-speed like I had originally planned. Kevin, I haven't
read of any verified accounts of Ted trolling at Western,
but it defies credulity that he didn't. It's a straight shot
up I-5, maybe 1.5 hours or so from Seattle.

What I find interesting about this, is that during this
period of the Washington State murders, no one knew about
Ted Bundy, nor of his occasional use of a false mustache
when he engaged in abduction. That alone, in my view,
gives this a bit of credibility it otherwise wouldn't have,
as we know specific times Bundy used a false mustache,
including the abduction of Debra Kent from Viewmont High
School in Bountiful, Utah, after the aborted abduction of
Carol DaRonch.

Dawn's observations continue:

I told him I was a psych major, so it's likely, being a
psych major himself, he suspected I was dissecting him
*as he spoke. He **did** try to scare me a couple of times:*
By feigning concern, when I knew he also intended to
induce fear by slyly smiling almost flirtatiously while
saying things like "I imagine an attractive young
woman such as yourself must be afraid knowing
'Theodore Bundy' is on campus." Or his pondering
out loud and watching my face react, "it must have
been a terrifying nightmarish experience for the
missing young women." At some point I corrected Ted
as he kept saying "the missing young women" and
I responded "They aren't missing women, they are

dead. Their bones were found on Taylor Mountain."
At which point he deflected to how he "didn't know the
details of the case", but bragged his friend 'knew more
about the case than even the investigators did' as "she
was writing a book about it, and she was convinced
of my innocence." He was referring of course to true
crime writer Ann Rule.

I was never actually directly confrontational with
Ted or anything, I knew it was all a mind game, but I
really wanted to look Ted in the face and say her name
to him" (Naslund), which is what I did when I said
"I knew Denise Naslund". He offered his awkward
*empty platitude "I feel sorry for the **genuine** friends*
and family of the missing young women ..." and it
immediately struck me how the saying is normally "I
*feel **genuinely sorry** for the friends and family." So it*
seemed Ted misspoke his empty rehearsed line ... and
because of his artifice and lack of sincerity, he didn't
feel or notice the empathetic difference!

It's clear Dawn was sizing up Bundy from the moment
she first saw him.

I closely observed Ted Bundy gleefully wolfing
down a hamburger and spinning a lot of baloney to
his companion, brazenly perching himself right at
the center of his favorite hunting grounds (U of W
Undergraduate Library cafeteria), while the rest
of world seemed not to notice. Well, I noticed. And
Ted noticed that I noticed. Could that man really be
Ted? Would he really have the guts to come back on
campus? His nerve truly stunned me. But more than
that, I was angry. I had known Denise Naslund because
she worked as a receptionist at Graybar Electric with
my then boyfriend. She was such a sparkly, vivacious,
pretty, smiley young girl. So full of life. And her mother

was totally destroyed by her murder. To see him laughing and smiling and enjoying a burger was pretty nauseating to watch. I wanted to observe how he spun his web, and dodged and weaved and turned on the charm. I noticed the artifice in his choice of words, trying to say what normal people say. Trying to mimic compassion. He wore leather gloves and was fidgeting, winding the loose ends of the cloth belt of his over-sweater around his hands, again and again. I watched his actions and thought 'strangulation'. At that point in time little was known (or at least released) about cause of death. But the way he subconsciously moved his hands ...!

A quick mention: I'm correcting here a statement in *The Bundy Murders* where I state that Dawn had a brother who was a Seattle Police detective; something, by the way, that I received directly from the record and which is clearly a mistake. It was actually her cousin who was the Seattle Police investigator.

When I got home from school and told my parents I talked to Ted Bundy, my father was (understandably) furious. "What!? All that smarts and not one ounce of common sense!" We immediately called our cousin Al Schrader, who had been a Seattle homicide detective. Al got Detective McChesney etc., the info and the detectives came out to my parents' house to interview me. Also, a side note that came from my cousin, Seattle Detective, Al Shrader: Ted had told me he was studying at the Undergraduate Library that day precisely because he'd been asked to leave the Law Library (located elsewhere). In fact, Al Schrader told me, Ted was kicked out of the Law Library days before and was simply coming back to campus day after day to prowl.

Lastly, Dawn touched upon a central theme of Bundy's life – his search to be seen as something special; a "greatness," if you will, that Bundy—a constant user of people—would experience through the work and success of others, and in this particular case, his lawyer.

He also bragged about having John Henry Brown as his attorney. Brown was a youngish, dapper dresser with a theatrical flair and was a bit of a local celebrity lawyer, mostly due to his style and ability to retain higher profile clients. Ted seemed to relish the limelight, and it seemed that Ted felt Brown was one more example of how special and important Ted was.

CHAPTER SEVENTEEN

DR. AL CARLISLE

Back in the spring of last year (2018), Al Carlisle, the clinical psychologist who evaluated Ted Bundy after his incarceration in Utah, passed away. It came as a bit of a shock to me, as Al appeared to be in the peak of heath, and his death was sudden and unexpected.

My connection with Al Carlisle began after my friend James Massie contacted Al on my behalf (they'd been friends for years), asking if we could talk, and Al, true to his friendly nature, told Jim it was fine if I contacted him. At the time this occurred, I had only very recently decided to write a book about Bundy and I knew Al would have very good information even beyond that which I could locate in the official reports. After receiving the go-ahead, I called Al in the summer of 2006, in preparation of my trip to Utah for research purposes in August of that year.

Unfortunately, our schedules could not align themselves to allow us to meet face to face during my trip, but we did contact each other by phone and email as he assisted me in understanding what it was like dealing with Ted Bundy. And in very short order, we became friends. So much so, that we kept up with each other over the years, and we'd often send each other signed copies of our books whenever a new one was released. I'm very grateful that he took the time to write several books, for by doing so, he's left us a great deal of knowledge pertaining to Ted Bundy and killers in general. For those of you who've been traveling along with me through the years as I penned the first, and then the second, and finally, the third Bundy book, you'll notice that Dr. Al Carlisle plays a part in them all.

What follows is an email Al sent me in September 2006, only several weeks after he began working with me. I had sent him a number of questions which he promptly and succinctly answered.

Sent: Monday, September 11, 2006 10:53 p.m.

Subject: Ted Bundy

Kevin. Here are some answers to your questions.

1.—My first impression of Ted was that he was an intelligent, assertive person who had an air of confidence.

2.—If Ted had not been apprehended in Florida I believe he would have continued killing. He was out of control and I don't believe there was any chance that he would have been able to get control back. He was wanted by the police, he was separated from his family and the area he was most familiar with (northwest) and he couldn't go back to college and major in law. I believe that he knew that he would always be looking over his shoulder to see if there was a cop or someone who knew him. In essence, he was "free" but he was a person without hope.

3.—I believe that Ted felt remorse quite frequently for what he was doing. Bob Keppel in The Riverman film talks about Ted driving away from a crime scene, almost in hysterics because of what he had done. I believe he wanted to stop but couldn't. Instead, he built a defense mechanism in an attempt to shut off the guilt before it reached the level of consciousness. Ted was intelligent enough to be aware that sooner or later he would be caught and he knew he would be giving up everything he wanted out of life if he was caught. The issue here is: Was he feeling genuine guilt or was his remorse out of a fear of being caught? I believe there was a little of both. Ted built his life around being in control and I'm sure it bothered him when he wasn't.

4.—*This conversation occurred in the hall outside one of the interview rooms. Ted asked if I felt he was guilty of the Washington crimes. I wanted to say I knew for certain he was guilty but I felt that if I did say it, he would say that I was biased in my report. Ted paused, didn't ask why I thought that and he returned to his cell block. He didn't show any anger here.*

5.—*I didn't feel there was any time when Bundy was reaching out for "help." There were times when he would reach out for contact, both with me and with others.*

6.—Author's note: my question to Dr. Carlisle had to do with Bundy's statement to the writer Stephen Michaud about how he was able to refrain from killing a particular young woman, and jokingly said that he was in his "reformation period." *Regarding Bundy's statement to Michaud, I believe that Bundy's statement was probably more of a wish at the time of the event that he could get rid of his need for violence.*

7.—*There were only a few times that I saw Ted really angry. For the most part, he wanted to appear cooperative, in control, and not guilty. He knew that if I saw anger in him it would go in the report.*

8.—*I didn't sense any body odor changes in him. Regarding the eyes, I have had other women tell me about the eyes of the person about to attack them. There is a difference which is likely due to some form of temporary neurotransmitter changes when a person is in that state of mind.*

The relationship between Ted Bundy and Al Carlisle is fascinating to observe, albeit from the distance of many years from when the actual events occurred. From Al's perspective, he understood Bundy was a blood-thirsty psychopathic killer who was responsible for the nightmarish deaths of many women. And yet, on a day-to-day basis, as he interviewed and conducted tests, he also began to see a likeable man and, in turn, it's clear Bundy liked the doctor as well. Of course, Carlisle understood he was only seeing the well-crafted façade that Bundy had worked so hard to create, so he was never "fooled" by his tactics. But in a human sense, under such controlled circumstances, Ted Bundy could be that likeable fellow. It was this charming outward demeanor that caused his family members and friends back in Washington state to stand by him—it just couldn't be their Ted— even after he was revealed to the world as the monster he ultimately became.

It is of interest to note too, that these friendly interactions between the two men would continue long after Bundy had ceased any official dealings with the psychologist. After Bundy was turned over to the Colorado authorities to stand trial for the murder of Caryn Campbell, he managed to escape from the Aspen Courthouse one spring day by jumping out of the second story window (no easy task, as it's a twenty-five-foot drop to the ground). After his recapture, close to a week later, he made it a point of calling Carlisle to discuss it, and this conversation was wisely recorded. And from the joviality one hears in Ted's voice, it's very easy to imagine that two close friends were simply catching up with one another.

PHOTOGRAPHS

*The Campus Crier newspaper at Central Washington
State College, depicting a composite drawing of the
man who abducted Susan Rancourt, and attempted
other abductions at the college, on April 17, 1974*

Susan Elaine Rancourt IS MISSING

SUSAN ELAINE RANCOURT
WHITE, FEMALE
AMERICAN
DATE OF BIRTH
10—12—55

HEIGHT: 5'2"
WEIGHT: 120—130
EYES: BLUE
HAIR: BLONDE
SHOULDER LENGTH
AGE: 18 YEARS

$1,000.00 REWARD

FOR INFORMATION LEADING TO HER PRESENT WHEREABOUTS AND RETURN

SUSAN WAS LAST SEEN WEDNESDAY EVENING AT 10:00 p.m. SHE HAS NOT CALLED HOME, HER RESIDENCE HALL AT CENTRAL WASHINGTON STATE COLLEGE, ANY OF HER KNOWN FRIENDS, NOR HAS SHE BEEN SEEN WITH ANYONE SINCE WEDNESDAY.

SHE WAS LAST SEEN WEARING A YELLOW COAT, YELLOW SHORT SLEEVE SWEATER, GRAY CORDUROY PANTS AND BROWN HUSH-PUPPY TYPE SHOES.

IF YOU HAVE SEEN SUSAN OR ANYONE CLOSELY RESEMBLING HER PLEASE CALL C.W.S.C. (COLLECT) (509) 963—1111 OR THE NEAREST POLICE DEPART MENT OR THE WASHINGTON

The Missing Person's poster of Susan Rancourt

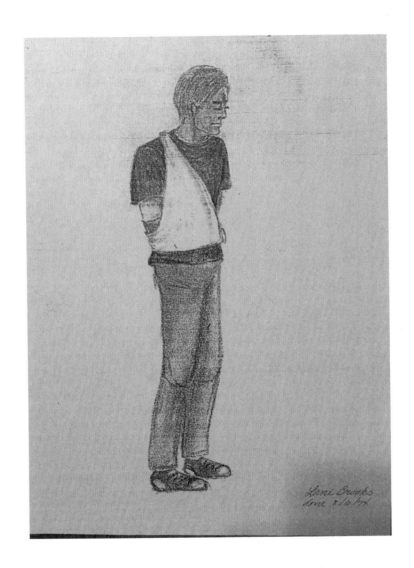

A rarely seen composite drawing of the
man (Bundy) with his arm in a sling

A shot of the walkway that Bundy and Susan Rancourt traveled down at CWSC. Bundy and Rancourt came from the front of the library and rounded the far corner of the building on the left. The bridge that ran over the pond was situated where the newer walkway is seen, and as they stepped off the bridge they stayed on the asphalt and angled off to the right of the photo to a deserted spot on campus by a railroad trestle

On the evening of May 6, 1974, Kathy Parks and Lorraine Fargo, both Oregon State University students, spent a few minutes talking on the sidewalk area seen in the above photo. Afterward, Kathy crossed the small street and entered the Memorial Union Commons by way of the steps seen on the right. Bundy would lead her away from here about 15 minutes later

*Sackett Hall, where Kathy Parks was a resident, was
only one block from the Memorial Union Commons*

Alameda Middle School in Pocatello, Idaho. It was here that Ted Bundy rolled up in his VW and convinced Lynette Culver, 12, to leave with him. He would murder her back at his hotel room at the Holiday Inn by drowning her in the bathtub.

$10,000 REWARD

to anyone having information leading to the
safe return of Jayleen Banker, Age 10

4'6" Tall

60 Lbs.

Brown Eyes

Long
Light Brown
Hair

Fair
Complexion

Small Scars
at hairline,
left side

Abducted
Aug. 23,
1974
from
Rawlins,
Wyoming

Please Contact
CARBON COUNTY SHERIFF'S OFFICE
Rawlins, Wyo. 82301   Call 307-324-2776   C.W. Ogburn, Sheriff

*Jayleen Banker, one of the victims of
the Wyoming Rodeo Murders*

A portion of the rear of the Chi Omega Sorority house, as seen in the summer of 2008. Undergoing restoration at that time, the stacked doors to the right of the photo are classic 1970s design

Chi Omega, summer 2008

Dawn Kraut, who had a revealing conversation with Ted Bundy in the cafeteria at the University of Washington

Leslie Parmenter, 1979, only one year
after her encounter with Ted Bundy

ACKNOWLEDGMENTS

It is impossible to write nonfiction books without having a number of people to thank, and this book is no exception. First, because I've used a large portion of the official record, I would like to thank those institutions that have diligently housed what has come to be a voluminous amount of material that make up the Ted Bundy case file. And for the Bundy case there are two: The King County Archives in Seattle, Washington, and the Florida State Archives, in Tallahassee, Florida. Without these fine institutions, writing about the Bundy murders would be extremely difficult, and that difficulty would only increase over time. Of the many thousands of pages that I retain from my days of writing my first book on the case, over 98% of this material came from these two archives. Once again, I would like to give a nod and a tip of the hat to these two fine institutions, and the wonderful people who run them! Although Utah has never shown any interest in housing any materials from Bundy's reign of terror in Utah and the surrounding states, Jerry Thompson, the lead detective for the Bundy case in Utah, was kind enough to share his files with me, and for that I'm extremely grateful. Indeed, I'm extremely grateful to all the investigators and other participants who so kindly worked with me throughout the writing of this series. Without their active and dedicated participation, a great deal of valuable information would have remained hidden, and ultimately lost forever.

I would also like to thank the following people who assisted me with this book:

Shirl Sipperley DiGugno. Shirl not only assisted me in locating two of the interviewees for this book, but was very helpful in securing contact info for other individuals as well. Knowing how difficult this process can be, I very much appreciate her efforts; Amy Merka, a Facebook friend and fellow traveler in the field of true crime, for introducing me to Bundy victim, Kathy Kleiner, whose testimony appears in this book. Without her efforts I would never have had a chance to interact with Kathy, become friends, and interview her for this book. Thanks goes also to Vince Lahey who, while digging through the archive in Aspen, Colorado, found an article containing important information from *The Aspen Times* and passed it along to me, which I've used for this book.

My thanks go out to all of those who've allowed me to interview them for this book. In doing so, they are contributing to history, for wherever valid and accurate testimony can be saved and placed on the printed page, it will be of great benefit for future generations. Each and every story is like a television screen allowing us to look back into the past, and I'm grateful for each one of you: Francine Bardole and her son Larry Bardole; Kathy Kleiner; Robert Cook; Andrew Valdez; Laurie Anne Hulse and her son Tom Hulse; "Maggie" from Tallahassee; the woman who wishes to remain anonymous, but was nevertheless close with both Kathy Parks and Lorraine Fargo; and the late Lorraine Fargo, who contacted me after *The Bundy Murders* was published. Lorraine, like so many of the family and friends of the women Bundy murdered, carried deep emotional wounds stemming from that time. But through our communications, little by little, she began to open up, and it wasn't long before she mentioned that what was now happening in her life, was actually proving to be cathartic for her. And then, within a year, Lorraine passed away.

Thankfully, her exceedingly important testimony has been preserved in my book, *The Trail of Ted Bundy: Digging up the Untold Stories*.

And last, but certainly not least, I'd like to thank my editor at WildBlue Press, Jacqueline Burch, for all her efforts and skill that makes every book she edits a much better book than what it would be otherwise. She also has a great deal of patience. I know she does, as she's worked with me on my last two books!

Other Ted Bundy Books From Kevin Sullivan and WildBlue Press

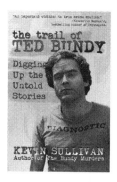

The Trail of Ted Bundy: A look into the life of serial killer Ted Bundy, from those who knew him, to those who chased him, and from those who mourned his many victims. The Trail of Ted Bundy: Digging Up the Untold Stories, is a journey back in time, to a world when Ted Bundy was killing young women and girls in the Pacific Northwest and beyond. You'll hear all the revealing stories; many of them coming to light for the first time. *wbp.bz/trailbundya*

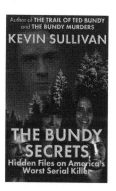

The Bundy Secrets: The hidden files of the manhunt to find and stop Ted Bundy, as well as the investigations into his depredations, gathered from official and unofficial sources from Washington to Florida, as well as contemporary interviews and author commentary to flesh out the details. A must-read for true crime students of Ted Bundy. *wbp.bz/bundysecetsa*

More Great Reads From Kevin Sullivan and WildBlue Press

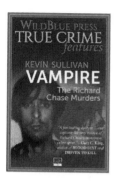

VAMPIRE: The Richard Chase Murders is the tale of a diabolical, homicidal madman running amok, mutilating and murdering the unsuspecting residents in the quiet neighborhoods of Sacramento, CA. His diabolical and unrelenting desires, not just to kill his victims but to drink their blood, unleashed a terror within the city unlike anything the residents had ever known. *wbp.bz/vampirea*

Kentucky Bloodbath: An excursion into the weird and the bizarre: from a medieval-esque murder in a small town museum to the jilted boyfriend who decided that his former girlfriend needed to die on her twenty-first birthday. Then there's the demented son who returns home to live with his mother and stepfather, and one night in their beautiful mansion sitting atop a high bluff overlooking the Ohio River, slaughters them. Each case will keep you on the edge of your seat. *wbp.bz/kba*

SAMUEL L. SOMMER
CHRISTOPHER JOSSART

RAILROADED

FRAMED FOR MURDER,
FIGHTING FOR JUSTICE

RAILROADED by CHRISTOPHER JOSSART

Read an excerpt next

1.

Stolen in Suffolk

Three men in sharp suits briskly walked toward Sam Sommer's car. Sam looked down at the D on his automatic transmission console inside his Chevy station wagon, grabbed the door handle with his left hand, and poised his right hand atop the horn. His vehicle slowly coasted with one foot on the brake. He wasn't sure whether to squeal out, park and run, lay on the horn, or just keep coasting and jittering.

For someone who made a living making decisions that affected dozens of people each day, Sam couldn't decide what to do in a flash for his own good. His 150-pound furry backseat driver did a better job on demonstrating some damn decisiveness than he did. Sam figured the hell with indecision; it felt better to freeze and hope they would go away. He parked the car—stopping just inside a driveway from a well-travelled street. The unorthodox position of the vehicle appeared foreign to structured rows of parking stalls that filled the lot.

One of the men shouted, "Sommer!" This was all business whomever these good ole' boys were, and the unfolding encounter made Sam realize it included a one-sided agenda. One guy looked familiar from a recent civil, yet macho-style encounter he experienced with a member of Suffolk County law enforcement almost a week ago.

Sam quickly caught a glimpse of an unmarked car parked on the other side of the lot near Walter Court, which runs next to Long Island's busy Jericho Turnpike. The observation of the car parked away from everything else made Sam's already sweaty predicament even more of a salty horror.

He pulled into a Dunkin' Donuts parking lot adjacent to the freeway in Commack, New York, with his big St. Bernard dog. The 2073 Jericho Turnpike establishment opened in 1964 and was a favorite destination for a blossoming community. It was within blocks of Sam's house. The donut shop still stands today near the long-running Mayfair Shopping Center.

Sargent started barking wildly at the sight of oncoming strangers. Sam squinted out the window in an attempt to muster some last-second negotiation to slow the men's collective pace. The way the men marched spelled trouble.

"Who are you and what do you want?" Sam contended. Nothing but steps for an answer, now a few feet from his car. The pleasant distraction of sweet dough aroma in the air moments earlier was now history. It was replaced with the stench of something dirty going down around 8:10 p.m. on Wednesday, May 22, 1968.

Sargent's momentous fit temporarily distracted the three intruders from their pursuit. The hiccup in an imminent showdown of three-against-one (plus canine) gave Sam an attempt to slide across the seat and exit the passenger side. It was too late for man and best friend. One of the three men had already swung around that side of the car to guard the passenger door.

The man who was shouting "Sommer" identified himself as Detective Thomas Gill with Suffolk County Homicide. The officer, a bit older than Sam, commanded him to join his men in going to the homicide division fourth precinct in nearby Smithtown.

The guy that Sam believed he met days earlier was another detective, Thomas Mansel, who piggybacked Gill's command. "You heard him, Sommer, let's go." Mansel was with the County's Homicide Squad as well.

Sam boldly said he wasn't going anywhere until he learned why.

"Let's go, Sommer," Gill said. He and another man opened the door before Sam could roll up the window and lock his vehicle. They clutched him by the shoulders.

Two men yanked Sam out of his idling station wagon head first in waning daylight at Dunkin' Donuts. Sam thought for a second that the orchestrated grab-and-go was a bad joke somehow tied to a call he received around dinner time to meet someone at the donut shop. He winced in pain from the deep grabs that latched into his sunburned skin. The men rolled Sam to his side on the concrete and cuffed him.

"What the fuck?" cried the thirty-one-year-old family man and business pro in feeble resistance to a kidnapping. Sam's five foot, eight inch frame fell prey to two taller kidnappers. "Stop!" A chorus line of pleas continued during the out-of-the-blue confrontation. While resisting he received a kick in the back of his knee from one of the detectives while being prone on his side for the wide open target. The men quickly dragged Sam across the parking lot toward the unmarked car.

"All right, all right," Sam yelped. Mansel and the other detective following Gill let go of Sam. They lifted him up and let him walk on his own toward their vehicle after a hard shove from Mansel. Sam resumed the journey to the police car voluntarily.

It was still bright enough to notice a man being dragged against his will. Some teenagers had been hanging out in the store for quite some time. Less than a minute before the men left their car from across the lot, Sam entered the Dunkin' Donuts property to meet another man for a meeting concerning one of his business associates, a family relative. The man had not yet arrived, but Sam arrived expecting to wait for him.

Sam slowed his pace toward the car and glanced at the men, expressing concern for Sargent. The dog was left alone in a running car with the driver's side door partially opened. A response came in the form of another shove forward. Sam looked back again toward his station wagon without breaking his stride to catch a glimpse of Sargent. The car bounced like a modern-day pimp mobile from Sargent's display of protection toward his master.

Within feet from the unmarked vehicle, Sam switched his cadence from a defensive tone to one of cooperation. "What's this all about? Please, stop."

Gill opened the back seat door and the other men chucked Sam into the car. After avoiding a brush with his head against the far side door, Sam tried to roll on his back. He was instantly lifted up to a sitting position and buckled. While vehicles zoomed next to one of New York's busiest thoroughfares, a group of men allegedly sworn to serve and protect were stealing a man's freedom amidst the roaring engines.

The door closed to the back seat while Sam realized there were no inside handles. His capturers were in a hurry. The car instantly hit the turnpike and in no time it merged with traffic.

Sam was shaking too much to play eye games with Mansel and Gill, who were seated on each side of him. He just closed his eyes and prayed for the best—whatever that meant. The car quickly exited the turnpike and within a few blocks ended up parked in what seemed like a bumpy lot right next to a main road. That made Sam breathe a little better knowing he wasn't going somewhere far—a self-fulfilling means of fabricating hope.

The driver got out, and Sam asked Gill what this ordeal was about. Gill said he'd find out soon enough and told him to shut up. The driver came back and in less than five minutes the journey to purgatory resumed. No more freeway. Sam arrived in what appeared to be an alley by the narrowing of a street between two lit buildings. He then realized he was at the police station in Hauppauge, a suburb of Smithtown to the south.

It was dusk when the three men placed Sam to his feet in the parking lot of the back entrance to the Suffolk County Fourth Precinct. The whole thing about being around cops suddenly didn't feel right. Sam was supposed to find comfort at a police station; yet, he felt increasingly scared while the three men assertively escorted him toward the back entrance. Once inside, they led Sam down a long hallway to a room on the right.

The average-sized room, about twelve by twelve, was filled with some office equipment, a stool, a couple of chairs, and a square table. It resembled an interrogation room but with a more office-like feel to it. The men immediately shoved Sam against the table and then dropped his fumbling body onto a hard wooden stool and removed his cuffs. They seemed to be setting a tone of play along or it's gonna get physical. The three men convened with a fourth badge from the station outside the room while the door remained open. Sam mulled the connection of a few dots.

How in the world does one go from hooking up with someone in a parking lot to finding a home in a Suffolk County police station in the snap of a finger?

He tried to link learning about the sudden death of his business partner and relative, Irving Silver, to the current madness. Sam flew home last Wednesday, May 15, from Florida by himself while his family remained vacationing with both sets of in-laws. Sam had to deal with a dilemma Silver was having with Sommer's businesses, in particular a man named Harold Goberman.

Goberman was the one who called Sam around dinner time to meet at Dunkin' Donuts regarding Silver's death. Sam recently hired Goberman, who went with an alias of a Harold Masterson, to do some work at his deli in Commack, the Deli-Queen. His hiring was the result of a recommendation from Silver to help Goberman get reacclimated into society. He retained a vast criminal record and was out of prison on parole. Sam wanted to give the man another chance at life.

Detective Mansel rather forcefully asked Sam to help Suffolk County police identify Silver's body on the afternoon of Friday, May 17. Silver was apparently killed during the early morning on the same day. His body was found on Wheatley Road, a rather unfrequented rural artery off the Jericho Turnpike southeast of Commack.

"You're going to confess, Sommer, right now," instructed Gill in the interrogation room. No identification given of the other men. No reading of any rights concerning a kidnapping called an arrest. The door slammed from the hallway and the same two men who nabbed him plus another stood behind Gill in the crowded room.

"About what?" Sam inquired, still cuffed.

The new man on the scene from the precinct grabbed Sam under his arms and lifted him off of the stool. Gill then pushed Sam head first into the wall and proceeded to shove him onto the floor. Still cuffed, Sam was then harshly seated and punched across the left eye by another officer. His sunburned skin absorbed the beating with needlelike pain.

Another greeting with the concrete floor. Picked up again and placed on the stool, Gill got in Sam's face.

"Want a lawyer, Sommer, or you gonna fess up?"

"For what?" Sam shouted.

"Killing your business buddy," Mansel shouted. "We know you wacked him with a lead pipe and then ran him over. Son of a bitch."

Stunned by what he heard, Sam offered a left-to-right head nod that suggested a nonverbal "No" in reply to the men's accusations. Bewildered with the name Harold Goberman taking over his mind as the centerpiece part of a jigsaw puzzle, Sam started to describe his phone call to Gill tied to a meeting at Dunkin' Donuts.

"A Harold Goberman is behind this" … stars—a galaxy of pain. A thump on the head by an undetected detective from behind with a telephone book while Sam was held down on the stool blurred his vision. Another whack on the neck from the phone directory ensued in what seemed to be a one-sided conversation. The Goberman mention obviously set off the detectives.

More pounds from the phone book behind Sam's head continued until his ability to sit upright in the stool gave way to the hard floor. Sam laid with his hands over his head and shook enough to trip a Richter scale. His fear couldn't muster any words.

The persuasive techniques used in the basement of Suffolk County's Homicide Unit didn't stop. The men of the badge kicked and yelled at Sam while he curled up on the floor. Realizing there was no other choice but to possibly die, Sam begged to tell the officers about the Goberman phone call. They would have nothing to do with the Goberman thing.

The four men huddled together as if it was fourth-and-goal on the one-yard line and Sam was on defense all by himself. Too pissed off to think about a lawyer, Sam wanted to fight the assholes head on. It was evident there was no more hope for textbook interrogation procedures; it was now all about survival—in a damn police station.

Further beating might have killed Sam. Why didn't they just kill him? That question is still debated today by people who know and love him. God's grace allowed for his story to be told for the benefit of others in the name of justice, Sam offered in retrospect.

"Think about what comes out of your mouth before we come back, Sommer," asserted Gill. The men then left the smoke-filled whipping chamber to the hallway with the door still open. In a cloud of chaos sat a man who a couple of hours earlier left home to learn something to aid in the case of a loved one.

The origination of Sam Sommer's fateful trip to Dunkin' Donuts came with risks and uncertainties in dealing with Goberman. The disgruntled Goberman set Sam up, or so it appeared.

To this day, dear friends Phil and Susan Cirrone from Long Island remember that day more than fifty years later. Philly, as Sam coined the nickname of his close friend, detailed the circumstances leading up to the kidnapping and subsequent aftermath.

A personal recount of horror:

I got a call around 8:00 from Elaine Sommer to come over earlier than planned the evening of the twenty-second of May. We were going to leave shortly anyway to see Elaine's parents visiting from Florida, but Elaine said it was important. We heard earlier in the week that a family member died unexpectedly.

Susan and I are the type of friends to Sammy and Elaine that wouldn't question them in a time of need. We got a babysitter in light of the urgent development and headed to their house.

Upon arrival, Elaine greeted us by the front door. We could tell something was up. She told us that Sam didn't return yet from a meeting at Dunkin' Donuts near the freeway. Elaine didn't have time to go into detail. All she said was that Sam had been involved in trying to find out what happened to her uncle, Irving Silver. She was beside herself; Susan and I were barely inside the door.

Sam was going to meet some guy who had information about Silver at a donut shop. She said Sam drove the station wagon to Dunkin' Donuts with their dog and that something felt wrong.

We didn't know Irving Silver, but Elaine quickly filled us in about his connection to her family and that he was dead. Regardless, friends are friends, and there was no need to pry at the moment about what happened to him. Shocked and saddened by the news, we kept listening. Her parents hugged us and just remained silent the whole time.

Elaine asked me to kindly take her to check on Sammy at Dunkin' Donuts. Of course Susan and I agreed, but first I told Elaine to call the store. She did so and learned Sam wasn't inside the establishment. We then left, determined to find out where he was. Her parents remained at the house for the kids.

The three of us arrived at a nearby Dunkin' Donuts off the turnpike and immediately saw the Sommer's vehicle barely inside the lot from the road. We cautiously circled the car to get a pulse on the situation and noticed their dog going berserk in the back seat.

Creepy shit, yet we remained calm for a horrified Elaine. The lot was well lit and a couple of cars were parked near the store's entrance. Elaine jumped out of our car and yelled to us that Sam's vehicle was still running. We could see, too, that the driver's side door wasn't closed all the way either.

Unquestionably, this was a spine-chilling scene. The dog increased its barking likely from recognizing Elaine. Susan and I both hesitated to go near the car. We advised Elaine not to touch anything and told her that we were going inside the donut shop to see if anyone knew anything. Susan and I sped to the entrance of the donut shop and ran inside for answers.

Inside the store we couldn't find Sammy, but we found the sight of curiosity all over the joint from the way a couple of workers and a group of kids looked at us. They all appeared dazed.

I was working as a corrections officer at the time and learned a few things when it came to reading people. Susan kept an eye on Elaine while I asked the manager what was going on. Sweat drenched my shirt. Where in the hell was Sammy?

A few teenagers congregated around the counter in front of the manager. He said the person in the car who parked weirdly in his lot was taken by some guys. One of the teens chimed in and said the man he thinks we were talking about was dragged out of his car and taken away (pointing in the direction of the turnpike). Another teen described the dog in the back seat running around so wildly that the car bounced.

Susan and I grabbed hold of one another. "What?" we collectively bellowed. "Like kidnapped?" I piggybacked the disbelief with a question to continue the inquisition. We froze with jaws on the floor. The first kid said they were like gangsters and asked if we knew the guy who was taken.

The store manager indicated that the men, unable to recall how many for sure—a few he proclaimed, looked like a bunch of wise guys. Another teen said that they looked like bad asses and one of them carried a gun. The same youngster believed there were three men working together against one victim.

I asked the manager if he called the cops. He said no. I got the impression he wanted to look the other way, so to speak. The kids were kind enough to wish us well and they split, too, likely not wanting to stick around much longer. The described mobster-type men had everyone on edge.

On the verge of calling the police, I noticed a cop car pull into the lot. It felt comforting, yet odd. If no one called the police how would they know what was going on? Maybe someone else around the neighborhood or store called, I thought. Anyway, Susan went outside toward Elaine, who quickly grabbed the officer's attention for obvious reasons. I made a quick call to a lawyer friend of mine to explain what was going down and then joined the commotion outside.

The front driver's side door was part way open. A slimy mist, like dew, covered most of the windows, probably from the dog's cries. It didn't look like Sammy was around. All eyes fixated on the cop for answers. Car running. Dog freaking out. No Sammy. The officer then did a quick search of the car.

Elaine then left with the officer to go across the way a short distance to the Mayfair Shopping Center to use a phone. We just stood by the car trying to comfort the dog without being able to touch anything. The biggest thing we couldn't touch was reality. We were scared and more so for Sammy.

The officer said that he and Elaine would be back in a matter of minutes. Their poor dog's barks grew hoarser. I told Susan that I called Joe Scibilia, and that he might be able to help Sammy from a legal standpoint, if needed.

Like the officer promised, he returned with Elaine. She looked as mad as she did worried a few moments ago. I asked what was going on. The officer informed us that he called the station to see if there was anything on Mr. Sommer. I could tell Elaine was pissed. She then insisted that her husband was kidnapped. Just hearing that word sent shivers through my body.

The officer said that she would need to fill out a Missing Persons Report at the police station in Hauppauge. He told Elaine that she could take the car home (for perceived concern about the dog). The cop's intention appeared heartfelt toward the dog; yet, I found it strange that he would release the car back to its owner so quickly. Theoretically, this location and the vehicle itself could still be considered a potential crime scene, I thought.

Here's what else seemed screwed up. The officer didn't write anything down up until this point. From my years in corrections, documentation means everything. Writing something down gave an impression of importance and focus. How do you dismiss a running car with the driver's side door left open and a dog going nuts in the back seat as anything not related to foul play?

http://wbp.bz/railroadeda

**AVAILABLE FROM SUSAN FENSTEN
AND WILDBLUE PRESS!**

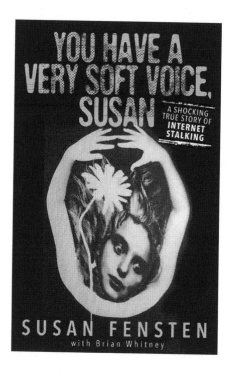

**YOU HAVE A VERY SOFT VOICE,
SUSAN by SUSAN FENSTEN**

Read an excerpt next

http://wbp.bz/softvoicea

PROLOGUE

I've Seen Where You Live, I Know What You Eat

A tremor went down my spine the day I heard that Leonard was planning to sell his ranch-style house in the New Jersey suburbs and move to my neighborhood, Williamsburg, Brooklyn. It was a gray, chilly spring day, fittingly gloomy. The dank weather compounded my mood and lent itself to a scene from a grainy noir movie, dilapidated factories in stages of decomposition everywhere that he could hide, stash a weapon, stash a body. Stash me.

It seemed that Leonard thought a loft might better suit his lifestyle. Leonard, the schizophrenic child math prodigy, who had blossomed into a wealthy swinger, painter, and collector of sexual paraphernalia. This wasn't a good sign since his present residence had apparently been suitably outfitted for his bacchanals for quite some time. He claimed he wanted something bigger, hipper, something located in an area where he wouldn't stand out quite as much from his cookie cutter neighbors in New Jersey. But I knew that wasn't it. His wealth could have easily afforded him lofts in SoHo, Tribeca, or Chelsea—all within striking distance of the downtown dungeons and secret after-hours places. The real attraction for him was his new "cousin Susan." Was he intent on intensifying the deviant nature of his parties with me as his guest of honor?

I'd never met Leonard, but I knew a lot about him. I knew that he had been charged but never convicted of rape and kidnapping. I knew that he had a lavish psychiatric history and that he often went off his meds and had been repeatedly hospitalized. His doctors had decided that he was mentally competent for release. He had been able to keep down his Wall Street job, at least well enough to amass a fortune. Leonard had the knack of appearing so normal at times, so non-descript. If he wanted to, he could look like an ordinary person. He was just an *ordinary* person, one who just happened to be obsessed with me.

I fearfully imagined him dazed, wandering the streets searching for me. The area could readily conceal someone like Leonard by virtue of the eclectic mix of people it attracted. Much to the chagrin of natives and old timers, the "weird folk" had moved in and found that it suited their alternate lifestyles all too well. Williamsburg. It was a forgotten New York neighborhood with exotic, dark alleys; a Mecca for artists, musicians, yuppies, skinheads, and those of the tattooed persuasion. The hulking smokestack of the Domino Sugar factory belched out an aroma of burned brown sugar that draped everything with a sweet, invisible mist. It was a hipster zone, where a chameleon like Leonard could crawl unobtrusively from building to building, from playground to lounge. Leonard, a master of stealth to begin with, might find that Williamsburg rendered his avant-garde lifestyle and morbid moods virtually invisible.

Early spring in New York City can be depressing, and the gloomy weekend served only to fuel my imagination as my mind's eye saw Leonard examining lofts and surveying the neighborhood. He was near, possibly peering through the window from the back seat of a Town Car as it rolled past clothing stores, cafes, delis, a subway stop, the Salvation Army, the Domino sugar factory. He was examining the landscape, beads of water sliding from the glass to the shiny black exterior of the car. These images sliced through my mind like sharp, piercing screams. Had he come to the conclusion that *all* Williamsburg residents were creatures of darkness and decay? Or was it just me? Did he believe that I was a perfect match for the side of his personality never seen by his Wall Street clients? Did he picture me in his harness?

The cold gray rain made me feel only more desolate.

***

It wasn't long after Leonard's trip to Brooklyn that he let his observations be known by updating his Yahoo! profile. It now featured a graphic close-up photo of a vagina tattooed with a fanged red devil, a shiny metal earring piercing the clitoris. He knew I would see it. He knew he had scared me so much I couldn't stop looking. On his new profile, below a list of his favorite torture and rape websites was a taunting poem:

Dear cousin, my cousin, Oh cousin so sweet.
I've seen where you live, I know what you eat.
I want to see your eyes when we first meet.

He was getting closer, I could feel it. He was emerging from my email inbox, coming out into the real world, my world. He was going to get a closer look at me, see me on the street, go by my house, and run a finger along the gate. And I had nowhere to go.

CHAPTER ONE

Information Not Released to the Public

Murderers are not monsters, they're men.
And that's the most frightening thing about them.

—Alice Sebold

After an hour of questioning and getting nowhere, one of the detectives pulled out a photograph. He looked at it, placed it on the table, and with his index finger, slid it toward me across the metal desk. My heart constricted like a convulsion of sharp pins. Fearing it might be a crime scene photo I braced myself. But then I recognized it immediately, it was a simple color photo of Jennifer Whipkey in life, one of two images that I had seen in internet news reports about her murder. Her beaming face seemed to hover ghostlike above the cold steel desk, lying in front of me, looking at me. A presence that was chillingly real. Her cheerful expression was frozen in time. The atmosphere in the blue lit room felt like a morgue. A mere one hundred pounds, she perished under a frenzy of sixty-three stab wounds.

Feeling helpless, I thought of her young child, motherless, like my nephew when my sister died. Death and sorrow—my uninvited twin companions, the feeling was always the same—my soul touching the third rail. I wondered what the detectives thought of me. They seemed like any other overworked cops following up on leads and hitting dead ends three years and counting. Could they really hold suspicions that I was connected to murder? Or were they hoping for just a shred of detail that could point them in the right direction and spring the case back to life? I told them that I felt horrible about her death, about the nature of this extremely violent crime, and how terrifying it must have been for her. That I had heartfelt sympathy for what her family was going through. I knew all about how the violent death of a young woman decimates the surviving family. My words felt futile. I wished that there something I could do to help them, but I knew nothing.

The meeting was long and unsettling. It was obvious they really wanted to solve this case which almost seemed personal for them. They had to answer to her family and her community. Their labor, frustration, and emotion were coming through in their questions about my life, my social life, how I came to know about Jennifer Whipkey's murder. The killing wasn't highly publicized outside of the small New Jersey Township of West Deptford. They wanted to know why I had information about a crime that wasn't made public. Of course it would draw the immediate attention of homicide detectives; that was completely understandable. But I was far removed from the terrifying deed and had only been pulled in by a net of lies as complex as a spider's web.

When it concluded, I thanked Special Agent Waller. I had the feeling I would be seeing him again very soon.

I was escorted to the elevator by another FBI official. I passed once again through multiple security checkpoints, each time fishing out ID from my wallet. All the while I reflected back in hopes of finding some sense in it all, while at the same point realizing that there are some things in this world that will never make any sense, things that you are forced to accept. Like actions with no reason or purpose, minds without conscience. In the thick glass that seemed to be everywhere, I caught a glimpse of my transparent reflection. It was still me, at least I looked the same, which surprised me as my life had been bluntly interrupted and thrown around like rag doll. I waved 'thanks' to the last security guard who buzzed me out and pushed through the revolving door. Out into the financial district, the city sunlight and street noise brought me back to normalcy. My town, New York City; ever moving along, never stopping, and reverberating in a million directions. It reinvigorated me.

It was a relief to re-join the ordinary world. I had emerged from the underworld, an 'other' realm, an unpretty world where bodies washed of their evidence are posed in caked puddles of blood. A world of chaos and order where square-shouldered law enforcement personnel dutifully knocked on doors, chased down witnesses, and presented evidence to prosecutors. Most of the time they wrapped up their cases, but tragically sometimes not, moving on to the next one in a ceaseless cycle of reward and frustration. I was left with the indelible knowledge that there were butcherers traveling the highways and lurking in back yards never to be found. Maybe even in my own backyard.

At the core of this saga is the reason I was here in the first place. This very strange thing that I had encountered had affected me in ways I could not have imagined. It had been almost two years since this all began in 2003, like a carnival of cracked mirrors with a quicksand floor with phantoms reflected in the distorted glass. I had to shake off these images and get back to my desk at Rizzoli International

Publications just a few stops away at 22nd Street and Park Avenue South. I had missed enough time already.

My life started out unsheltered, I was spared little in the bad old days of New York, but it was now all about books and publishers, authors, tours, media lists, and high expectations. A book publicist is essentially a salesman, a pitchman with an idea clutching a roster of ambitious authors and anxious editors. It's at times a waltz on a high wire, at others glamorous, yet bone-grinding hard work. I hopped on the uptown subway immersed in a reel of thoughts of how I came to be exhaustively questioned by two New Jersey Homicide Detectives at One Federal Plaza, FBI Headquarters in New York City.

How did I get here? How did an otherwise normal everyday New Yorker who did not operate in the world of crime, wind up at FBI headquarters in downtown Manhattan now being vigorously interrogated about an unsolved brutal murder?

CHAPTER TWO

Into the World

*There is always one moment in childhood when
the door opens and lets in the future.*

—Graham Greene

In the cab, my sister wouldn't even look at my mother. She stared straight ahead in a fury on the way home from the hospital. It was just hours after I was born. Upon news of my arrival, my father almost fainted because he had another daughter. Less than a day old and already my reception into the world was fractured. My father and mother met in a Greenwich Village café. He was twenty-four and an aspiring actor; she was nineteen and had moved to New York to study fashion illustration at Parson's School of Design. My father, John Fensten, studied at the Actor's Studio with Lee and Susan Strasberg (Susan, my namesake, visited mom in the hospital when I was born). He landed a role on *Playhouse 90*, the acclaimed ninety-minute live TV series that ran from the late fifties to the early sixties. One would think that such a couple, blessed with talent and connections, could look forward to a happy life together. After my parents married in 1961, however, things unraveled almost immediately. The years that followed would be tough—at times grueling—for my mother and father and their children, my sister Ilia and me.

Still, I love to think about the early years of my childhood even though they don't represent an idyllic time of innocence or white picket fences. My parents lived on the Upper West Side when I was born in July of 1962, but by the time I was two, we lived on the Lower East Side, moving from apartment to apartment just one step ahead of the rent collector. My father began to disappear for weeks at a time, occasionally landing in Bellevue Hospital. We had no clue as to his whereabouts during these disappearances. He was generally unemployed except for a brief stint as an insurance clerk, and my mother worked as a waitress, standing on her feet eight hours a day for thirty-five bucks a week.

Despite the hardships, there were good times. Desperation had an air of excitement and surviving in the streets of Manhattan conferred unspoken badges of honor on Ilia and me. Life in Fun City, New York's nickname before it became known as the Big Apple, was gritty and hard. Films like *Midnight Cowboy*, *Taxi Driver*, and *Mean Streets* could have been documentaries about life in my neighborhoods. My mother had come from an upper-middle class home in New England and didn't find living in survival mode so enchanting, but my sister and I loved every minute of it. Uptown or downtown, there was always adrenaline in the streets—junkies, gang fights, or a naked woman walking down Lexington Avenue—the island was ours. Life was raw, never dull. Our apartment on St. Mark's Place in the East Village was burglarized nine times. Our missing things were found in the junkie's apartment upstairs but the detective investigating the crime wouldn't make an arrest unless my mother agreed to sleep with him. She didn't and we moved out soon after.

Things weren't much different when we moved uptown to Spanish Harlem in 1967. It was the summer of the race riots. Bottles and metal garbage cans rained down from rooftops within days of moving in. Upon the discovery of a woman upstairs in the hallway who had been stabbed, my mother quickly ushered us into our apartment door. There were used syringes and burned spoons of heroin addicts outside of our apartment door on the way to school in the mornings. Fires routinely flared up across the street when junkies shot up in dark rooms of abandoned apartment buildings, the matches used to cook heroin igniting the filthy mattresses they slept on. We could feel the intense heat on our faces while leaning out the apartment window, lurid yellow flames lighting up the night as they licked the brick and mortar.

While waiting to be buzzed into our building one night, Ilia and I were held up at knifepoint by a teenager who threatened to cut our tongues out. The thief got all of twelve dollars by shoving his hand in Ilia's pocket. It was a good trade. He got the cash and we kept our tongues, although Ilia, normally full of swagger and attitude—"Ya gotta get tough, Susie!"—cried like a baby when we got upstairs. I, on the other hand, was fascinated. I wasn't scared. It was neat and fast, over in a few seconds. His hand movements were light and quick, and he knew exactly which pocket to grab. Despite the threat, I knew we weren't going to get hurt. He wanted fast money for drugs and got it. It was part of the city's pulse which we lived every day—a pulse I had mastered. Our neighborhood was all color, life, movement. Small repair shops, corner groceries, sirens, brawling—I drank it all in.

***

My mother, Nancy, was strong, talented, beautiful, and fiercely optimistic. She had movie-star good looks. A tussle of blonde hair, lipstick, a cigarette, black miniskirt and boots —that was my mother. Endlessly resourceful and creative, she made our dresses and clothes, knitted sweaters, hats, and mittens, and even made our stuffed toys and animals using scraps of material and patterns that she drew herself. She held us together, literally and figuratively, collecting soda bottles to get the five-cent return in order to pay for the subway to work every day. Each morning she grabbed that long train ride from the East Village to the World's Fair in Queens to sling hot dogs and beer to the crowds in the sweltering New York City summer heat.

She continued waiting tables until she got her start in animation, hand-inking and painting animators' drawings onto cels for TV commercials at Stars and Stripes Studios. She went on to work for Academy Award-winning Hubley Studios, helping create both short and full-length features for PBS. She also worked on such classics as *Schoolhouse Rock*, and while at Cel-Art Studios she did the inking and painting for classic television commercials for Hawaiian Punch, Hostess Cakes, and Cheerios. Much later, in the 1990s, she worked on MTV's animated series, *Beavis and Butthead* as well as the 1996 full-length feature *Beavis and Butthead Do America*. In a very real sense, cartoons saved us. We always got a thrill watching my mother's handiwork on the old black-and-white television, the one with the bent coat hanger for an antenna in our railroad apartment uptown.

http://wbp.bz/softvoicea

More True Crime You'll Love From WildBlue Press

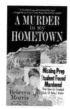

A MURDER IN MY HOMETOWN by Rebecca Morris
Nearly 50 years after the murder of seventeen year old Dick Kitchel, Rebecca Morris returned to her hometown to write about how the murder changed a town, a school, and the lives of his friends.

wbp.bz/hometowna

THE BEAST I LOVED by Robert Davidson
Robert Davidson again demonstrates that he is a master of psychological horror in this riveting and hypnotic story ... I was so enthralled that I finished the book in a single sitting. "—James Byron Huggins, International Bestselling Author of The Reckoning

wbp.bz/tbila

BULLIED TO DEATH by Judith A. Yates
On September 5, 2015, in a public park in LaVergne, Tennessee, fourteen-year-old Sherokee Harriman drove a kitchen knife into her stomach as other teens watched in horror. Despite attempts to save her, the girl died, and the coroner ruled it a "suicide." But was it? Or was it a crime perpetuated by other teens who had bullied her?

wbp.bz/btda

SUMMARY EXECUTION by Michael Withey
"An incredible true story that reads like an international crime thriller peopled with assassins, political activists, shady FBI informants, murdered witnesses, a tenacious attorney, and a murderous foreign dictator."—Steve Jackson, New York Times bestselling author of NO STONE UNTURNED

wbp.bz/sea

Printed in Great Britain
by Amazon